WHAT DOESN'T KILL HER

Women's Stories of Resilience

Edited by Kerry Garvin & Elisabeth Sharp McKetta, Ph.D.

H&S Books
Cambridge, Massachusetts

harridanandstrumpet.com

Cover and layout by Sarah Tregay.

Cover photo (tree) by David Cornelius.

Dedicated to women everywhere who tell their stories.

Dear Jessica,
we had the power
all along

Jede

Praise for *What Doesn't Kill Her*

"In ancient times the Sacred Feminine was revered. The woman was seen as 'The Giver of Life.' Through history the voices, stories, and the beautiful energy of the Feminine have been suppressed, oppressed, and forced into hiding. But the truth refuses to remain hidden. In this profound book, a compilation of sixty powerful individuals exude the courage and bravery required to push through the invisible chains of millennia of suppression to speak out. Each one adds her triumphant voice to the chorus representing the Feminine in all its Divinity and our need to restore it to its rightful place of reverence."

— AnnaLynne McCord, Actor and Activist

"Now more than ever we need to listen and learn from the voices of women. What Doesn't Kill Her *whole heartedly embraces the stories of sixty different women in very different situations and showcases their resilience, their strength, their creativity, and generosity of spirit. You cannot fail to be moved by their voices, and you cannot fail to be inspired to end the injustices that these stories so eloquently recount."*

— Cherie Blair CBE QC,
Founder of the Cherie Blair Foundation for Women

"When someone is ill, many old cultures say that they have lost their story. I believe that reading the stories in What Doesn't Kill Her *will help each of us to trust and tell our own."*

— Gloria Steinem

"I am inspired. This treasury of stories by women of courage is an important and necessary book. What Doesn't Kill Her *will make all of us stronger."*

— Barbara Morgan, NASA Astronaut (ret.)

*"*What Doesn't Kill Her *is a unique window into many brave women's lives. Their life stories are here to tell us we are not alone."*

— Adria Petty, Film Director

Table of Contents

i   Introduction

1   **Zara Ali | "Ignorance Is Not Bliss"**
As I pinched my skin, I looked down and examined my arms and hands. For the first time, the brownish color of my skin had never been so distinctive.

7   **Rebecca Andrew | "Sometimes You Need to Walk Away"**
Don't believe people who say you can't run away from your problems; the Atlantic Ocean that stood between him and me during that period was my sanctuary and my fortress, an enormous calming moat of safety and protection that went to the horizon and beyond.

13   **Leonora Anyango | "Maragua"**
"Menyera!" Kibe bellowed. I feared him even though I did not know what he had just said. It was just my second day at this school, and I did not have the courage to contend with him. Yesterday, he had waited until the teacher had left the classroom and he had led the rest of the boys into a chant of "mono, mono..."

19   **Sunshine Valus Arnold | "The Stranger I Know"**
One big bad thing can ruin your life if you let it, but if you find a million small things to celebrate, you can be happy and keep going.

23   **Eli Beagle | "Made in China (中国制造)"**
I had been barely welcomed into the world when my birth mother left me at a nearby school. Two students had found me, took me to a teacher, and probably went home that day with an interesting story to tell their parents. I, on the other hand, went to an orphanage, where I remained until being adopted at the age of ten months.

27   **Shersy Kerstin Benson | "Big Fires and Little Superheroes"**
We waved goodbye to the home we hoped would survive the fire... I drove for miles in the midday darkness, sweating under the stress of the mask, heat and recirculated air. Soot darkened the sky, and what was left of the sun peeking through the smoke burned a brilliant red.

33   **Sherry Briscoe | "From Teardrops to Raindrops"**
It was sink or swim time. I saw a glimmer of light piercing through the surface of the water. Here's your chance, I thought. Do something. Take action. Swim.

38   **Michele Brito | "Put in the Time"**
For my champion, my mother, work was a scattered and necessary activity that brought no joy. It wasn't meant to. It was meant to bring money.

41   **Dawn Brockett | "Enough"**
The potential that fills you, seeps out through your generosity, it is yours to direct, to fulfill and at times when you must, to abandon. This living is an act of creativity, not of control.

46   **Laura Bruno | "The Phoenix of the Polo Grounds"**
Yet, even with all of the falls I've lived through, I have always put that left foot back into the stirrup, hopping back into the saddle every time—no exceptions, even if it hurts.

50   **Nancy Buffington | "The Two Jizos"**
I realized finally that I was wrapping myself in grief like a thick winter coat, not wanting to feel better, as that would require separating myself from those babies.

53   **Lindsey Byars | "Self-Love"**
I stand in front of the mirror every morning naked, examining the carnage of nearly forty years and giving birth to three children.

60   **Kate Canute | "The Messiness of Perseverance"**
I don't always have total confidence in myself, and I struggle with the changes I have endured, just like anyone who has dealt with a catastrophic illness or a life-altering event. But there is one truth that remains—I am still here, and I choose to move forward.

65   **Ana Cristina Cash | Resilient**
You are the architect of your own destiny. / Who made anyone else the warden of your dreams? / You are resilient.

68   **Rachel Cassidy | "Sploosh"**
I vomit until sunrise. My lawyers and the thug will be here at nine.

75   **Patricia Chamburs | "To Love and Be Loved"**
It seems I've lived two different lives, and I believe the experiences in our lives help our true selves emerge, if we're lucky. What I've learned is that love is extremely powerful and my mantra—to love and be loved—is what life is all about.

79   **Emily Charles | "The Pretend Mother"**
*I wish I knew what was the actual turning point in my life and when I developed a voice that I finally realized was my true voice. It was most likely always there—just never uncovered until I reached a point of desperation when I realized that my family, under my roof, needed me more than the others who had come before them.*r

83   **Natalie Clark | "Head North"**
There's an irony to the fact that when I moved from Scotland to Hollywood, I discovered that the reality of 'living your dream' isn't the way it's portrayed in the movies. Life isn't a movie. 'Living your dream,' or at least the pursuit of such, is in reality hard, sometimes terrifying, and sometimes downright ugly.

88   **Darla Eden | "Doubt"**
The most difficult obstacle in an emotionally abusive relationship is doubt. It's the weapon most effectively used by the abuser, and the main reason those being subjected don't leave.

95   **Alane Ferguson | "Resurrection"**
To live, die and then live again makes me an unnatural creature of this world, yet I feel that is what I am. One thing I learned is that coming back to life is not the trick. Discovering how to be alive again is the true triumph.

100   **Lauren Flores | "Keep on Keeping on"**
Grief. A five-letter word with five stages. An endless road with no direction. That's how I felt sitting on the cold concrete steps of my apartment on the morning of March 8, 2018, searching for a reason why my twenty-four-year-old brother committed suicide.

104   **Kerry Garvin | "Rescue"**
I would survive because I told my story, I entrusted others with my pain, and on the other end was an echo, a collective of people who'd been through the same pain, who'd survived, but who hadn't stopped feeling or remembering, because to feel, to remember, and to unburden our weight when we're too weak to carry it is what makes us strong.

115   Sarah Graalman | "The Silence After Bad Nights"
When I was twenty-five, I had a bad night with a man I'd just met. I referred to it as a one-night stand, but "not a good one." That was all I ever said about that night for nearly a decade. No one ever questioned me—not even myself.

119   Janelle Gray | "My Crown, My Fire"
There was an activation for action in my DNA that happened when my country sanctioned the murder of my people. My fire has not only been ignited, it is constantly being incited and stoked by all of the injustices to my people.

123   Kristiana Gregory | "Rescuing Jeff and David"
Out-of-Print is heartbreaking to an author. It means the publisher has given up on selling, promoting, and caring for a title despite vigorous fan mail. It always comes down to sales. I grieved this loss deeply, noting in my journal, "I wrote these stories to be read, not just to collect an advance."

127   Gillian Hill | "All In"
I remember leaning forward so the nurse could give me the epidural and her laughing with surprise that I was so flexible. I didn't say that the thing that made her job so easy, my tiny bump, was because this baby was not supposed to be coming out today.

132   Diane Hughes | "Don't Call It a Comeback, I've Been Here for Years"
I thought I had been down this road before—the one with the blind curves. And I can tell you with 100% certainty that the fear is in the not knowing. Not knowing what is going to happen, what you will have to endure, what you will have to give up, and what will simply be ripped out of your control.

138   Elizabeth Hunter | "From Homeless to Healthy"
I will never allow myself to forget what happens when I don't face my fears or emotions. I am still not precisely sure what caused my mental break, but I do know that I had gotten a divorce, been laid off from my dream job, and lost

145   Natalie Komlos-Zeiler | "The Kestrel"
she saves herself to a needle-covered tower / and waits. / are you coming?

147   Kristine Hope Kowalski | "The Event"
Was I having a stroke? Was my mom going to find me? Since when was there a trailer park in my urban town?

152   Amber Paige Lee | "How Disney Brought Me to Life"
Like a princess under a sleeping spell who gets awakened, Disney brought me back to life. Only instead of Prince Charming waking me up, I awakened my own soul. Now that I know what self-love is, the clock never strikes midnight on my adventure.

156 Rochelle Lierz | "Now I Know"

Only a narrow slice of the human tribe knows what walking each other toward death really means day-to-day. Only a few take heed of that reality. They know that each sunrise brings a new opportunity to love. They know that heartbreak is part of the deal. They know that choosing to love again is the way through the pain.

162 Bethanie MacDonald | "Essay on Resilience, Take 38,474"

It was a humid morning when I met the ambulance carrying my husband home from the battlefield hospital. Men standing around me told me I'd not want to see him in the condition he was in. I looked at them strangely: how could I not be there to hold my husband's hand as he was taken off the ambulance bringing him home one last time?

168 Angela McCall | "The Common Denominator"

How did I get here? The truth is, I dug this hole for nearly seven years. Seven years. That's how long it took me to reach the rocks at the bottom. No one helped me. I actively and knowingly participated in every bad decision that led me to where I am now. I am the common denominator.

172 Elisabeth Sharp McKetta | "Robber Face"

When I was a child, I read a fairy tale about a robber who wished to marry a well-bred girl. He knew nobody would take him with his robber's face, so he used stolen money to have a mask made—a perfect face, virtuous and innocent and trustworthy.

179 Isla McKetta | "The Legacy of my Great Grandmother's Diamond"

In the hours before her February memorial service, my family gathered in her apartment in Austin while the women prepared to sort through and divide Baba's jewelry. It was a day my grandfather had orchestrated involving a hierarchy, rules and a stop watch.

183 Mage McManus | "Romancing Risk"

There's no way to know why I fell and it cracked that one time. I lay there stunned, while everyone rushed around me telling me with pale faces not to look at my leg. I felt no pain, just confused and scared and desperate to convince these people that they were wrong—I was in the best shape of my life...

188 Breanna McPhillips | "The Van"

From the outside, I had everything anyone could ever want. Life should have been perfect and I should have been happy. However, I wasn't. And I was in even greater pain and inner conflict than ever. The gender dysphoria worsened as I aged. My feelings hadn't disappeared—they'd intensified.

195   **Melanie Mendenhall | "The Thread of All Sorrows"**
Those losses have tied me, inextricably, to what I once thought of as a huge rent, or fissure, in the world. The poet Naomi Shihab Nye calls it "the thread of all sorrows."

200   **Kelly Mercer | "Mosaic Woman"**
I lost my father in an unreal tragedy, I lost my younger brother to the judicial system, and now I was losing my wife ... I realized that every day I woke up, I was alive and I had survived another day; I realized that twenty-four hours were an amazing accomplishment and I needed to acknowledge that small success.

206   **Kathleen Miller | "Everything Changed"**
I went to touch his hand and his tiny fingers instantly wrapped around mine. I stood there for the longest time as he fell back to sleep. I was so scared I would wake him up.

213   **Matiwonesa Munyaradzi | "We Were Never Meant to Die"**
Nothing is perfect. I still have family. I still have my mom who is everything. There are days when I feel the emptiness like I belong to no one. Is this what it feels like to have no family? Here, but not here. Existing, but not actually being anywhere at all.

219   **Liz Nance | "Our Secrets Keep Us Sick"**
Reading Mama's notebooks and journals opened my eyes to the wild injustices within our family and to a woman who was living in silent terror. She would leave small cries for help in the margins. She wrote the words "quiet strength, inner turmoil" in such beautiful handwriting that you would think it contained a lovely message of hope.

224   **Puma Perl | "Running the Obstacle Course"**
I have not cleared all of my obstacles, but I've survived and even thrived despite them. And I need to remember that on a daily basis—for the rest of my life.

228   **Taylor Richards | "Bent Not Broken"**
Research indicates babies barely remember the first year of their life. I am glad I left while my daughter was still young. My daughter has no idea of what I've been through and I wish to keep it that way.

236   **Erin Riley | "The Long Road Home"**
Yet, through those extremely dark times, I found that I had so much support and so much more strength than I ever thought imaginable.

241   **Elizabeth Rodgers | "The Bad Guy"**
This wasn't the first time I had trouble when I spoke up for myself. I've had differences with lots of people and have argued plenty. It's in my DNA. I never had a problem in college—we were there to argue. The trouble came after college when the men (always men) I argued with were not having as good a time as I was.

249 **Jasmin Rodriguez | "Devoted to My Magic"**
I defied the odds. The universe conspired. I now know that this is what I was always meant to do and I hope that the universe will continue to help guide me on the right path. I can only hope that through my own struggles as a Latina designer, I can pave the way and inspire other people of color to be fearless in pursuit of their dreams, of their magic.

253 **Monique Rojas | "Surviving the Underworld"**
I was never going to let anyone abuse me ever again. I had had guns pulled on me by boyfriends, I'd been beaten, I'd done the beating, I'd been cheated on, I'd been nearly killed by an ex. And none of it killed me. I can't be destroyed—I am my own guardian angel and I am the only one who can cause myself to fall.

261 **Aurélie Rose | "The Crossfire"**
As far as I can recall I have always wanted to be a mom. When my sister was born, I was only five years old, but when I held her in my arms for the first time, I felt I had a responsibility towards this little girl who had just arrived in my life.

268 **Emily Rose | "I Am Not a Writer"**
I sat down weeks ago to write about "bottoming out" and wound up discovering momentary stories wrapped in lifelong stories—breakdown moments triggered by lived-in lies, built upon other moments that marked my character and after tens of thousands of words transcribed, identified me as the woman I am today: not a writer.

270 **Cheryl Slavin | "Surviving Myself"**
I've been told that mental illness recovery takes two years. I am a notorious overachiever. I did it in about five. It's been over a decade since I was hospitalized. This is some of what I remember.

274 **Jessica Steindorff | "Lotus"**
These children are beyond grateful because their basic needs are met: food, water, shelter and access to education. It's that simple. Because they have those things, everything after that is just a gift. They have taught me a new way of thinking. I love myself. I love my life. I found my purpose.

277 **Mary Stewart | "Bardo"**
Do not pity the bereaved mothers for they are as adept at losing as they are at having it all, and sometimes scarcely know the difference.

279 **Samantha L. Taylor | "After All, She Deserves a Celebration"**
May we celebrate the woman who has fought many battles and regardless of battle scares, comes out victorious.

282   **Awet Teame | "Innie"**

When my family finally asked what I want, I told them, "I want what Oprah has!" They said, "Oprah?" I said, "Yeah, Oprah." They said, "OK!" I thought, "OK? They're okay with the whole long-term non-marriage thing? This is great!" They misunderstood. And found me an Eritrean who looked like Stedman. I said, "That wasn't what I meant." But it was impressive, so I put in an order for an Eritrean who looked like a Allen Payne, Blair Underwood, or Denzel.

287   **AK Turner | "Frank"**

I receive a phone call that my ex-stepfather has died in a plane crash. Relief washes through me in warm waves. He is gone. And I am relieved.

291   **Erika Warner | "Spilt Milk"**

I had been in school all of my life, but these people were new to the whole school thing. They were blue-collar workers, grandmothers, homemakers, adults who had not even finished high school. They put so much effort in their learning; I fell in love with their resilience. That was the day I found my vocation.

296   **Christy Wicks | "Luck to Cluck About"**

Even though my shelf-life has been revised, I'm not ready to be discarded quite yet.

301   **Mae B. Yu | "I Promise I'm a Friend"**

Could it be that the solution to your turmoil—the harmful urges, the endless arguments, the loss of half your days—was small enough to fit on a Post-it? The thought made you laugh through your tears.

306   **Contributors' Biographies**

Introduction

In late 2018, in the wake of the Me Too Movement and the United States' midterm elections that saw an unprecedented number of women elected to Congress, we—two Harvard-educated women who write, edit, and teach creative writing—felt heartened and inspired to see so many women feeling empowered to share their stories in the public world.

We began to dream of a collection of essays—a collective memoir of sorts—dedicated to the strength and resilience of women from all walks of life, a book we could pluck from our shelves during times of adversity in our own lives, or that we could lend to a mother, sister, or friend enduring hardship.

And so we sent our wish into the world—in the form of an email to more than fifty women, inviting each one to write an essay about one of the most trying times in their lives, a time when they felt they had hit rock bottom. We asked these women not to focus on the descent to their lowest point so much as their ascent back up. We wanted to understand how they were able to grow stronger, wiser and more resilient in the face of adversity.

Not a task for the faint of heart.

One after another, their stories trickled into our inboxes. But they shared more than their stories—these women shared our call to action, and more and more women wrote to us stating that they had a story to tell of rising from their own particular ashes.

As we pored over the essays that arrived in our inboxes throughout the spring of 2019, we realized that a force even greater than courage drove these women to write: the force of empathy. Each of the women included in this collective memoir wrote with the hope that other women—and men and non-binary people—might find something there, some useful lesson, some wisdom to pull and carry on their own journeys forward. Each woman offered her story as inspiration, holding it high like a lantern to guide others through darkness.

With the sparks created by increased dialogue about the importance of inclusivity and intersectional feminism, it seemed right that so many women would feel empowered at this point in history to come forward and share experiences that have marked their lives. We exist in an especially poignant moment worldwide, in which we all must summon strength to determine what the coming world will look like—not only for women but for everyone.

Now, in 2021, the book is finally complete, and the world has changed yet again. Nearly two years after our original call-for-essays went out, the need for not only dialogue, but the act of listening to and truly hearing others—particularly Black people and people of color—has gained much-needed significance, as well as life and death stakes. The global COVID-19 pandemic highlighted wide disparities in healthcare by disproportionately affecting Black people and people of color. Furthermore, the tragic murders of unarmed Black men and women in the first-half of 2020, from Ahmaud Arbery to Breonna Taylor to George Floyd, have brought to national prominence a long overdue discussion on the enduring racism in policing and our justice system. With Black Lives Matter fighting to change where power lies, and in the wake of the turbulent 2020 presidential election, amid dire predictions about the future of the earth we inhabit, it seems that all of life hinges upon the strength and collaboration of all women to lead the charge in healing the world's wounds.

Resilience—how and why we must summon it—is crucial to the conversations that all of us must have in this day and age.

Within this collective memoir are sixty triumphant stories by a diverse array of women. Sometimes triumph is a soaring achievement in the face of adversity. At other times, it's getting out of bed and putting one foot in front of the other. Phoenixes arise from ashes of all sorts—even bed sheets.

Each essay ends, as most memoirs end, with some form of either courage or acceptance: the courage to change one's situation or the willingness to accept one's own life, whatever its lopsided "happily ever after" might hold. These stories vary greatly, and what is hard for one woman might feel second nature to another. Some stories are straightforward, some dramatic, some subtle, some poetic. Each woman views her survival differently. As one writer in this book describes it, there is a distinction between being broken by adversity and becoming a rich mosaic—colorful and storied.

To be a woman at any point in human history is an experiment in survival. Women experience constant adversity due to institutionalized misogyny, widespread sexism, and rampant inequality. For Black women and women of color, the adversity has been—and still very much is—compounded exponentially.

But women are innate survivors—both in myth and life. Penelope was patient. Persephone learned to live underground. Medea killed one litter of children when she learned that her home would not be a secure place for them. Women carry children and stories, culture and community. It is the work of women, throughout history, to do the ordinary daily work to ensure the existence of our species. It is no wonder then that survival is built into women.

Women persist—not broken or unbroken—but as mosaics with enduring lives and stories to piece together and pass on to others.

Many of the essays feature culturally relevant topics such as advocating for healthcare as a woman, surviving sexual assault, reconciling female genital mutilation with the mother who made the decision to cut her baby girl, battling body dysmorphia, working in the sex industry, overcoming breast cancer, motherhood after miscarriage, losing a husband on a battlefield in Afghanistan, and transitioning from male to female. These stories do not espouse political or religious leanings but aspire to show, on a broad scale, the experience of being a woman in the twenty-first century.

Some of the women included in *What Doesn't Kill Her* are professional writers and academics. Most are not. Women's stories deserve to be heard at an equal volume and with equal dignity, regardless of socioeconomic standing, academic background, race, religion or sexual orientation. The book features a diverse group of voices, ranging in racial and cultural backgrounds from African American, to Latin American, to Asian American, to European American, to Europeans, Africans, Asians, and South Americans; ranging in sexual orientation from gay to bisexual to straight; ranging in gender identity from transgender to cisgender; ranging in age from teenagers to seniors; ranging in career from writer to exotic dancer to entrepreneur to homemaker; and ranging tremendously in subject material and tone. As editors, we chose to be light-handed, preserving each woman's voice and story so that it felt truthful to each writer.

In closing, we wish to extend our heartfelt gratitude to all of the intrepid writers who contributed this collection. We hope that your experience as a writer has been as profoundly transformative and cathartic for you as it has been for us as editors. You exemplify what this project set out to accomplish: telling stories that show not only the ways women experience adversity, but the ways women summon strength and rise, lifting others as we take flight.

With admiration and gratitude,
Kerry Garvin & Elisabeth Sharp McKetta

Ignorance Is Not Bliss

By Zara Ali

Fears are fascinating concepts. They can develop from heart-stopping, jaw-dropping incidents or even from the smallest, seemingly insignificant events. I had common fears and phobias that most children develop: the dark, spiders, heights. Those fears came from my wild, unconstrained imagination. I used to think that spiders had the ability to grow exponentially in size and that their pincers would lift me away from the clutches of my parents. And that if I were to drop from a height, my flailing limbs and turbulent body would spin eternally and fall and fall—even if that height was five feet. But my greatest, most unexplainable fear was the city.

I distinctly remember my five-year-old self looking wide-eyed at the extensive humanity of people that passed by me during a visit to New York City. Some donned sharp, slick suits, and as they rushed off to work, they left behind their pungent perfumes. Others jogged in their bright, neon shorts and t-shirts, while a handful sat on the pavement carrying their most prized possessions in plastic bags with their palms facing upwards. One would think that such diversity in people would have been fascinating to a kindergartener, but it was quite the opposite for me. As I craned my neck backwards to find the ends of the skyscrapers that pierced through the white, fluffy clouds and deep blue sky, the feelings of discomfort and unfamiliarity were incredibly daunting.

What made me so afraid of the sea of people in Times Square or of the miniature version of that same scene in Boston's Faneuil Hall? The reason was that I had only ever lived in a small, isolated, safe town: Holmfirth, Massachusetts. It was familiar and uniform, and cities weren't.

Ten years after my trip to New York City, Holmfirth remained my home, and I thought it always would be. I couldn't imagine living anywhere else other than in a New England suburb. Cities are too unpredictable, too different, almost too foreign. In Holmfirth, I would greet the same neighbors I knew since I was born, I lived in the same house I played in since I was little, I surrounded myself with the same friends I went to daycare with. It was a very familiar, similar lifestyle. Everyone dressed the same, we all seemed to channel a nautical style crossed with urban preppy and if you're feeling particularly daring, add a hint of vintage style. Everyone spoke similarly, Everyone spoke similarly, in a New England dialect, though I did develop a Boston English accent, which was immediately repressed the moment I pronounced the word "car" as "cah" and said "wicked." Essentially, to live in Homforth was to follow the town's norms—so much so that the only noticeable difference was physical. For instance, most of my friends had paler complexions while I had a tanner one.

Although we didn't necessarily look the same, we still felt the same. Some of us went to church, others went to the temple, some to the mosque, and some didn't go anywhere at all. But it was irrelevant because I felt no different than my peers. Besides, "different" was frequently looked down upon, which was why I often thought of Holmfirth as the closest America would ever get to a utopia. Everything there must be the same for the town to function perfectly and flawlessly. The world in my town was only black and white, no grey, or color, for that matter. Admittedly, Holmfirth wasn't a town for everyone because of the difficulties of conforming to it, but it was the place for me. Or so I thought.

"Goodbye, Mother!" I sarcastically shouted back and waved absent-mindedly while walking on my regular path to school. It was 2010, and I was thinking about the wonderful party I would be throwing that evening for my sixteenth birthday, with spectacular lights, food and entertainment. The thought of it filled me with excitement and exhilaration. I was inviting everyone from my school—quite literally *everyone*. Even the new kids, which was an exception that my friends were shocked I made.

Cars pulled into the parking lot as they arrived at the venue for my party. Dressed in a sleeveless white gown covered in shades of blue swirls that mimicked the soft rolling of waves, I greeted my friends and directed them inside through the halls. After what felt like hours of standing outside in the humid weather to welcome guests, I returned to the festivities and music. As soon as I made it past the doors, it felt like I had entered a separate world. I saw people I knew talking, dancing, eating and laughing. Moments such as those strengthened my love for consistency and sameness. Growing up in Holmfirth had intensified my fear of variation, dissimilarity, and cities.

"I am happy here. I'm happy everyone is here," I thought.

Through the corners of my eyes I saw a brown-haired girl wearing a bright pink, flowy dress. I had an eerie feeling that her eyes were following my every move. Even though I had not commanded it to do so, I felt my head slowly turning to meet her watchful, scrutinizing eyes. I did not recognize her immediately, so I quickly deduced that she must have been one of the new girls. She slowly glided toward me with a look that sent shivers down my spine. In that instant, I thought I heard the music die down, conversations come to an end, and the laughing stop as hundreds of eyes turn toward me.

"You're not like us. You're different," she said as I stood there awkwardly, feeling confused.

Quietly and nervously, I asked, "What do you mean?" I felt another fear arise—a fear that I had never experienced before. A fear of being unmasked, discovered, and caught lying. Not lying to others, but lying to myself. Lying about myself and who I was.

"Haven't you noticed? Look at your skin. Look at your beliefs. Look at you. You're probably related to Osama Bin Laden. You'll bomb the entire school or something."

I opened my mouth, but I had nothing to say. Instead, I gulped and shut it again. There was a sensation of shock that ran through me. I felt like I was deaf to every noise in the world but my own heart-beat. What was first a steady, light thumping in my chest became a rapid, fluctuating one. The sound of my heartbeat was getting louder. And louder. Breathing seemed strained and difficult. I stumbled back-wards and tried to grab hold of the back of a chair for support. But my suddenly clammy hands slipped, my legs began to give away and I fell. It was almost like time had stopped and there I was, in midair. Then I crashed.

Even if nobody had noticed the devastating seconds before, I had everyone's attention once I was sprawled on the floor. The seconds ticked by, and everyone was staring. The deadly silence was inter-rupted by a nearby friend coming to my aid and lifting me up. As I made an effort to regain my composure, a throbbing headache emerged, mixed with lightheadedness. I wanted to cry and let all my frustration, confusion and anger out. But I didn't like to cry in front of people. I never had. To keep the tears from overflowing in my eyes, I pinched my arm and bit the insides of my cheeks so hard that they become insensate.

As I pinched my skin, I looked down and examined my arms and hands. For the first time, the brownish color of my skin had never been so distinctive. I became aware that the pinching failed, and my face was stained with tears. I felt the color drain from my cheeks and my heavy, quick breathing turned into hyperventilation. No matter how much oxygen I filled my lungs with, it did not feel like it was enough. I was drowning. And as my vision darkened, I saw my dear parents rushing to hold me in their arms.

I slowly opened my eyelids and saw the silhouette of a woman with a stethoscope looking down on me. She had been talking with my parents. "A doctor?" I wondered. Where was I? I surveyed my surround-ings and met my parents' concerned eyes. They hugged and soothed me, in spite of the fact that my body was full of Benzodiazepines and no longer needed to be calmed.

"We had to rush you in an ambulance to the ER. You began to hyper-ventilate and suffered a severe panic attack," my father trailed off.

As the doctor turned to leave, she explained, "Don't worry about it. She should be all right, but it seems she had quite a shock. It's a shame that racism is so apparent at such a young age."

Racism. A sharp, savage word I only ever heard when referencing communities where people didn't fit in. Where certain people entertain the idea that they are superior to others because of the way they appear.

I knew exactly who Osama Bin Laden was. I knew what atrocious crimes he committed and the innocent lives he took while carrying out his acts of terror. And wrongly doing it all in the name of a religion that does not condone his actions. To be compared with such a human being because of my appearance and religious affiliations was the most terrifying and hurtful situation I had ever been in. My skin was the same color as before. The only thing that changed was that it made me feel different. The girl was right. I did look different, and in Holmfirth, apparently that was not acceptable. I began to wonder if that was what the world really thought of me? Were they friendly out of fear? Was that all they could see in me—a budding terrorist?

As I mulled the questions over and racked my brain to find some answers, I began to see Holmfirth in a different light. And I began to ask myself different questions. How many times had I bought clothes while keeping in mind what other people in my town would think of them, rather than if I actually liked them? Had I really wanted those peanut butter and jelly sandwiches every day, even though I hated peanut butter, or was it just because those were the kinds of lunches my classmates brought, and I was too afraid to bring what I liked? Did I really surround myself with genuine friends who had accepted me for who I was, or did I change myself to become someone they could accept? I allowed myself and others to diminish the real me through self-consciousness and fear of uniqueness. Wanting to fit in is a typical feeling for most teenagers but where do we draw the line before we fall too deep into the comforts of uniformity?

My sister was anxiously waiting for me as I returned home from the ER. I knew that someday she would grow up and realize that she was different, too. In that moment, I felt a strong sense of duty and responsibility toward her, as an older sister, to guide and teach her that it's okay to be different, contrary to what I once believed. She had no reason to be ashamed of her family, her heritage, or her religious beliefs—and neither did I. I wanted to save her from the brutal awakening that I had just experienced.

That day, I may have turned a year older, but mentally I felt like I had aged years. I now understood that the uniformity of Holmfirth, which I was once so comforted by, led to racism as soon as I had failed to conform. My first interactions with racism were far from ideal but they helped me overcome my fear of cities—diverse, dynamic, accepting, unprejudiced cities. New jobs and colleges have, since, taken my family farther from Holmfirth than I could have ever imagined. And though I closely hold my hometown to my heart, I have learned to accept change. In fact, I welcome it. It has been said that time heals all wounds, but several years have passed since the fateful day of my sixteenth birthday, and despite some mends and scabs, there are other parts of me I know will never quite recover. There are still scars, some visible and some not as much, that will never disappear. And those hurting, scarred parts will tell you that ignorance is not bliss.

Sometimes You Need to Walk Away

By Rebecca Andrew

"**Sometimes you need to walk away.** Not to make someone else realize how worthy you are. But for you to understand and realize your own self-worth."

I don't recall where I first came across those words. It may have been an "empowering" quote posted on Facebook by a near-forgotten school acquaintance. Or, perhaps it was one of those "thoughts of the day" scrawled in uneven hand on tatty, stained once-whiteboards in London's tube stations—someone's attempt to add deep and meaningful inspiration to the worker ant commuters' daily trudge. The source doesn't really matter to this story. What matters is that those words managed to pierce through the toxic, swirling fog that permeated my brain. On the 28th day of August in 2015, at precisely 5:45 p.m. according to the note I carefully typed into my iPhone, it felt vital for me to write down those words, to remember them.

In reality, it took me until the 3rd of March the following year to summon up enough strength (or, perhaps more accurately, to lose the last bit of capacity and will to keep battling) to finally walk away. That was the day I texted my friend Katie: "I just cannot cope anymore."

After work that evening, I went back to the flat I shared with him

(I deliberately don't use the word "home"), packed a suitcase (small enough to count as a carry-on), stepped outside into a waiting taxi, and left for an address in South London that wasn't my own. I felt a deep, leaden sadness. There was no victory in leaving. I didn't look back as I closed the door.

I cancelled the holiday that he had meticulously planned. I applied for a visa to India with a drained and grey photo booth mugshot. At 6:30 a.m., the day after the visa was approved (despite the serial killer photo), I booked a flight. Four hours later I was on my way to Goa and an unknown path that I had no map to navigate.

The weeks that followed are a blur of angry calls and texts filled with accusations of betrayal. I had broken his heart and ruined his life. Loving words. Hate-filled words. And questions as to my mental state: "There are times I've considered whether you have had, are on the verge of, or are susceptible in the future to a breakdown or some kind of similar episode."

In some odd way the idea that I was simply unhinged seemed to comfort him. He was a man who had an obsessive-compulsive desire for every aspect of his life to be regimented and controlled (from the way he folded his clothes with crisp, starched, military precision, to the way he would check-check-check that the front door was always locked). My apparent madness was the only explanation for my sudden departure that his mind could begin to compute. He couldn't have been expected to make this relationship work, as this wasn't his failing—I was broken. I was mad.

In my darker moments, there were many times that I questioned my sanity. Sometimes, I still do. Was it possible that he had some insight into my mind that neither I nor any of my lifelong friends had unearthed? He certainly had evidence of my many failings—after all he had been an observer, a friend and a confidante when my last relationship came to a sad but unremarkable end. Could it be that he was the only person who really understood me after all these years? He used this proof to chip away at me—subtly but steadily. Gradually, the edges between his thoughts and my thoughts blurred.

The onslaught was relentless: Why did I suffer from M.E. (myalgic encephalomyelitis, also known as chronic fatigue syndrome) during childhood? And wasn't that some made-up illness anyway? Could that be a sign of some mental vulnerability? Was I abused? Why, as a sixteen-year-old, had I drawn a portrait of a woman with her ribs showing? (I tried to explain that I was simply a lanky teenager, but under his tutorage that picture shape-shifted from a dreamlike representation to a distorted house of horrors reflection of a deeply troubled young woman).

Why did I wear lipstick when I went out with my girlfriends? Why was I so desperate to impress people who weren't really my friends anyway? Why was I so needy? Was I so pathetic? Small insecurities became bigger and louder and all-defining.

When was I going to get out of my going-nowhere "career," and why was I trying so hard and prioritizing that above him when it was a dead-end job anyway? I thought I was so important, but I should remember that I would soon find myself trapped—I was over-promoted and overpaid.

Why was I so illness-obsessed, wallowing after a recent cancer scare? It was clear that I wasn't coping, I was fragile—just look at my recently developed alopecia. Maybe I couldn't really cope with life after all. But I was lucky. Lucky to have someone who understood me and would be there for me. I didn't need to go out late with my friends. I should just stay at the flat with him and look after my body. He would take care of me. It wouldn't matter if my hair fell out, because I wasn't on my own; he would still be there for me. It wouldn't matter if no one else thought I was lovable or attractive anymore because I had him. And so the warped incantation went on.

The way I spoke had the hallmarks of a woman in an abusive relationship. This is what the counselor told me.

But it was not the sort of abuse that I expected or understood: I wasn't beaten or punched, my ribs were not cracked, I didn't have to tell anyone that I was a woman who walked into doors. Part of me, a big defiant proud part, likes to think that if I had been subject to that form of abuse, I would have left long ago. Violence is more black-and-white.

And yet, I—an intelligent, educated, rational woman, a woman with friends and a good job and who liked to laugh—stopped laughing and forgot how to smile. I found myself trapped, 10,000 feet in the air, trying to get to the other end of a never-ending tightrope with a storm howling around me.

Looking back, with my feet now on the ground, it feels strange that I let him treat me that way. I'm angry with him, but I'm also bitter at what feels like my own complicity. But at the time, I felt no more able to leave than I would be able to stand stationary on train tracks with a locomotive hurtling toward me. And yet, my prison was not one of iron or steel, of lock or key. I had the physical ability to walk away at any point and yet for some reason I couldn't—be it guilt, or fear or some warped sense of loyalty, I couldn't walk until I was pushed to the precipice of exhausted insanity, as though his prophecy was coming true.

Around a month after I walked away, having returned from Goa and made a start at putting the basic building blocks of a normal life back together, we met up to talk. His dad hadn't been well. He said he needed my support as a friend, that I owed him that much after everything. That was the first day I found my anger, after two years of tiptoeing around him, frantically empathizing, desperately trying to do better and trying to understand my own failings.

And so, I raged. I raged at him with a previously unearthed, unknown ferocity. I raged that he had systematically torn apart and undermined every single aspect of my life and confidence. Alas, my mind and body betrayed me, and I promptly suffered my first panic attack.

As my lungs gasped for air like a helpless drowning fish on the shore, a sense of panic overwhelmed me. He was nice. That made it worse. I was a traitor to myself and let him comfort me. For days afterwards, every breath created a deep ache in my chest as my body taunted me for daring to try to stand up to him, for daring to be strong.

I don't look at either my outburst of rage or my packed carry-on bag as defining turning points or empowering moments of epiphany. It is hard to feel that way when I still hear his voice in my ear, reminding me that I'm mentally unbalanced, that my friends aren't really my friends, that I only have my job because I flirt and smile. Those whispers become dark and twisted roots, like a pervasive, damaging, deep-rooted Japanese knotweed that is still anchored in my mind.

The clever and the cruel impact of someone who questions the very foundations of your mind, your identity, and every facet of your life is a resultant lack of trust in your own judgment and even the perceptions of others around you. My initial reaction to deal with the second-guessing was an almost obsessive need to provide evidence, to seek validation, and for others to agree that yes, I was emotionally abused. He was the mad one, not me.

For a long time, I wanted him to see what he had done, I wanted him to admit it--what perfect closure that would have provided. But it has become apparent to me over time that we have two different truths, and I will only find peace from accepting that he will never see or acknowledge mine.

It is coming up to three years since I walked away. Some days, I still wake up from nightmares where he has talked me into giving the relationship another chance and I am trapped (sometimes physically bound) all over again.

That fear of being trapped led to me very nearly sabotaging my next relationship completely. I first met Chris the following November. He was kind and consistently open, confident and heartfelt in articulating his feelings toward me. In return, I was consistently cagey, non-committal, and held him at arm's length. I rejected the "girlfriend" label as though it was something unpleasantly contagious. It gave me a deep sense of unease. I dealt with this unease by accepting a secondment to New York City and even suggesting he could date other people whilst I was away. There was nothing I could fault him with, yet the idea of being back in a relationship petrified me, and it seemed to be the only reasonable and fair thing to do.

There isn't an overnight miracle cure to those thoughts and feelings. I couldn't just pull up the dark parasitic roots caused by an abusive relationship. But being brave enough to say "yes" to the secondment was one important step in finding my way back to being me. Almost a year later to the day after I first walked away, I found myself packing up my bags and life once more (although this time with three large suitcases—progress).

On the 11th of March 2017, I found myself sat on British Airways' flight 185 destined for New York. Whilst waiting for take-off, I read an email from HR warning me of an impending blizzard and reminding me to pack my snow boots. I didn't own any, and it occurred to me that after the safety blanket of living in London for the last eight years, I was not remotely prepared for my new life. I barely knew a soul in New York. I was terrified that I was going to get found out at work. And I had a genuine concern that I would spend the next three months' worth of Friday nights watching Netflix and feeling lonelier than ever.

Fortunately, my fears did not materialize and my time in New York provided an opportunity for catharsis (and turned out to be far more effective than therapy). Don't believe people who say you can't run away from your problems; the Atlantic Ocean that stood between him and me during that period was my sanctuary and my fortress, an enormous calming moat of safety and protection that went to the horizon and beyond. After being told for years that I was weak, I found steel in doing something terrifying and coming out the other side happier and alive. I'd be lying if I were to say that a stint in New York washed away the sense of doubt and restored me to whom I was before, but little by little I have found that the more space I make for positive people and experiences, the less headspace I have for the shadows.

Against all odds Chris, as of a week ago, asked me to marry him and I said "yes"—three times, to be exact, as he kept checking. And whilst I love him wholeheartedly, this story isn't meant to be a love story. Instead, it is hopefully one of healing. The steps towards my own healing have come in many forms and from many places. Healing can come from an otherwise trite slogan on a tube board, which tells you to know your own worth. It can come from a friend who (weeks before getting married herself) puts a roof over your head, pours you a bath and feeds you wine and pizza because you are homeless, desperate, and don't know where else to turn. It can come from flying to India (very Eat, Pray, Love) and learning to stand on your head at a yoga retreat in the dazzling Goan sunshine as the beams warm your skin and quietly soothe your wretched soul. It can come from a stranger flirting with you, and making you laugh, and remembering what that feels like. It can come from drinking wine (and whiskey) in Manhattan into the early hours with new friends that you will hold dear for life. It can come from someone who tells you that they don't have much, but everything they do have, they will give to you. And finally, it can come from yourself—from walking away so that you can begin to learn your own worth.

Maragua

By Leonora Anyango

"Menyera!" **Kibe** *bellowed.* I feared him even though I did not know
what he had just said.

It was just my second day at this school, and I did not have the
courage to contend with him. Yesterday, he had waited until the
teacher had left the classroom, and he had led the rest of the boys
into a chant of *"mono, mono..."* My cousin had mentioned this word,
saying that it was a derogatory word for new students at her boarding
high school.

"Menyera!" Kibe repeated when he realized that I had been standing there, petrified, saying nothing. I was not going to say anything.
The last two days had already taught me that you do not mess with any
of these boys. My walk home was also long enough, and I did not want
any of them to find a reason to send me running all the way home
after school as was the tradition for the mean boys. If they promised
to "end the school day with you," they would wait until you started
your journey home. Then they would run after you, two or three of
them, just to torment you.

I stood there, not blinking my eyes even once, staring at Kibe,
motionless. Short and skinny, he was probably the smallest boy in

13

standard 6C, the class I had been placed into. His deep, loud voice was a far cry from his calm eyes that displayed a false meekness. I wondered what it would be like if I had met him anywhere in the streets of Maragua away from this school environment that he seemed to rule with an iron fist. Perhaps he would not even look at me in the eye and scream, *"Menyera."* Perhaps I would be the one who would be sending chills down his spine with a stern look he would never forget. Perhaps, just perhaps.

"Mono!" My thoughts of false courage were interrupted by a soft voice from behind me. I turned around. Nyakio was standing there, tall and slim, composed as ever. My first thought was how much taller she was than Kibe. Nyakio had pushed Kibe away yesterday when Kibe had tried to torment me. Her smile revealed her straight milk-white teeth that enhanced her face and gave way to a look that did not show her tough side. Her brown eyes radiated a shine that warmly betrayed the fact that she was ready to embrace me as her new friend.

"Nyah-kee-ooh!" I said haltingly. Her name was still new to me, and being of a different language, it was heavy on my tongue.

"Nyah-keh-o," She repeated, correcting my pronunciation. I wanted to be her friend immediately. I knew that she would teach me the language, and I would learn a lot from her, even tactics that would help me protect myself from Kibe. "Do you know why I called you mono?" she continued. I had wondered why, but I could not figure out a reason that would make her use this word that I had come to loathe.

"No," I responded without hesitation. The urgency in my voice was unmistakable. Talking to Nyakio was nothing like trying to face Kibe. I had not said anything to Kibe so far. Yet even though my answer to Nyakio was a short one word, I felt comfortable saying it, and I knew then that I sensed no ill intentions in her, even though she had used Kibe's mean word.

"I wanted to see if you would look at me," Nyakio said sternly. I knew she was driving at something, but she was circling around it in a way that made it even more mysterious. I could tell she was relishing the blank look on my face.

"Why?" I asked with my now signature one-word response. I did not speak Kikuyu, and while she spoke English, her sentences were sprinkled with some Kikuyu words that I did not understand.

"Don't let them!" Nyakio said with resolve, pointing at Kibe. She did not mind that Kibe was looking squarely at her. "When they call you anything other than your name, don't look, okay?" Nyakio was a tough girl, I could tell. Her "okay" was not a request, neither was it a command clothed in a request. It was a straight command, with her voice rising high up while she said it, and her mouth widening emphatically at the end of it.

"Okay!" I replied. I thought I sensed more than a hint of resolve in my own voice.

I was not wrong, after all, that Nyakio would teach me more than Kikuyu. She would bring out the true, courageous me to the forefront, to fight Kibe and his cronies. They—Kibe and his crew—were the ones in trouble, not me. I could not wait to tackle them. Tackle was tackle in any language, and I was going to say it, mumble it, murmur it, or do it anyhow.

That evening on our way from school, Nyakio asked me to pass through her home with her and wait for her to walk with me. She would change from her school uniform and go to her father's canteen to help her father out.

"I go there most days after school," she said.

"That's good," I replied, surprised that I had used two words.

I could not wait to learn Kikuyu and talk as much as I would have wanted. I wanted to ask Nyakio about so many things. I wanted to ask her why she was not as timid as the other girls. I wanted to ask her why she did not think anything of Kibe, where she found the courage to face him, and why she seemed comfortable and carefree. I wanted to ask her what she thought of me and if she thought we would be good friends. "But more so, I wanted to ask her why Kibe always yelled "Menyera" at me."

This last one could not wait. As we wound our way down the dusty road from Kiiru village, our footsteps almost unified in sound, it felt as though we had always walked on this rugged road, Nyakio and I. I could not believe that only yesterday, I had walked this road for the first time ever in my life, to and from school. This morning, silence had engulfed me as I hurriedly walked to school, hearing only the chirping of birds in different tunes as the sun forced its rays between the trees. The bushes on each side of the road were so thick that it was hard to see the homes inside the banana plants beyond them. I had never dreamt that I would walk five kilometers to school and another five to go back home. I wondered why my parents had chosen this school, instead of Maragua Primary, where our neighbor's children went. But Nyakio was in this school, and it made all the difference.

"Nyakio!" I called as we trudged along the dusty road. She must have thought I was calling her attention to something I had seen on the side of the road.

"*Iiii!*" She responded with the Kikuyu response that I had to get used to immediately.

"What is *menyera?*" I asked with a tone that displayed genuine concern. I was surprised that I did not stumble on the word.

"Anyah-go!" She called my name without answering my question. I noticed that she had not really pronounced the "n" sound in my name and realized that we would both be getting used to new accents from each other. I did not correct her pronunciation of mine, as I had already asked her the question that I considered most urgent. I wanted both of us to stay focused until she had answered my question.

"*Iiii!*" I finally responded, imitating her in the precise way she had said it. I knew that I was beginning my journey toward learning Kikuyu.

"*Hiii!*" She gasped back. She could not hide her surprise! "Only yesterday! You will know Kikuyu very quickly!" Her voice was full of pride. I was enjoying her Kikuyu accent that was distinctly audible in her English speech, which was in itself half Kikuyu. She seemed not to be bothered that I did not understand most of these words yet.

"So, what does it mean?" I asked again, without showing openly that I was impatiently waiting for the answer. I had to know what Kibe was trying to tell me all this time.

"Oh, *menyera!*" She started and did not give me the long-awaited answer for a while. I waited.

"Yes!" I did not want to repeat the word again because it was filling my mouth without offering any taste. I no longer wanted to say it if I could not attach any meaning to it. What if it was a bad word and Nyakio did not even want to tell me the meaning?

"Get used to it!" She finally responded. I was stunned. She was not going to tell me the meaning of this word.

"What?" I asked, almost obviously showing my agitation.

"Get used to it!" She repeated. I decided not to be silent anymore.

"Will you please tell me?" I implored, hoping she would read my pleading voice.

"Get used to it, yes." She said with finality. It was her turn to be impatient.

"Is that what it means?" I finally asked, almost sure that I was wrong.

"I said yes. Get used to it."

Okay, I thought, that was the meaning. What did Kibe mean? Did he want me to get used to the school? Or was it the language, or the people? It became more puzzling after knowing the meaning of the word.

"Anyango, the shoes," Nyakio said, pointing at my feet.

"What about them?"

"Nobody wears shoes in school." That was her answer. When I looked at her with questioning eyes, she continued, "Kibe and his friends will bother you if you continue to wear your shoes. Nobody wears shoes. Even children of big people with money. They don't. Get used to it!"

This was my second big lesson. Nyakio was my social studies teacher. Nyakio would lead me through life in Kiiru. Nyakio would help me to survive the rugged terrain of this new school. She would sharpen my skills of how to survive Kibe and his friends, and how to make sure I fitted into my new school community. She would teach me what to do and what not to do.

Still, I was not sure how she was going to teach me the art of walking ten kilometers without shoes. Was that even possible? I thought of how, after what had started as uniform steps, I had struggled to keep up with her as we walked after school. She had started to walk so fast that sometimes I was half running to try and keep her pace. Yet, she had no shoes. Her feet did not seem to shy away from making firm and complete steps as she surged forth, and not once did she seem to be troubled or hurt by the occasional little stones on the road.

"It is so far!" I broke the silence. We did not seem to be getting closer to our destination.

"Menyera!" Nyakio quipped. She did not even glance at me. She kept walking briskly, and I had to stay apace. I laughed loudly. She stopped and looked at me. Then she also laughed.

We laughed and laughed for what seemed to be one full minute. Our worlds, even with their two languages, had melded into one. Right now, we were fine. Right now, I felt I would be the one to warn Kibe to watch this space! *Menyera!* Right now, I felt that I would indeed get used to it, to this new place—and that I might even like it.

The Stranger I Know

By Sunshine Valus Arnold

I had always thought the hardest part of my life was when my father was diagnosed with cancer and passed away when I was only twelve years old. It changed my life completely. I could not have imagined anything worse in the world. It's funny how when you are going through a hard time, you can't see a way out or how anything could possibly get worse. It can be a very selfish thought—things can always get worse. Soon, a type of genetic imagination would show just how naïve I was as a child. Little did I know then that my life and my family's life would truly change forever because my other parent had a secret that no one knew.

My mother had always been the kind of mom you saw in a magazine, the mom most girls wish they had. She was absolutely beautiful and always looked perfect from head to toe, not a hair out of place. She never missed anything. She made my costumes. She hugged me every day (at least eight times, to be exact). And she said I love you more than I thought I needed to hear. She was a college-educated stay-at-home mom whose children were the center of her world. Her laugh and smile were infectious, and she was always the prettiest, happiest woman in the room.

But one day, it was like someone from above flipped a light switch. The woman smiling and laughing slowly began to disappear from my life. It started small. She would forget things. She would lose her temper and yell. My adolescent mind created an explanation—my mother was heartbroken and lost without her soulmate. It seemed reasonable enough to me at the time. My father was the sole bread-winner and had taken care of all financial responsibilities during their marriage. So, it seemed logical these new responsibilities were difficult for her to handle on her own. There was no other explanation for the sudden changes in her personality or her behavior.

As time went on, daily activities became increasingly difficult for her, and she spent more and more time at home and alone. My once-social butterfly mama had clipped her own wings and would only leave home to attend my school or sporting events. Through my high school years, there were glimmers of the woman who had raised me as a young girl. I came to think of my own mother as "the stranger in our home." It seemed she was able to contain the stranger inside of her mind most of the time back then. But when the stranger would appear, she would first grow angry, even sometimes violent, and then very sad and confused, trying to figure out what was going on around her. I remember spending many days at Haslam's bookstore in dowtown St. Petersburg, Florida, with my mother. It was perfect for us because the self-help/psychology books she spent hours reading were right next to the kids' section. I didn't realize it as a child, but she was truly trying to figure out what was happening to her mind and her body—she was searching for an answer.

This was the life I became used to—grieving for my heartbroken mother and what the loss of her love had done to her mind. When I wasn't sad, I was angry and embarrassed. I was angry at my father and family for leaving us all alone, I was angry that she couldn't just snap out of it and take care of me, and I was angry I was stuck taking care of her and covering up for her behaviors. Eventually, the stranger made more frequent appearances and began to take a stronger hold of her mind and her physical body, as well. My mother would stumble, unable to control her movements. Her once-beautiful handwriting now looked like a child's. And her speech slurred so badly that she would be accused of being drunk.

When I was in my early twenties, the stranger was finally given a name: Huntington's disease (HD). My mother was plagued by a disease best described as having Lou Gehrig's disease (ALS), Alzheimer's and Parkinson's—*simultaneously*. Pretty terrible, right?

Don't forget, I said earlier things can always get worse. Huntington's disease is a "family disease." Every child of a person with HD has a 50/50 chance of developing the disease. By the time my mother was diagnosed, she had four adult children and eight grandchildren—all at risk for the same fate. Over the remaining ten years of her life she lived with my own family and continued to deteriorate. There is no cure for HD. There is no grief like grieving someone who is not yet dead but begging for their suffering to end. Like all who suffer from HD, my mother eventually lost her ability to reason, speak, and move. Eventually, the stranger spent more time with me than my mother did. I would stare into my mother's eyes, begging her to return, to let me see her, if only for a moment. My mother was set free from the stranger inside of her in 2016, when she returned to my father's side.

This disease, in many ways, has ripped my family apart. My siblings and I all struggle in different ways with the disease. We struggle with the decision to get tested or not, a struggle for all families living with HD. To test positive is to know that the stranger is hiding in your shadow and will eventually make itself known. To test negative may give some temporary relief to the individual, but then the guilt sets in. It's hard getting up each day knowing what monster may be waiting for the people you love most. It can consume you, if you let it. There are days when I am still angry, days when I hate the world, days when I ask why my family deserved this fate. For so many years I felt helpless and powerless against Huntington's. I couldn't stop it from slowly taking my mother away from me, and I can't stop it from taking any more of my family.

But I have found hope and power in educating others about HD and advocating for those who have it. My family had never heard of HD until my mother's diagnosis. We were blindsided. Many professionals in the medical field have never helped a person with HD. I will continue to tell anyone and everyone who will listen about HD to ensure that HD families are treated with dignity and respect.

Finally, I do what my mom would have done—she always remained positive. One of her favorite songs was "Don't Worry, Be Happy." Her HD doctor always remarked that she was one of the most positive HD patients he had ever met. Remaining positive during a difficult time is not an easy feat, and it takes practice. I am grateful for each day of my life and each happy moment I had with my mother. Practicing gratitude is how I keep my thoughts positive and from drifting too far into anger and hopelessness. Gratitude is the true key to happiness. I have realized that the greatest joys are often found in the smallest of things. One big, bad thing can ruin your life if you let it, but if you find a million small things to celebrate, you can be happy and keep going. Happiness cannot be attained without hope and effort. I look at each new day with great intention and for reasons to be happy. My mother's favorite color was yellow and she absolutely adored butterflies. Cloudless Sulphur butterflies are abundant in Florida, and were always one of her very favorite. Now, each day, I look for one to remind me of this woman I love and admire so much—my mother, not the stranger. I don't always see one every day, but the days that I do remind me to keep going because this is not the end.

Made in China (中国制造)

By Eli Beagle

I had been barely welcomed into the world when my birth mother left me at a nearby school. Two students found me, took me to a teacher, and probably went home that day with an interesting story to tell their parents. I, on the other hand, went to an orphanage, where I remained until being adopted at the age of ten months.

In my family, I never once questioned my validity, place, or purpose. My parents raised me in an environment that was open-hearted and honest about adoption. But behind the scenes of my little world, behind the thick curtain my parents had placed between others and myself, people were unkind and ignorant, and they spoke things they didn't really understand.

"Are you going to have your own children?"

"Does she know her real parents?"

"We want to adopt, too—after having a few of our own."

"Is she really yours?"

My parents adopted two more girls after me and tried their best to keep us from hearing these things. Of course, I was a child, and sometimes what other adults said didn't really concern me. Rather, it was what other children said that made me anxious or mad. When they learned I was from China, their first reactions usually ranged from apathy to dislike, with a bit of confusion mixed in as well. Kindergarten and elementary school were two of the main places I realized others were not like me. Some were kind; some were not.

Most Asian kids—especially those with biological parents—can relate to the snide comments about "eating dogs" and "speaking ching-chong," or watching classmates purposely squint their eyes and laugh. Looking back, it surprises me that I was bullied so much, as my school was diverse and had many Asian-American families. But I suppose that numbers don't really matter if your heritage is seen as weird and foreign.

However, I do understand the bullying I received was quite mild compared to those raised in a traditional Chinese family. I didn't bring *Xiaolongbao* to school for lunch, nor did I have parents of the same race to walk me to class. My own mother is White and works at my old elementary school as a teacher. To my classmates, the bullying wasn't directed toward my mannerisms or food, but rather stereo-types perpetuated by the media and my own physical traits. And I suppose adults were like this, too. Some would call my parents "noble" for adopting me, as if adoption was some kind of heroic action that required higher morals. To them, it wasn't *normal*. It was different and foreign. At other times, they acted out the comments above, asking my parents if I was really theirs or questioning my mom's infertility as the reason behind my American existence. And deep down, I know that many of them meant no harm. They were just regular people saying regular, ignorant things. But it reflects the societal idea that adoption is lesser than having biological children, or that adopted children aren't really part of their families because they don't share blood. And sometimes, due to those comments, I felt like a second choice.

Yet, it wasn't just the ignorance of others that caused conflict. My parents seemed to notice that the rift between my past and present was growing bigger, and in an effort to keep my heritage alive, they enrolled me in Chinese classes. I walked into school, equally nervous and excited. I saw my mom and dad talking to the other adults. And I remember seeing the other children—all Chinese—speaking fluent Mandarin with a grace and fluency that I had never achieved.

It was around this point that I realized Chinese school wasn't necessarily geared toward adoptees, but rather kids born into

Chinese families. While they were born in America, they were not expected to know the language off the bat, but they were expected to speak and study it at home—an easy task, considering with whom they lived. My parents really did try, but what was new to me was also new to them. They couldn't understand enough Mandarin to practice at home, nor did they have much time to immerse themselves in the lessons. And this unique aspect of our lives showed in school. I was often grouped with much younger children—children who were already more skilled than me—because those my age were already in advanced classes. When I look back at this moment in my life, the first word I think of is inadequate. Maybe failure, too, or frustration. Still Chinese, but still *not*.

Despite these setbacks, I learned many things about my culture. We cooked mooncakes during New Year's and made Chinese crafts like lanterns and paper fish. I fondly recall practicing tai chi on our bright blue yoga mats and playing with the *jianzi* in the sports field. I also made friends. Family-friends, but still friends nonetheless.

But no matter how hard I tried to assimilate into Chinese culture, every day at Chinese school only brought more resentment. I hated not being able to keep up with my classmates or talk to the teachers in Mandarin. I hated not being able to understand what seemed to come so easily to everyone else. It was because of this that my parents eventually took me out of Chinese school, and whatever knowledge I had acquired there faded rather quickly. It wasn't until I was older that I finally began to really try again.

The high school language requirement acted as a catalyst for change. There were popular options, like Spanish, French, German and ASL. My dad told me to pick something similar to English— perhaps a romantic language. But Chinese caught my attention, and my desire to bridge the cultural rift I had felt appeared again. I enrolled in an online class the next week, more hopeful and optimistic than before. My lessons were no longer limited to a classroom. I had the whole of the Internet at my disposal to do research as well as apps to talk to Chinese students who were studying English.

However, some things are harder said than done. I immersed myself in Mandarin, but the syllables sounded unnatural as they fell from my mouth. I cringed as the words filled the air—every tone seemed wrong, every noise seemed different. When I played back the recording, my voice was hesitant—a reminder of my mind's struggle to remember the proper saying and a sharp throwback to the conflict I felt during my younger years in Chinese school. It wasn't just the language, either, but not having anyone to help bridge the widening cultural rift I felt inside. My sisters are both Chinese, but they had no interest in learning about their past culture; my high school, though diverse, only had two other Chinese students. Apps for conversation between other Chinese-speaking students were hard due to the fact there's a 12-hour time difference between China and the United States. The confidence I once had about this new chapter in my life started to shake, and I wasn't sure I could continue. I spent a lot of time reflecting on what I wanted, on what I gained from stumbling on this unknown road, and I'm still honestly not sure, other than a mysterious longing of the first home I can't remember.

About a year ago I started joking to people that I was Made in China. Made like the toys you find in Walmart, made like the clothes you wear from Target. Except, of course, there's no tag indicating my origin or label stamped across my neck. There's just me and my story.

I was made like all of China's 1.3 billion citizens. But sometimes, it seems I'm more of a product than a person. I wasn't *raised* there. In fact, for most of my life, I've never really grasped the concept of being Chinese. Of being *me.* At times, I feel like a manufactured product— something made only to be sent halfway across the world for another purpose. I don't regret my parents adopting me. It's because of that choice I'm where I am today. But it's weird—this cycle of dislike to yearning: from being young and angry about my past, to desperately wanting to regain some semblance of my culture; from an almost perfect assimilation to a stumbling, backward transition. I suppose this is my adversity—not just the cultural gap I can't seem to close, but also the conflict of my own personal identity. I'm still trying to find a sense of who I am. Maybe I don't even need to. Maybe I'm just one of many things, all jumbled up and mixed: an adoptee others don't consider real, a Chinese immigrant raised American, a teenager learning to speak the language of her blood.

And a woman, still piecing the two opposite ends of her life, in hopes they'll cross the rift together.

Big Fires and Little Superheroes

By Shersy Kerstin Benson

"This thing is just coming down off the hills," Captain David Zaniboni said to the local Noozhawk reporter. "The smoke is horrific," Zaniboni added. The Fire Captain and Public Information Officer of Santa Barbara County urged anyone still in the mandatory evacuation areas to leave immediately, even though no one was left to leave. The flames had smoked out even the most stubborn residents in the Montecito foothills. At the time, the Thomas Fire would be the largest fire in California's modern history.

As my toddler son and I walked the couple blocks from our house to the beach, I understood Captain Zaniboni's warning firsthand. Normally, we would wear a light sweater at night. But on this night, we wore respirators, goggles, and windbreakers to cut through the smoke and ash. We perched ourselves on the beach bluffs overlooking downtown Santa Barbara and watched our hometown's foothills become engulfed by flames. The flames were seeping down the mountain range, about six miles away. The sky lit up in long strips of fire across the mountainside, making the town glow an eerie orange. It smelled like summer bonfires by the lake. Sirens and helicopters pierced the silent crackling glow in this quiet upper-class beach town.

Depending on how quickly the fire would spread due to the gusty Santa Ana winds, we would evacuate the next day.

Santa Barbara is an upper-class beach town nestled in the California Central Coast—an eclectic convergence between the tech giants, artists and colorful culture of San Francisco, and the entertainment industry and gridlock of Los Angeles. It's where people buy a home when they finally make a name for themselves. Celebrities want a small-town feel where they don't get stopped for autographs all the time, and a commute that's easy enough to get to their activity hub. I made a name for myself here, by supporting the ultra-wealthy. I started bodyguarding firms and consulted with the elite on how to keep their indiscretions discrete. And now, the empire I was building for my son was being jeopardized by unstoppable flames inching closer hour by hour.

I held my son's tiny hand in my palm as we walked back home. We were dressed for the apocalypse, but he seemed to enjoy playing dress-up. Ari Raphael bounced and played with the falling ash like snowflakes, unaware of the state of emergency or the evacuation orders for our friends and family. He is an unusually happy two-year-old. Nothing makes him happier than pretending to be a superhero by wearing a cape and shield. He loves oatmeal, Disney movies, and his special superhero cape. As we returned to our home, I sealed all the doors and windows, checked our flashlights, and turned on the HEPA air purifiers before putting Ari Raphael to bed.

The next morning, I woke up to a phone call from Lisa Campbell, a former colleague and protection specialist whose partner specializes in lung disease litigation, urging us to evacuate.

"We really don't know what is in the smoke now," said Lisa, using her professionally stern bodyguard voice over a choppy cell connection. "This isn't like the other fires. The fumes aren't just forest fire; they are from oil fields, from manure and agriculture fertilizers, petroleum products, automobiles, homes brimming with asbestos and chemicals. Get your son out. He could get permanent damage."

The air quality rating was the worst it had ever been, with hazardous ratings blaring from every television and emergency alert on our cell phones. I decided to use what little funds I had scraped together over the year for Christmas presents to buy a hotel room out of the smoke zone. Others were experiencing a lingering cough and exhaustion from the prolonged smoke exposure. As a single mom in an expensive town, it was a harder decision to make than I'd like to admit.

In the end, I chose to forego Christmas for the chance at fresh air.

The morning sky was black and raining thick chunks of ash as I briskly packed the car. The smell of bonfires and burning plastic filled our nostrils and worked its way into every crevice of even the most tightly sealed homes. I had spent my life traveling and thought I was an expert at packing in a hurry, only to end up forgetting my toothbrush and packing eight pairs of pants and only one shirt for my son when the evacuation alarms started ringing. At least I remembered the precious superhero cape. It was the only cherished possession my two-year-old had—his precious orange and gray superhero cape, lovingly sewn by his grandma for protection in all battles and adventures wherever his imagination could take him.

The car was finally packed, my son was buckled in, and with our N-95 facemasks and glasses on, we waved goodbye to the home we hoped would survive the fire, heading north to safety and breathable air. I drove for miles in the midday darkness, sweating under the stress of the mask, heat and recirculated air. Soot darkened the sky, and what was left of the sun peeking through the smoke burned a brilliant red. I let my son watch Moana on the drive, a welcome distraction that kept him from fidgeting with his facemask in the heat.

It took two hours and over 150 miles but finally the sky cleared, and the angry clouds were gone, resting behind the gentle new mountain range I never bothered to notice in previous travels. The Nine Sisters are a chain of volcanic peaks stretching to the Pacific Ocean, forming comforting new ridges and peaks that stretch to the sky and guarded us on our journey.

Hotels were filling fast with waves of refugees being driven north. I found a seaside inn with a vacancy in the quaint town of Shell Beach, California. It was an old but tidy mid-century beachfront hotel with a few funky art deco buildings scattered around a parking lot, burrowed between the main highway and beach cliffs. They cut their prices for evacuees and even upgraded us to an oceanfront suite with a fireplace. But I couldn't bear to turn on the fireplace—I had my fill of fire. Dogs and cats mewed and howled that night, muffled by the closed doors and ocean waves, as the front desk overlooked their "No Pets" policy for evacuees. With a suitcase and a sigh of relief, we moved into our new home.

That night, we listened to waves and pretended it was a vacation, comforted by being so close to the water and clean air.

The next morning, I woke up to a chipper toddler in complete darkness. It felt like it should have still been night, but my phone read 9:00 a.m. I opened the blinds to see the billowing clouds coming towards us once again.

"Let's get breakfast," I said in a light tone. Ari grabbed his cape and shield then searched for his final accessory. He found a mighty sword—a plastic spoon from the cheap coffee display in the hotel room. With his outfit complete, he marched bravely beside me as we walked down the outdoor steps and through the parking lot toward the lobby. We were both struck by the lighting. It was as if night and day happened at the same time. To the left was a bright sunny morning, and to the right were dark and looming clouds seeping over the peaks of the Nine Sisters.

We walked a few steps from the parking lot to the edge of the ocean cliffs and saw a black smoky cloud swallow up the sky again as it moved closer to us. My son stared at the black smoke and spoke up in a squeaky voice.

"Momma, cape off."

He lived, breathed and slept in his cape. I had never heard those words come from my fearless crime fighter.

"Oh, ok. You want your cape off? Why is that, honey?" I paused pensively.

His head sunk low as he muttered, "Cape off, Momma. Tefiti too strong."

I stood there stunned. This tiny human believed the evil lava monster from Moana was coming to get us. He did not think he had the strength to fight such a big force, so he no longer wanted to be any superhero at all.

"You're strong, my love. Fire can be scary. Fire can be big. We must always be careful around it. You are strong. This is not Tefiti, but it is big and things are different right now. Mommy and Ari will be okay; we're just going on an adventure, so we don't get near the black clouds. Those black clouds make us cough."

He didn't believe me. He clearly saw the clouds and darkness coming and thought the major battle of his favorite movie was coming. He felt so ill-prepared.

"You are strong, my love. Momma is strong. Let's go get breakfast and see what we can do," I urged him—with no luck. He kept telling me to take off his cape.

Just then a couple walking by paused when they heard his tired and overwhelmed pleas. The woman could have been a grandma. She had long lanky limbs and a frizzy red mane of hair. She let go of her husband's hand, walked over to Ari, and kneeled down—completely unconcerned that she was pushing the knees of her white pant legs into the sand and dirt.

"Well, hello there, superhero." She smiled wide and looked him in the eye. "My, you look big and strong today. You have a beautiful cape."

Ari looked down at the ground, then up at her, with big quivering eyes.

She continued looking straight into his eyes and said with a warm smile, "I just wanted to say thank you so much for protecting us. Thank you for protecting all of us. We are grateful to you, my super-hero." She touched the corner of his cape, looked back into his eyes for a moment, then quietly got up and left, grabbing her husband's hand and winking at me as she continued her morning beach stroll.

My eyes filled with tears. I stood there, unable to speak or thank this wise woman for her ability to inspire my child in this difficult time. He ran toward me and wrapped his arms around my leg. "I love you, Momma," he said.

"I love you too."

"Momma?"

"Yes?"

"Can I have da waffles wid cream?"

"Yes, Ari. You may have waffles and whipped cream."

We marched proudly to the lobby, with his spoon sword held high. He never asked for his cape to be taken off again.

Thank you, stranger. We were all brought together on that day by this woven blanket of smoke, fire, and anxiety seeping up the California gold coast. In the midst of chaos and uncertainty, some of the most beautiful human gestures were revealed amid our fears and panic. Thank you, stranger, for finding the words when I couldn't. Thank you for giving us all a little more superhero strength on that dark day.

From Teardrops to Raindrops

By Sherry Briscoe

After one semester of college in Florida, I decided to come back home to Idaho. Florida is a great place to visit, but I missed home, the changing of the seasons, and my family. I packed up my Volkswagen Beetle and headed out for a week's worth of adventure on the road: Disney World, the St. Louis Arch, and miles and miles of America passing by. Springtime in the northwest is beautiful. Vibrant green hillsides, bushes and trees exploding in brightly colored petals. But my little sister wanted me home for her birthday on May 24, so I had a timeline.

In my family, all the women got married young. No one went to college. They didn't explore careers or travel the world. In my family, you were no one until you were married. Your husband established your worth. I felt an urgency inside to be someone of value in my family's eyes. So when I met a wonderful man who fell in love with me and wanted to marry me, I knew I was on the right path. After three months of dating, we were wed! Getting married was exciting, blinding, and fun. The following June, our first child was born. We were a family. Soon we were four—now with a son and a daughter. Life was complete. I was someone now in my family's eyes.

I always thought of men as being the strong ones. Strength in physical and emotional arenas. And I needed that, being the insecure introvert that I was. At that time in my life I didn't know how to properly communicate with my husband. I couldn't express my feelings, my fears, my doubts. I couldn't tell him when I was upset or unhappy. Instead, my emotions bottled up inside me, gallon upon gallon. I needed his strength.

But my husband was not the man I thought he was. He was insecure, just like me. He felt threatened every time I did anything out of his total control. He told me what to wear, what to do, how to fix my hair. I couldn't buy a hamburger for lunch without his prior approval. He told me I was to stop seeing my family. His family was my family now. He took away the checkbook. I didn't have any credit cards. I had just enough money for gas. We always did our shopping together, whether at the thrift store for clothes or the grocery store for food. And again, he approved every single purchase.

I was lost. I was no longer in charge of my life. I was his wife.

He wanted to move to the Oregon coast because his brother and mother had moved there. So, we sold our house, packed up the kids, and left my family in Idaho behind.

A year later my little brother was graduating from high school with top honors. He was the Brainiac of the family. He was getting a full-ride scholarship to the college of his choice. I was so proud of him. My husband didn't want to go back to Idaho for my brother's graduation. In fact, he didn't want me to go either. And then he threw out the threat, like he always did, that if I did this thing he didn't want me to do, he would divorce me. If I went home to see my little brother graduate, I might as well stay because my husband would divorce me. And of course, it came with the added bonus that he was keeping the kids.

So, I stayed. And I missed my little brother's graduation. I missed my family. I missed my life. But I was his wife. Additional gallons of bottled-up hurt gathered inside my soul.

My mother-in-law moved to Spokane, Washington. My husband, predictably, insisted we do the same. Once more we loaded up the kids and moved inland. We bought a large turn-of-the-century home in Spokane. It was beautiful, but it needed a lot of work. My husband and I were both handy and did much of the repairs ourselves. It was a fun project. I was bored, and it gave me something to do. But the projects were not enough. I really wanted to go back to work. He finally consented, and I found a great job as a receptionist at a very large law firm downtown.

Another spring day. I got off work and admired the new summer outfits on the child mannequins in the department store windows. My husband and I were both making good money. We had practically no debt—he didn't allow it. And without even thinking, I spontaneously walked into the department store and bought each of the kids a new outfit. Nothing extravagant, nothing expensive. Just a cute pair of shorts and a top to match. I had the cash. Besides, I realized that our kids had NEVER had a new outfit. All our clothes were either something I had made or from a thrift store. Which is just fine, mind you, but every now and then, you just need something new.

With excitement, I displayed the kids' new clothes. One outfit each. Bright spring colors that matched the smiles on their faces, especially my daughter's. And then, I looked up to see the look on his face. Fury blazed in my husband's eyes. He accused me of having an affair. Why else would I do something so irrational?

What?

He yelled, "If the kids needed new clothes, you should have told me. We could have gone to the thrift store."

My spirit sank. My shoulders slumped. He didn't understand, and I didn't know how to explain it to him. Communication at a time like this was my biggest weakness. I stood silent. But he didn't. He roared at me that I might as well file for divorce. There it was. That same old ugly threat rearing its head again. Divorce. All I ever wanted was to be happily married. To be his wife. To share a home and raise a family together.

Another gallon of bottled-up emotions poured into the reservoir of my soul. I walked into the other room and cried.

Then the dam broke, and the floodwaters crashed through. It was sink or swim time. I saw a glimmer of light piercing through the surface of the water. *Here's your chance,* I thought. *Do something. Take action. Swim.*

At work the next morning, I filed for divorce. After all, I worked for one of the largest law firms in the city. You can only push a girl so far. When I went home that night and told him what I had done, he dropped into a chair with a look of shock. He said he never dreamt I would actually do it!

What in the hell did he expect? Years of threatening me with divorce anytime I looked like I was going to turn left when he wanted me to turn right. Don't tell a woman who works at a law firm to file for divorce unless you really mean it. Lesson one!

Divorced. Single parent of two. Low wages. Day care. Car payment. Rent. My family was over four hundred miles away. I was drowning again. Scared and alone. Lost. I didn't have my husband, and I didn't have *me* either. I hadn't stood up for myself ever. I didn't know how. I didn't know what I wanted, or even who I was. I was his ex-wife. What was that?

I forged on. Two-bedroom apartment. I knew I should move back home, but I didn't even have enough money to do that. I still had a job here. A good job.

On my way to work one Friday morning, I saw a bumper sticker on the car in front of me that read Expect A Miracle! A wonderful feeling washed over me. And all through the day, I reminded myself to expect a miracle. It gave me courage and hope. At quitting time, the HR Manager called me into his office and said they were doing some reorganizing and needed to let me go.

I couldn't breathe. *What do you mean you're letting me go? I'm a single parent with rent due. I need my job!*

I drove home in a daze, still not believing what had happened. "God," I said, "we need to have a clear definition of miracles! This is not what I expected."

I sat in my small apartment as the kids played. My brain was numb. I dared not ask for another miracle—that was for sure. I called my girlfriend back home and cried on her shoulder over the phone.

I had nothing. I was invisible again. No husband. No job. No money. I couldn't wade back home through the muck of disapproval and disappointment.

Three days later my girlfriend and her brother showed up at my door in a U-Haul truck. "Pack up," she said, "we're taking you home. Back to Idaho."

Back to family and friends. Back to me. Time to reinvent myself. As scared and unsure as I felt, I had an ocean of possibilities of who I could be and what I could do.

I could buy a hamburger with no prior approval and no punishment. I could stand in the storm and be cleansed by the drenching rain. I could stay there as long as I wanted, face up to the sky, arms spread out wide, twirling wet and free. I was *me* again.

Put in the Time

By Michele Brito

For my champion, my mother, work was a scattered and necessary activity that brought no joy. It wasn't meant to. It was meant to bring money. Between home and whichever hours she worked off a future debt, Mom seemed to amass a guilt relieved only by narrating her trials to us—my brother and me—filtered through an immigrant meme of sacrificing time and passion to fulfill needs and responsibilities. I could never let her in on how rocky my foundation got. In my twenties, I was financially unsteady, but I knew that if I let her know, she would urge me to return home from California and I might even be low enough to accept.

So I told her my success stories, such as once getting surprised by a job offer when a friend called out of the blue to ask if I'd do social media work for a startup. I told her that it was a job with a salary, not a paycheck. I shared stories of witnessing people younger than me make hay in the digital-sun. How it felt like we had no bosses, just clients. How we all felt like collaborators on a great project. How I flourished in this work environment, getting two promotions and a raise in five months.

But other details I did not share: how the open-plan office

space—the kind that sets all politics on a stage—was filled with competitive twenty-somethings nurturing a gossipy reality-show-style atmosphere in which personal issues became professional obstacles and underhanded sexist remarks grew into blatant violations of Title IX.

The truth was what I didn't tell my mother. At the startup's first Christmas party, the youngest of the CEOs, age twenty-three, asked me to follow him to the far end of the office where nothing we said could be heard. "We're firing Harry," he blurted. "You can have his job." Harry was this CEO's childhood best friend. I thought if Harry wasn't safe here, who was? He saw my hesitation and said, "It's just business."

I knew it wasn't just business. But I also knew what my answer would be. I accepted the position because it would be more than I had ever earned. Within a month I cleared my debt, padded my bank account, and flew to New York to fill my mother's empty apartment with furniture.

And suddenly I was the only woman in the C-suite. I was the campaign manager. My job essentially consisted of protecting the CEOs from their own bad decisions and convincing the company lawyer to dismiss the sequential copyright infringements. The men in the room, with their sneakers propped on the desks, crudely discussed the drugs and models they enjoyed the night before. The CMO, who received his cues from social media, encouraged this party behavior as Influencer or Disrupter Culture. The CFO casually commented on fudging numbers because he wanted the reports to be impressive. The CEO had a habit of cornering employees with personal questions or riddles, just for fun. I tried to maintain relationships with my original group of trusted co-workers—the women who'd kept note of sexist remarks and general violations of human resources—but found that I was now a boss, and our lives and schedules didn't sync up anymore. It was a hideous culture, and I was in the center of it, earning plenty of money, but watching my workdays fill with trials that I could narrate to nobody.

When the nascent company finally hired someone for Human Resources, I asked for a meeting. But first, I called a lunch of trusted co-workers, women I'd leaned on and helped, to meet in a safe space where we could share grievances and be one another's witnesses.

Though the lunch held the tension of a brewing spectacle, I was the only one who voiced a complaint. Was there fear among the group? Or was I just like the rest of the C-suite: morally malleable and untrustworthy?

It was 8 p.m. on a Tuesday, and I was at a supermarket, paying no attention to the fruit or to my husband, who was making excellent suggestions for meal prep. I shuffled my feet behind him, staring at the blinking ellipses on my phone. The CEO was processing what I had just sent him. My question: "Am I good at my job?"

My husband asked why I would send such a question.

But to me it was important. Even before I pressed "send," I knew the answer: I was very good at my job. But I didn't want to be good at it anymore. I spent my days apologizing for the bad behavior of my young male colleagues, providing them with outs, justifications, and often giving them the wherewithal to continue breaking whatever rules they deemed unnecessary. I was an enabler. Sending that message, I realized that the CEO's answer didn't matter to me. The question has answered itself. I refused to be good at this job anymore.

I have often heard the refrain "You've got to put in the time." I recognized that night that in my career I was giving up not only my time, but worse. I was giving up my values. Our values are priceless. In losing them, my lowest point had come with my highest paycheck.

I decided to make a change. I would put in the time with myself.

With a padded savings account and no new bosses lined up, I restored my prized commodity: time. I handed in my resignation, and I took back my time and my skillset, putting them to a use that I actually cared about—figuring out how to do work that brings both joy and money, that satisfies passion and responsibility. One generation after my mother, I can tell a different story.

Enough

By Dawn Brockett

Let's get this out of the way: anorexia is not about control. Anorexia is like trying to bake a tall, round, crusty, pocketed loaf of bread when you have been given frigidity and salt to feed the yeast instead of sweetness and warmth. The anorectic, working with the wrong ingredients before she is savvy enough to know the difference, arrives at the table with a hard, dense, inedible brick, and then is beaten to a psychological pulp for this failure by the very voices and thoughts that tricked her into believing that she had enough—all that she needed and plenty to share.

Anorexia is about shrinking to accommodate the space that you have been allowed to take up in your life, the exact amount of space that you can hold without making anyone else uncomfortable. Healing from anorexia is an act of insubordination, of self-defense. You must fill the space that you have been denied—the space that someone else thinks belongs to him. Be assured, he will fight back, accustomed as he is to taking up all the space that he desires, unquestioned, unchallenged.

The widely accepted social narrative holds that anorectics are perfectionists, risk-averse, and controlling. On the first two, I surrender.

Yes, layers and complexity are collapsed into convenient labeling, but all sides of the argument end in nearly the same location, in subtleties not worth dissecting here. However, with the control claim, I take singular and serious issue. It is a label not merely of convenience, but of false identity, a tool to minimize, a corrupting blame misplaced. The 'anorectic as control freak' accusation is a straw man argument: false, evasive of the real problem, easy to destroy.

So, if a person's goal is to simply destroy her—to define the identity of the shrinking person, to shape her agency in the way that will best reflect onto him, to excise her hope of finding the will to take up a column of self-sustaining space in the world—he should carry on with this self-serving attack. Label her controlling; walk away; feel superior. She will shrink further, and he can puff himself up into the space that she surrenders, feeling deserving about his bloated sense of self-worth, further buoyed by the twisted kindness of the illness: her guilt for having inconvenienced him by simply *existing* will drive her to exist less, ever smaller.

It is not true that I was happy to learn that my father is a narcissistic sociopath—it is just that the relief of the diagnosis coming from a licensed, tenured, respected psychologist was so profound that it was nearly indistinguishable from a certain kind of happiness. Knowing this one thing sans doute clarified so many disparate parts of my life. It was the puzzle piece I was missing, without which my experiences felt random and cruel and deeply disconcerting.

I love my dad, almost as much as I can't stand him. Ours is not a standard-issue father-daughter story of angel and demon behavior, of wit and charm, frustration and rebellion, followed predictably by reconciliation. Truth is, I don't really know what a standard-issue father-daughter story is. I have seen some from a distance. They look a lot like Disney to me: delightful but terribly unrealistic under the laws of my natural world, where there is no daddy-daughter dance—there is only destruction. Ours is an oilfield aflame—a wealth of possibility turned toxic, irrelevant, and permanently mind-altering.

This is not a love story—at least, I don't think it is. I am too young to pretend to know how large a narrative love can hold. Unlimited, you may say. Love underscores the plots of epic sagas. It holds the extremities of human existence. It soothes the unnamed condition. It heals all things. But you don't know my father.

In the words of Euripides, the great Greek playwright, "To a father growing old, nothing is dearer than a daughter." Aristotle considered him to be the most tragic of the playwrights, likely because his works shifted the focus from gods to man, driving the tragedy deeper into the core of daily living. He was among the first to allow for intelligence in slave characters and depth in female characters.

My father could learn something from this man, who lived nearly 1500 years ago. My father, who is now growing old without the dear benefit of his daughter. My father, who laughed at and dismissed boundaries. My father who took up every square inch of space in the room, in my world, in my mind. He believed that it was his to take.

My dad gave me the outdoors and a love of nature. He trained my eyes to catch every small deviation, to move through the world as resilient prey—a dangerous assignment, evermore so given that the hunter lived within. In defensive mode, I am quick to spot an animal from only a flutter or a subtle shade difference deep in the neutral woods. I notice the texture of the snow and how long it has lain undisturbed on the ground since a living creature tread upon it. I am comfortable in a wide range of temperatures and conditions. I need little preparation, adapting like the alter ego of the pea-disturbed princess. I move silently. I prefer low light or darkness. My trust is earned with great difficulty.

Despite feeling hunted throughout most of my life, I prefer solitude. I am not a pack animal; I do not embrace the protective comforts of community. Deep, quiet, enduring aloneness rejuvenates and strengthens me, prepares me to outrun the monster, to outwit the master, to say "no" to the tyrant.

This I have learned: to defeat the demon, you must hold your ground and appear large. You must fully inhabit your space. You must stop depriving yourself to feed him.

He will try to make you look crazier than you already feel. Someone is going to get hurt. Someone has taken squatter's rights on your sanity. The moment that you know for certain that the space is yours, and that you are willing to defend it, you can know that you are going to win. No doubt, you will lose many battles in this war but, in the end, you will win by inhabiting the place in this world that rightfully belongs to you.

The potential that fills you, seeps out through your generosity, it is yours to direct, to fulfill and at times when you must, to abandon. This living is an act of creativity, not of control.

Refuse him the right to write his failed life story on your bones. Your story is your own to craft, in your beautiful handwriting, your open prose.

Anorexia wrote several chapters of my life story. My closest consort for many years, the most lethal of the scientifically classified mental illnesses, I know her intimately. In moments of overwhelm, I still wish to disappear, to fade into stardust. Nagging physical pain or emotional discomfort distract and fatigue my awareness. Fortifying routines become compromised. My guard lowers, and the punch lands. Dizzy, and with thoughts like stars circling my field of reality, I begin to believe the voice finding fault with my simple contentment.

In harsh tones, the internal voice of anorexia tells me that I would feel fundamentally different if I weighed remarkably less, if I denied myself one thing or another, if I cinched my discipline corset an inch, preferably more. The voice holds incredible power; it drove me to a cacophony of outrageous decisions that ultimately resulted in my physical body weighing half of the lowest recommended healthy weight for my height. The voice sneers that peace lies in dimming the lights of the world to black, evaporating obligations and responsibilities and ties that bind. "Tuck in for a very long, cold nap," it offers. Eyes lower, then clench, breathing all but ceases, a sort of compensatory hibernating paralysis holds me in its clutches until something breaks the spell.

Anorexia nervosa isolates and kills, like the true predator that it is. Yet, contrary to typical predatory behavior, it seeks the strongest, the brightest, the kindest, and the most capable. Anorexia craves the best. First, it must weaken its prey with the most powerful weapon of all: thoughts. Anorexia usurps the logical processes of the mind, generating a Moebius loop of self-loathing. Starvation is merely a method, one that can further warp the mind with its endless counting, denial, craving, restriction, allowances, guilt, confessions and penitence. It is a complex death march of religious proportion.

What breaks the spell? Space and healthy connections (you'll recognize these by their easy respect for your boundaries). Breaking commitments that hold you to unrealistic terms. Taking extraordinary risk. Cultivating a feeling of being enough. Sensory saturation, touch, hot coffee, physical activity, gentle and benign words that cannot be easily twisted or strained. Love with loads of space.

The world turns upside down, then right side up again. The sun bursts through the clouds, revealing a way forward. A scene of possibility emerges into view. Something substantive, strong and solid stitches and patches the battle wounds. It feels like self-respect, and it provides more strength and sustenance than any father—or any other person to whom society recommends I sublet my unique human value—ever could. I stand now, with less fear. Having scrambled up this treacherous mountain to defeat the predator that feels too often inseparable from myself, the distinction at times impossible to make. I wonder. What other powerful solidity lies within reach from this place?

I gave up on the bitter illusion of perfection. To release this false hope is to slay the dragon. Healing is a human feat fueled by self-reflection: name and remind yourself of your boundaries in order to claim and reinforce them. You may, as I do, forget and surrender them a hundred times. Reclaim them for the 101st time. Do it again and again. To shift out of prey vulnerability, know your strengths and your enemy's kill points. They are one and the same; as you grow in strength and stature, as you hold the boundaries of yourself, you force him out of your space. You must leverage everything that you have within you. You have more than you realize, all that you need. Enough. You are worth the effort.

The Phoenix of the Polo Grounds

By Laura Bruno

I know when I'm falling off a horse. It usually starts with a stretch: I've either stretched too far out of the saddle or I've put my weight too far ahead on the horse or too far on one side. That one side is usually my right side, the side on which I carry the mallet.

Then, there's the moment when I know I'm off balance. I know because my hands are in front of me, trying to rebalance myself with the neck of the horse. It isn't a great idea because the horse, feeling the pressure on his neck from the imbalance while knowing the rider's body language, will try to get out of the pressure. The horse will lift his head to push the rider away like a branch, or step sideways to avoid the imbalance, or even run harder because he's now scared of the imbalance the rider created.

If I'm off balance, it's usually because I'm either not following the horse in a turn, or the horse didn't follow me in a turn. Whichever the reason, I'm off balance and falling, knowing I'll hit the ground coming at me like a Viking with a huge hammer, and I close my eyes. Then there is nothing. Except for a big thump.

I'm a very proud person and I almost always spring back up on my two legs, if I've fallen on any body part other than my own two feet. For the record, I've only fallen on my feet once. Falling on your feet is the least dangerous way to fall yet the most difficult to accomplish. Only once has the air escaped from my lungs. It was serious. I just couldn't breathe air back in. It was scary. Yet, even with all of the falls I've lived through, I have always put that left foot back into the stirrup, hopping back into the saddle every time—no exceptions, even if it hurts.

Even last week.

I travelled to Argentina to play polo and spend time with my partner and his family. He has faith in my potential in the saddle. I picked up my first mallet seven years ago. I'm now in my fourth season of playing polo at the Polo Parc Farms, in Montreal, Canada. In total, I've only played for about twelve months. And in those months, I've twice been voted most-improved player of the club. My learning curve is still on the rise.

So, here I was, in Tafí del Valle, Tucumán—a province in north-west Argentina. We had been playing every day that permitted, as you can't play polo in the rain. The prior week was no different from the rest. Yet, the mare I was riding, Tucumana, was too fast for my body. As soon as she would read my mind, she would turn swiftly, and I would lose my balance and fall.

The first fall, on Thursday, was my first fall landing on my feet. Tucumana turned one way and I went the other way. I tried to stay on, holding onto her neck, squeezing my legs. But nothing helped and I slid off her left side and landed perfectly.

"Are you okay?" the players asked.

"Yes, yes," I said, as I rushed back onto my horse.

At the end of the match, Pablito, one of the pros on the field, apologized, as if it were his fault. "No no, don't worry. It's okay. I'm okay. You don't need to apologize," I said as I winked and smirked.

Polo, especially in Argentina, is mostly a man's world. If there's a woman playing, they watch their language, which I'm not against, yet they sometimes let you hit the ball instead of playing normally. They can, for example, "check their horse"—meaning to slow down, in order to allow a woman or a beginner to hit the ball. I don't like that. If they don't play normally, how will I ever learn and better my game? Don't do that. Don't apologize as if you were in my way and it was your fault, I thought. It was my fault I fell. I lost balance.

The next day, I was back in the saddle. We were playing again. Rafa, one of my teammates, made a backhand hit and, according to him, I was so surprised by his beautiful hit that I fell off of the horse. I don't really know what happened—I only remember looking at Rafa as he was preparing his backhand shot. Then, I thought to myself, "We have to turn now." And, as if Tucumana had read my mind, she turned before I was ready. I lost my balance and tried to regain it but there was no chance. I was in the air. The ground was coming up quickly. I closed my eyes. Thump. And I was on the ground.

I sprang up, as I tended to do quickly, and in a matter of seconds I was back on Tucumana again. I must've fallen on my right shoulder because the next day things went wrong. Saturday, I hurt myself doing a wrong movement as I was going to hook one of the opposite team's players. It shouldn't have affected me but with the previous days' falls, the clock was ticking on my injuries.

Truthfully, I didn't want to play that day. I actually didn't want to play on any of those days, as I'd been quite down on my polo playing. I came to Argentina from Montreal to play polo, to better my game, and yet I felt as though I was not improving. I was practicing with my partner and he'd tell me all the bad moves and bad shots I was taking. I had lost the fun of playing.

I wanted go back home. I was coming off the field with tears in my eyes after every chukka (a period of play in polo, lasting seven to eight minutes each). I couldn't believe what I was feeling. Polo and horses are my passions. And now, I didn't feel like stepping on the field, let alone getting on a horse again.

All of these doubts came up in my head after each game. My partner was lending me his horses and I was supposed to help take care of the horses yet I felt useless. He'd lived his entire life around horses; my family was mostly scared of them. They didn't understand my passion—neither the game nor the fun and happiness it brought out in me when I was playing. My family was just waiting for me to hang up my polo mallets and get serious with my life. They wanted me to go into a "normal" profession and be done with polo.

Let me tell you, that Saturday, when I came off the third chukka and decided to double Tucumana, which simply means to play her two chukkas in one game, my right shoulder had begun to hurt. Being so proud and full of adrenaline, I got on my last horse and went out to play my last chukka. At the end of it, I could barely get off the horse. I was almost happy I was hurt and could not officially play the next day.

That Sunday was my low point. Seeing my partner get on his horse and canter onto the field for the first chukka, as I was standing on the side of the field, broke my heart.

That was my question: if I was going to come off the field with tears in my eyes, feeling like I couldn't play and better myself, then what exactly was I doing in Argentina? I knew that I was still there, where I felt I was supposed to be, and where I felt happiest. The frustration I was feeling was just, I hoped, a plateau I'd hit and overcome, even if it hurt. Just like writing about it hurts.

Being on a horse and galloping after a tiny plastic ball, with a mallet in my hands, is a unique feeling. Doing this with seven other players on a polo field is exhilarating. I can't get enough of these feelings.

So, being benched today, on the day I am writing, not knowing what my injury is exactly, means that I don't know if I'll be able to play polo in a while or maybe ever again. I don't know if I'll have a polo career. The only thing I do know is that no matter what, I'll get better. I'll get back on a horse.

The Two Jizos

By Nancy Buffington

It started with a miscarriage. After the blood, the pain, the unexpected passing of the fetus in the toilet, there was only grief, a great gasping hole in my world that refused to fill.

Months went by—enough time to have a second miscarriage. I realized finally that I was wrapping myself in grief like a thick winter coat, not wanting to feel better, as that would require separating myself from those babies.

But I had a six-year-old son and a husband; I was wanted back in the land of the living. The question became how to find my way back.

I felt I needed a ritual, but of course our culture hardly mentions miscarriage at all, much less offers a structured, communal way to mark this most tender of losses.

I needed an object, I decided. Something to remember these babies by—especially the first one, since I was almost at the end of my first trimester with that one, and in our innocence, we'd already told everyone about the baby and chosen its name. I'd lost them both before we'd bought clothes or toys, or anything I could cradle or enshrine. I needed something to contain my love and my loss: a focal point for what might have been.

And so, I turned to religious items. My family didn't go to church when I was young, but growing up in New Mexico made me a life-long cultural Catholic, a sucker for holy candles and scapulars, and a half-believer in Milagros. A santo, I thought—with the overabundance of Catholic saints, I'll find myself a Saint for Lost Babies.

I got online (this was in the earliest days of the internet; it was my first-ever attempt to buy something online). The search was slow and fruitless. I learned (according to that long-ago search, at least) that Catholics have patron saints for almost every malady—even indigestion and hemorrhoids—but not for miscarried babies.

So I looked eastward. My then-husband Clyde had lived in Japan for a few years before we'd met. The Japanese have a Buddha named Jizo, he told me, who protects pregnant women and babies—including miscarried and aborted babies. That was all I needed.

Clyde remembered he'd brought back a Jizo from Japan; after a couple hours of searching through thirty-odd Japanese cardboard boxes, he came back victorious. He held a small box covered in white and gray stripes. Inside was a beautiful, tasteful Jizo, but he seemed unapproachable: cast in metal, slim, with a serious face. Not for babies.

I didn't hide my disappointment—I really needed this to be right. Clyde, working hard to placate me, offered up his Jizo as a "placeholder" until we found a more comforting one. So I put Cold Jizo on my nightstand and got back online.

Many images of Jizo are on the cute side, chubby, round-faced and bald, as befits a guardian of babies. This is what I wanted: something almost cuddly, if a statue can be cuddly. I found what looked like just the thing on the Shasta Abbey monastery website: roundish and sweet, stone gray. I placed the order and started obsessing over each day's mail.

The package came about ten days later. I went in the bedroom, closed the door, sat on the bed and prepared for Cuddly Jizo to heal my heart.

Alas, it was not to be. Cuddly Jizo was mottled gray plaster, with a visible seam running up and down both his sides where plaster had seeped outside his mold. He was hollow. And leaned to the right when you stood him up. I cried a little, then packed Crooked Jizo and sent him straight back to Shasta Abbey.

On to Plan C. Clyde still had good friends in Japan. They fanned out in a great search, determined to find the Jizo that would finally be It. Dozens of emails and a couple months went by—this one was way too big, that one was way too expensive.

Finally, Clyde heard from a friend that she'd found "the one" in a monastery—the right size, the right price—and it had even been blessed by a Buddhist priest. "Let's do it," we emailed. And we started stalking the mail carrier once again.

When it finally arrived a couple weeks later, we waited until our son was asleep, then shut ourselves in our bedroom to unwrap it. Inside the package was a lovely card, and a small box with white and gray stripes. And inside the box—Jizo. Beautiful, tasteful Jizo: metal, slim, with the serious face. Identical in every way to Cold Jizo who'd lived on my nightstand this whole time. Even the box was identical.

I laughed and laughed—uncontrollable belly laughs I hadn't felt in months. The message was instantly clear to me: "the Buddha you want is the Buddha you already have."

It took me months, a worldwide search for statuary, and two identical Jizos to finally get me to understand: I'd been looking across the world for healing, and what I needed was at home, right next to me. My son and my husband, not to mention a whole world full of magic and mystery. My two twin Jizos, who still stand side by side on my nightstand seventeen years later, remind me of that every day. As does my sixteen-year-old son, conceived a year to the day after that first miscarriage.

Self-Love

By Lindsey Byars

I stand in front of the mirror every morning naked, examining the carnage of nearly forty years and giving birth to three children. The crow's feet kissing the corners of my eyes, the strands of silver in my hair, and the hundreds of freckles that seem to be joining forces to become age spots are not nearly as horrific as what's going on below the lines on my neck that grow deeper with each passing year.

My breasts are massive and now point toward the floor. They've always been large, but the once-firm melons are now squishy. If this were the fruit isle in the grocery story, these two would get tossed out. They're covered in silvery stretchmarks from the pulls and tugs of hungry babies. I will eventually pour them into a push-up bra and place my hope in the power of Victoria and all her secrets.

After my first natural childbirth, I decided pulling my vagina apart once was enough. I opted for a cesarean section with my second child. And when my IUD failed and I found myself pregnant for a third time, I told the doctor that he could use the same path and take out my tubes while he was in there. My C-section scar stretches across my lower abdomen, or at least I assume it does because I can't seem to see it anymore thanks to my round stomach that now sags below the incision. Imagine putting a marshmallow into the microwave, letting it puff up, and then turning off the heat. What's left is a lumpy pile of misshapen mess covered in squiggly silver trails all framing my worn-out bellybutton. My bellybutton itself could be the abandoned den of some small burrowing animal.

Take a baked potato and shove two baby carrots into it. That's my shape, a round torso held up by short, stubby, round legs.

If I really want to torture myself, I jump up and down to see what jiggles the most. I could blame media's portrayal of the female form for my utter disgust, but it's deeper. I'm raising two girls, and as much as I hate my physical form, I work so hard not to say words like "fat" or "diet" in front of them. We talk about health, portions, drinking plenty of water, and trying to recognize when we're hungry or just eating because it's there. It's exhausting, especially when I loathe my own body, but I'm determined not to let the voice of their mother shape any negative views of their bodies.

When I was growing up in the late 80s, Richard Simmons was sweating to the oldies, encouraging women to love themselves and dance away the body that held them back from happiness. I dug the tunes, but seeing overweight women dancing didn't inspire me. Denise Austin was the fitness queen, and her tapes lined our VHS collection.

To this day, I hate her voice.

I can remember doing millions of crunches, trying not to vomit, while the Barbie-type blond counted effortlessly, never sweating or losing her breath. I wanted to punch her in the face. While seeing the perfect bodies working out made me think I too would one day achieve such fitness, their ease doing what I felt was impossible just pissed me off. As a teenager, I felt like a badass round-house kicking with Billy Blanks, but never seemed to look like one. I tried yoga, purchasing a copy from the sale bin at Wal-Mart, but that was boring and I got lightheaded with all that breathing. I lacked the motivation to regularly adopt any workout routine, so I never seemed to get the results I dreamed of when I started. Getting that bikini-ready body felt impossible.

"You could probably lose ten pounds if you stopped drinking soda," my mother would say, often accompanied by "hold your stomach in."

She had been thin growing up, but childbirth and emotional eating had taken its toll, so whether it was Weight Watchers or Slim Fast, she was always trying the latest and greatest diet craze. She meant well, but I spent years wearing baggy tee shirts or anything that didn't touch my stomach, which evidently stuck out more than it should. I was not skinny like many of my friends, but I was athletic.

Looking back at pictures, I was small compared to today's average teen. But in the 80s and 90s, the goal was Cindy Crawford or anyone from the original cast of 90210 and I was nowhere close to their physiques. "How can I ever attract a man if I can't look like these women?" was the thought that consumed me, never taking into consideration that my health mattered. Looking good to men trumped any other reason to be physically fit.

In college, I got a Sam's Club membership just so my roommate and I could buy Slim Fast in bulk. I had a boyfriend, but I was still incredibly insecure with my physical form, especially when that form was buck naked. "Let's just keep the lights off" was the only thing that made me feel remotely comfortable during sex. When I graduated from college and got my first apartment, I cut out nearly naked pictures from People magazine of Jessica Simpson, who was to be the latest Daisy Duke. I taped them all over the inside of my cabinets where the snacks lived. The Atkins diet was popular, so for months, I lived on frozen hamburger patties left over from my graduation cookout and bags of salad. I pressed each frozen patty on my new George Forman grill, and within a short amount of time, I had lost quite a bit of weight, noticeable to my college friends who hadn't graduated yet and my boyfriend, turned fiancé.

The thing about a fad and being an emotional eater is that this type of progress will not last. No amount of weight loss could combat how I felt about myself, and gaining the weight all back triggered a depression that altered the trajectory of my career.

Adulting was not the adventure I dreamed it would be. I was working at a local news station as a producer, making a salary that qualified me for food stamps. I was paying bills for the first time and discovering things like personal property taxes, car payments, and rent. I had a schedule different from most of the world, so I was lonely. My best friends became Ben and Jerry, Samantha, Miranda, Charlotte, and Carrie. I watched Sex and the City in bed all night, living vicariously on the streets of New York, then slept until it was time to go into work at 2:30 pm. The weight came back, the stress increased, my clothes didn't fit, and the hate I had for myself impacted the confidence I lacked at work as a young, inexperienced person in the adult world. I decided maybe news wasn't for me since I was unable to handle the criticism from consultants who not only questioned my producing abilities, but the way I dressed, which evidently was not professional enough for the industry. I went back to school to become something different. I equated my lack of confidence in my career to the idea that perhaps I just chose the wrong one and needed to try again. In actuality, I wasn't comfortable with myself, so trying to find my place in the world was a struggle. This would not be my final career switch.

I eventually married my college boyfriend, barely squeezing into the wedding dress I had purchased six months before our wedding day. He loved me even when I didn't. This helped the loneliness, but now I was living with a man who could eat his weight in junk food and never gain a pound. I bought food and cooked to please him, and in turn, ate the portions he was able to eat. The first year we were married, I weighed more than I ever had in my entire life, and that number and the measurements I kept taking of every inch of my frame continued to increase as we welcomed our first child into the world.

At this point, you're probably picturing a contestant for The Biggest Loser, but as I stand naked in my bathroom, nearing forty and still recovering from the birth of my third child, I would kill for the body I couldn't stand to look at fifteen years ago. From high school well into my twenties, I wore anywhere from a women's size ten to twelve. These are not enormous, and today, the sizes are on the lower end of the national average. But all I could see were rolls of fat flowing over the top of my pants, the surface area of a chair my thighs covered when I sat down, the way my arm fat wobbled when I waved. Today, wearing a size fourteen, what I long for more than anything is the body shape I managed to achieve with the help of P90X and my husband's OCD dedication to working out and eating right.

By the time our first child turned one, I was in the best shape of my life. Ninety days with Tony Horton and my husband pushing me through moments when I didn't want to work out paid off. I was a size eight, smaller than I ever was in high school. Just when I was starting to feel comfortable in my skin, and as others around me praised me for my ability to get in shape, my husband said, "Well, we can always do better." I know in my heart he meant it as motivation to keep working, to feed the OCD demon he struggles with daily, but in that moment, my mind reverted back to hating my body, to never being satisfied with how I looked. As much as praise from others made me feel good about myself, his comment did the opposite, because even though I was no longer a girl child, I measured my beauty and my worth in the eyes of others. It didn't matter that I felt amazing; what mattered was that he thought we could do better, that what I had done wasn't enough.

Our firstborn is now ten, and raising a young woman has made me acutely aware of how she sees herself. Last year, she said to me on a walk, "Are my thighs big? They're bigger than most girls." Already, her mind was focused on what her body was not, and I wanted to cry. I explained to her that she was amazingly perfect.

"We are athletic women, not fragile flowers," I said.

We talked about the importance of working out to be healthy, and not eating too much sugar or more than a portion of something because it's bad for our health. We looked at my Fitbit and talked about calories going in and the energy needed to burn them—that you can't take in more than you're burning. I told her that while I was trying to lose weight left over from the birth of her baby brother, it was because it's not good for my heart to carry around all that extra weight. I want her to care about her body and her health, and while I said these things for her, I was also trying to convince myself. Still. All these decades later.

"Do I need to lose weight, Momma?" she asked. And I replied, "Absolutely not. You, my love, are perfect."

In a moment of self-loathing and longing for that fit frame of my late twenties, I broke out P90X. I am no longer in my twenties. As I sit here typing, I've pulled a muscle in my back after one day, yes one day of Tony torture. I cried, mad at my body for failing me. I am mad I still have twenty pounds of baby weight to get rid of. I'm mad that maybe it will take me longer than it used to. In some ways, though, my complicated relationship with my body image has changed. More than being skinny, I do want to enter these next decades of my life energetic, ready and able to climb mountains with my children, and hopefully one day, with my grandchildren. My husband still thinks my need to look a certain way hinges on his approval. "But I think you look great!" he says, like his opinion should be enough. And then his own insecurities creep in: "As long as you're not trying to look good for someone else." I honestly believe he prefers me larger and depressed because it means he won't have to compete with another man. But I am no longer twenty, so I tell him that I could give a shit if he or anyone else is happy with my appearance. I'm not happy, I'm not energetic, and I'm the one that matters most.

After teaching high school for eleven years, I happened upon a job that allowed me to work in education and public relations, writing and helping promote a university. In my late thirties I have stumbled on a different kind of confidence in who I am and what I am capable of, so I ended career number two and accepted the position. It's challenging and requires assertiveness that I never possessed in my twenties, and I love it. I traded my Vans for heels and cardigans for power suits. They're too tight right now, but I'm going to grant myself some grace as I work to get my body back into them. My back needs to heal, after all. And damn it, they make a power suit in a size larger than what's hanging in my closet, so I can always buy something new, because unlike my bank account of years gone by, there's some money in there.

I stand naked before my bathroom mirror with the lights on. What I'm looking at is a body that has gone the distance, lumpy like a topographic map with lines that stretch over mountains and valleys. This body has grown and borne three children. This body has carried me across many parts of Europe and the United States. I cannot completely silence the years of hating this body for not being like the bodies of others, but I try to tell myself that now is the time to be kinder to myself. How I treat this temple will impact how my children treat theirs. I don't want to tear down her walls and build a new structure. I just need to add some bracing to sagging floors and walls so she'll stand tall, confident. I need to restore the faith inside these temple walls. It doesn't matter if anyone else loves this body or desires this body. I need to love and desire being with myself. And maybe, just maybe, if I keep spending time naked before this mirror, remembering all the places I've gone and the many I have left to see, I'll learn how to drown the hate with respect, and hopefully one day, adoration.

The Messiness of Perseverance

By Kate Canute

The year 2012 was a banner year for me, in almost every way it could have been. My artsy electro-rock-hybrid band—my *raison d'etre* for as long as I could remember—released a full-length album in March. A somewhat-neurotic perfectionist, I had worked for the better part of a decade creating and fine-tuning the sound and lyrics, and had the good fortune to work with a record producer who was not only well connected, but one whose work I greatly admired as well. On the night of the release party, our favorite local venue was a packed house—fans, friends and colleagues mingled with curious neophytes who were drawn to the performance by radio ads and word of mouth. At the end of the evening, wrapped in bliss and the best kind of exhaustion, I drifted off knowing that I was on the precipice of something I had worked nearly my whole life to achieve.

The rest of the year was a whirlwind—rehearsals bled into lengthy drives to new venues in new towns, and subsequent performances to crowds of varying size and enthusiasm levels. A theater in Jacksonville with a large stage and an apparently non-existent marketing team produced few new fans but some high-pro photos, while a small-town dive bar (the audio engineer called my keyboard stand a "contraption" in exactly the deep-south accent you would expect) was an entertaining night with a raucous crowd. "Sleep It Off Sunday" became a weekly event—a day to recharge my batteries in front of the television and rest up for the coming week. I had always been an energetic person—some of my more blunt friends and acquaintances might have said I was "tightly wound"—and for once, this was more of an asset than an annoyance. There was plenty to do.

Then, in late 2012, something began to go wrong. The first signs of trouble came with a strange pinching feeling deep in my right hip during hot yoga classes. My teacher had a drill sergeant demeanor and was an excessively tan and wiry old curmudgeon who encouraged us to push through any uncomfortable sensations. This fed into my competitive nature in the worst possible way, and I ignored the pain and kept going. By the time Christmas arrived, the pain was no longer intermittent—it was a mind-numbing electrical zap that snaked down my right leg any time I put weight on it. It got so bad that I had to walk with a cane all of the time—fortunately, I had some theater-buff friends who lent me some very stylish canes to use during performances. I scheduled an appointment with a doctor recommended by a friend, who scheduled a series of corticosteroid injections that he insisted would improve my situation.

By April of 2013, I had been given three corticosteroid injections, and the pain in my hip (which turned out to be called Sacroiliac Joint Dysfunction) was greatly reduced. But in its place, a new concern arose. I began to suffer from an incredibly painful headache, one that was impervious to any pain medicine I took, and got worse every day. I had experienced migraines throughout my childhood and early adulthood, but this headache was a wholly different animal. It began with a pressure at the base of my skull and spread to my entire head over the course of the month. My eyes became blurry, and I was constantly nauseated. I kept telling myself it would get better, but it only seemed to get worse. The escalating pain and a weight loss of fifteen pounds due to vomiting forced my husband's hand—against my wishes, he insisted that I go to the emergency room.

I didn't realize it at the time, but I would not be leaving that hospital for 119 days. I had somehow contracted a very rare form of fungal meningitis that only affects the immunocompromised. When they found that my CD4+ count (often referred to as a "T-cell count" when discussing immune deficiency) was critically low, they tested me for HIV, the virus that causes AIDS. When the first test came back negative, they shook their heads and re-tested—five HIV tests, five negative results. Doctors were baffled, and I continued to get sicker. A neurosurgeon placed a shunt to pull excess cerebrospinal fluid from my skull, to ease the mounting pressure on my brain. A PICC line—a sort of semi-permanent IV—was placed in each of my arms, and I was started on a harsh anti-fungal medication called Amphotericin-B. I forgot how to walk. When I spoke, my words came out in senseless jumbles of word-salad. And I lived in a hallucinatory haze as my body and brain deteriorated.

And then something happened that saved my life—my main infectious disease doctor went on vacation. The doctor who took her place that weekend immediately recognized two important facts. First, I was having regular absence seizures caused by encephalitis, which was separate from the meningitis I had been fighting up until then, and required an addition to my medication regimen. Second, he recognized the signs of an extremely rare immune deficiency called Idiopathic CD4+ Lymphocytopenia (ICL for short). Somehow, this doctor who had, years earlier, been part of the first cohort of doctors to study the disorder at the National Institutes of Health, had ended up working at the very southern Florida hospital where I was dying of something my assigned doctors couldn't name. If I had been a religious sort, I might have called it a miracle.

This new doctor was positive that an old medication used to boost the immune systems of patients suffering from HIV/AIDS was my best hope to come out of this alive. When my insurance balked at the cost and complained about "off-label usage" and the hospital lamented the difficulty of finding and ordering this out-of-fashion treatment, the doctor didn't give in. He went around his supervisors and ordered the $24,000 per week medication anyway. When the medicine arrived, he began the treatment—a series of injections that occurred every other day, and made me even more nauseous than I already was. After a couple of weeks, my immune system finally began to rebound, and the anti-fungal and anti-viral medications I had been taking for over a month finally began to do their work.

I left the hospital in August of 2013, with an order to return daily for continued infusions of Amphotericin-B (or "Ampho-Terrible," as it is called by those of us who are unfortunate enough to have experienced it firsthand). I weighed a grand total of eighty-seven pounds—all of the muscle I had built up over years of exercise and careful eating had wasted away, leaving me confined to a wheelchair. I had lost the vision in my right eye when the pressure my swelling brain placed on my optic nerve was too much to bear, and my brain sounded and felt like constant AM radio static, as if someone was indiscriminately changing the frequency with the volume turned up to eleven.

In the movies, recovering from a serious illness or injury is almost always treated in the same fashion—a montage of relentlessly upward progress set to an inspirational power-ballad, ending in the main character's assured triumph. The hero is broken but unbending, and over three minutes they regain all of their old physical and mental abilities through grit, tenacity, and the support of their dedicated friends. The only perceptible change to our protagonist is a "new lease on life" (whatever that means), and a saccharine positivity that now radiates from their undamaged body. This vision of recovery is, at the very least, putting Vaseline on the lens. At the worst, it is utter bullshit.

Recovery sucks.

Recovery is not linear, and it is not predictable. I made slow progress over many months—re-learning how to walk, slowly re-acclimating to eating normal food, talking to people that I knew wouldn't laugh if I said "shit" when I meant "shirt." Recovery is a balancing act that requires both effort and rest. I was well-versed in the former, but had deficient experience with the latter. I had to learn to listen to my body and respect its limits by only doing what I could handle without pushing for more. Recovery does not have an end-date, which is simultaneously frustrating and encouraging. Although I did not know how long it would take for me to find my new sense of normal, I came to realize that as long as I still drew breath, I could work toward improvement. Even now, five years later, I still constantly ask myself what I can do to improve my health and wellbeing. I have not once concluded that I am done getting better, that there are no goals left that I am capable of attaining.

About a year after I was rushed to the emergency room, in March of 2014, my band returned to the stage for the first time after my hospitalization. I, of course, was scared senseless. What if I forgot the lyrics? What if I fell or passed out? What if I looked awkward out there? What if I just wasn't as good as I was before? The performance began with me, alone on the stage with the curtains closed, singing Pink Floyd's "Wish You Were Here." After the first few lines, the curtains opened, and I had to catch my breath—a sea of friends and fans spread out before me, each holding up a small lighted candle in a coordinated show of solidarity and support. My anxiety evaporated, and it was an unforgettable night.

We continued performing regularly until my CD4+ count began to creep downward at the beginning of 2015. At that point, I made the difficult decision to take an indefinite hiatus from live performance. I am not sure that I will ever return to the stage on a regular basis, but music is still a massive part of my life—I maintain a home recording studio, and I have even taught some voice and piano lessons at a school of rock that was opened by a musician whose band shared the stage with mine quite often. My career in music is very different than the one I envisioned for myself, but in the unpredictable mess that is life, adaptability is the name of the game.

Resilience comes in many forms, and just like life, it can be downright messy. My illness has changed me profoundly, both in positive and negative ways. I will never be exactly the same person that I was before April of 2013. Unlike some people who write about their tangles with ill health, I don't want to sugarcoat the difficulty that is inherent in living with a severe chronic illness. Being sick is hard work! It's not always pretty, and it's not always easy. Some days I feel almost the same as I did before—like I can take on the world with one hand tied behind my back. Some days I decide that the most I can handle is deciding on which Netflix series to binge-watch and what food delivery service to use. Most days are somewhere in between.

It is life's messiness and unpredictability that gives us the opportunity to persevere—to find the hidden reserve of badass that we didn't know we had, and to release it into the wild as we hang on for dear life. I don't always have total confidence in myself, and I struggle with the changes I have endured, just like anyone who has dealt with a catastrophic illness or a life-altering event. But there is one truth that remains—I am still here, and I choose to move forward.

Resilient

By Ana Cristina Cash

The spark is always there, no matter how they try to dim it
You are resilient

Their narcissistic glares have no power over you, for you will survive
this too
You are resilient

Like a palm tree that bends amidst the harsh winds of a hurricane,
you do not break.
You are resilient

Your brave soul will overcome darkness
Like steel that is forged in the fire,
You are resilient

Though they've betrayed you and spread falsities about you, do not
shrink yourself to make them feel better about themselves
You are resilient

When the world has been unkind, keep shining, as it will help others
    shine too
You are resilient

You've been underestimated, abandoned, abused and neglected,
But you rise above it time and again
You are resilient

They have labeled you as wicked and will burn you at the stake, but
    you will not perish
You are resilient

A child of God that was made in his likeness, and the best version of
    yourself
There is only one of you
You are resilient

You bring life into the world, for you are a woman
You have the world in the palm of your hand
You are resilient

You are not too old or too young, too underqualified, too big or too
    small to achieve anything
You are resilient

You are the architect of your own destiny
Who made anyone else the warden of your dreams?
You are resilient

Silence the negative voices
Harpoon their doubtful words
You are resilient

They may suck the marrow from your bones and dispose of you
    tomorrow, but you will get up again
You are resilient

You are a warrior, a hero, a female, a mother, a daughter, a sister, a
    wife, a friend, a colleague, a human
You've always had the power within you
You are resilient

Sploosh

By Rachel Cassidy

Sploosh.

It's pissing rain again, two in the morning, nightclubs thumping, and the sidewalk is slick as owlshit, I'm splayed out on the pavement four inches deep with running water, on my back in a puddle, and Fareed is doubled over with laughter. We're drunk, really drunk. Walking because we can't find an empty taxi in this weather, at this hour, in this waterlogged Mexican Caribbean town.

I need to be this drunk, right now, to forget for a few hours, and I need Fareed to pick my ass up out of this puddle, which he does, and notes proudly, "You didn't even spill your drink."

I examine it closely, take a swig. "Nope."

We stagger home, to my home, and I start to tremble as we approach.

"Please check and see if he's upstairs. Please." The house has a separate apartment on the second floor. I wait until Fareed comes back.

"He put a padlock on the gate to upstairs."

"On my fucking house?"

Fareed nods. "He's not there."

We go into the main floor and Fareed heads for the guest room, pats my head as he goes by.

"You OK?"

"Fuck no."

Sploosh.

I vomit until sunrise. My lawyers and the thug will be here at nine.

Arturo smelled good. He was a language teacher, and a writer, he said, over coffee. He had great arms and a hypnotic voice. A Chilango accent, educated, smart. We started to meet at the beach near my place for language lessons.

"What do you write about?"

"Sexuality."

Any sane woman, forty years old or not, should have run the fuck away. Fast. But I was alone, rebelliously post-corporate, living in another country, and the naughtiness of it sent a frisson down my spine. So I fell in love with him instead.

That sounds so cavalier, so carefree. And it was, for a while. Picnic beach concerts. Sharing books. Debating movies. Spending entire weekends in bed. What should have happened is that it stayed that way until I tired of his inevitable bullshit and moved on, like with almost every man in my past.

That isn't what happened.

We'd been together well over a year.

He'd finished writing his book, we'd traveled to Mexico City to do "book things," I'd set up a website for him, along with proper email identities and marketing tools he could use to promote and sell it. The launch party went off swimmingly and that long hot summer was full of celebration and promise.

But in the background, the economy was making rumbling noises.

Evenings with Arturo were great, but the afternoons were hell. The depression I'd struggled with sporadically over the years returned with a vengeance, same time, every day. I'd click vacantly on match-three computer games in the still quiet heat, sleep, drink. Zone out. Wait for him to come over.

I watched my savings and investments evaporate over a few short months. Money from the sale of the company I had built over twelve years, hard-earned as a female entrepreneur in a man's industry. I was numb, sure it would turn around any time now. But it didn't, not soon enough.

I was flat broke, in a way that wouldn't generate a lot of sympathy—I owned a house in the premium neighborhood of a Caribbean destination, and I could barely pay the electric bill. I moved upstairs to the studio apartment, tried to rent the main floor to tourists, but the tourists weren't coming. The house was for sale, but no one was buying—or even shopping—in the economic climate.

I needed to work. We discussed it, and he moved in. He would look after any holiday rentals that came through, and I drained the last of my funds and got on a plane to Canada.

Where there wasn't any work to be found. And it was fucking cold.

I spent the winter in a generous friend's basement in Calgary, searching for work in my field. It reeked of cat piss. Arturo and I messaged and Skyped constantly. He read to me until I fell asleep, cold and panicked.

I didn't recognize the name on the Facebook message. Marianne ____. She sounded American. Said I'm fucking her husband, who, by the way, isn't even named Arturo, which she thinks I should know.

I forwarded the message to him. What the hell?

He called immediately. "Well, yes. It's my pen name. I hated my name growing up."

I was dumbfounded. "So what is your actual name?"

"Guillermo ____. They called me Little Willie. I hated it."

I didn't know what to say.

"Look, if she's going to cause problems, maybe I should just move out. I told her you're just a friend I'm helping. And a lesbian."

I was frozen. I needed him there, in the house. "Why is she doing this? You were separated when we met two years ago."

He didn't respond. I knew.

"When's the last time you fucked her?"

Still no response.

I said no, stay, and hung up.

"Fareed, old friend. I have an interview for a maternity leave, in Vancouver."

"Well, come on over."

Fareed had a tiny apartment in an ancient house, with "inflatable luxury" for guests in the form of a leaky twin air mattress wedged against a wobbly bookshelf. It would deflate through the night so that my ass greeted the hardwood floor at dawn.

I got the job. I could go home to Mexico two weeks of the month, work remotely. The salary would just barely cover it, after paying recent debts. I had a hefty balance of airline points from my working days. I told Arturo I was coming home soon. He seemed happy about it.

I could feel the edges of my world solidifying again, and I would seize it and make it whole.

Arturo's laptop was pinging nonstop with message notifications. I was overtly not looking at the screen, but it was impossible—I was sitting right behind him. A dating website, with a photo of his book on a bed.

"It's marketing," he said. "Just marketing. They want to talk. Look." His profile was marked *in an open relationship*. He showed me conversations.

The next morning, we stopped for breakfast like we always did when he drove me to the airport in my truck. He was angry. Apparently, I refused him sex when I was still asleep.

I had admin rights to his author email. And a pretty good idea of what his password was for his personal one.

He never was good with tech.

I had a coat from before all this, a western-styled duster, thick ivory cotton with deep warm pockets. Fareed retrieved me from a rock at the waterfront.

"What's up?"

"Got whiskey in my pocket."

"Why?"

"He's picking her up at six. In my truck."

Sploosh.

He hauled me back to the apartment and I showed him the woman. Juana was partially disabled, an abuse survivor, desperately searching online for physical love, and vulnerable. They emailed back and forth for days, and Arturo had finally bestowed her with a gift. He would do her the grand favor of fucking her. He was going to take her to his fancy place near the beach and be her sexual god, her awakening.

In my bed.

I waited until I knew they'd be there, his laptop on the desk near the bedroom door. I started to message him with inane conversation.

Hey baby, what you doing? I miss you.

Ping. Ping. Ping. Ping.

With that, I justified watching his email account. Marking them unread when I was done. And I let it fester—had to, I told myself—until I could manage things without him. Just a few months of income, that's all it would take.

I started to fuck with him. Saying I'd video call at a time I knew he was meeting one of them. Messaging when I knew one was in the room.

Ping.

He arranged to meet one of them out of town. I messaged him. *I'm coming home, thinking of these particular days.*

He pushed back, had plans to meet college buddies in Mérida. *How about later, more time for us?*

I love Mérida! I'll meet you there!

Oh no, really, it's a guy thing, old friends, better to wait a few days and have all my attention.

My face was a grinning rictus as I agreed and signed off.

A few days later, Friday, guts churning, I breathed deep, and opened Messenger.

I want you out of my house by the end of the month.

My screen exploded with incoming video calls.

Decline.

Decline.

Decline.

I'm going offline now. Turning my phone off. For the weekend. How was Juana in bed, anyway? Go fuck yourself, Willie.

Ping.

Come Monday, the messages were piled up. He was enraged.

Bitch, you know I just spent all my money printing books.

You can't do this.

Through the following week, the texts, calls, and messages were incessant. He forwarded texts from women inviting him to spend an hour or a night with them, saying how unfortunate it was that I didn't understand him like they did. We had some terse conversations. I refused to engage or back down. Then the threats started.

Call me within 10 minutes or I'm going to report you to immigration.
I'm going to fucking sue you.

That's what he settled on—he decided he was now a property manager, was owed months of back pay, and had been illegally terminated. And he wasn't leaving—because that would be legally considered deserting his post.

From Vancouver, I placed panicked phone calls to every local law firm I could find online, and I found Gabriel. Steadfast, unflappable Gabriel. He listened, calmed me down.

"Come back. This is bullshit. We'll sort it out."

From the Mexico City airport, on layover with Fareed in tow for moral support, I texted Arturo.

I'll be at the house around 8 pm.

No response.

I was shaking as we arrived—to an empty house with a handwritten note on the door. Rain sheeted down from a low gray sky.

I think it's best if I'm not here tonight. My body sagged in relief.

In the morning, I met with Gabriel at his office. He brought in a family lawyer, and she brought along a thug. Arturo had been making scenes in the office, intimidating the receptionist, demanding they sign things. The thug was for security.

They had a plan.

"You need to remove him from the house. We're doing it tomorrow morning. Don't engage with him."

That afternoon, back at the house, the gate creaked open. Fareed went to the door, and I heard Arturo's voice. I winced.

"I want to talk to her."

"She doesn't want to talk to you."

I've never been so thankful for Fareed and his larger-than-life presence than in that moment. Arturo went up to the apartment, and left a while a later. Fareed and I went out and got stinking drunk.

Sploosh.

I text Gabriel early about the padlock. He's bringing a locksmith. They arrive at nine—lawyers, thug, a couple of young associates. Two police officers glide in on motorcycles. After a short conversation with Gabriel, they nod and depart.

Fareed is tormenting me a bit, trying for levity, but I'm hungover, exhausted, and terrified that Arturo will return before we finish what we're about to do.

The locksmith cuts away the padlock, and the associates go to work.

They throw Arturo's shit in boxes and garbage bags, pile it on the lawn. I answer questions—is this yours, is this his. I nod and point, numb. They discreetly empty the nightstand drawers of sex toys without asking, dispose of the sheets. A box of papers is dropped. Gabriel picks them up. An arrest record from Cuernavaca, with his real name.

Gabriel looks pensive. "What name does he have on his I.D.?"

"Arturo ____."

Gabriel smiles. "Good."

I leave a set of the new keys with Gabriel when he drops us off at the airport, and it is done. It's not until we're back in Vancouver and I go to my waterfront rock alone that I cry myself empty.

"The hearing was today. It didn't take long." Gabriel sounds satisfied. "He started ranting. I asked the judge to confirm who, in fact, it was we were talking to. Arturo ____ or Guillermo ____?"

"And?"

"The judge got curious, real fast... and he got quiet, real fast. It's over."

The email is from Marianne ____. I'm scanning the preview before the name registers. *His computer... found this... sex with someone... your house.* When it does register, it's a gut punch, even weeks later. I throw the phone at Fareed.

He reads the message. There's a video attached.

"Do you want to know?"

"No."

He deletes it.

To Love and Be Loved

By Patricia Chamburs

After nearly sixty years, the time has come for me to purge the cluttered, overflowing closet that occupies a dark room in my mind. It's not easy remembering the ugliness of my past, the shame and abuse I felt powerless against, never feeling worthy or confident or strong enough to escape. Mostly, I am ashamed not so much by what happened, but because I let it happen.

I was born in November 1944 and my mother died from leukemia in March 1947. I have no conscious memory of her.

My father was a smooth-talking, charming jazz musician. His life centered on music, period. He wasn't much of a father but he was one fun guy—a gentleman with a witty, interesting and entertaining demeanor. He was the sort of person you couldn't really stay angry at for long.

After my mother died, my father dropped me at my paternal grandmother's house. She was capable but distant, a devout Catholic, strict and no-nonsense. She still had three of her own children at home. I must have felt to her like just another mouth to feed. I attended Catholic school and mass every day and learned to do what I was told if I wanted to stay out of trouble (and not go to hell).

When I was six years old, my father remarried. My first memory of meeting my stepmother was running to hug her but not receiving a hug in return. She resented me and introduced me in this way: "These are my children and this is Frank's daughter." She once told me that our guests thought her children were cute but that I was a "showoff." A photographer came to our house when I was nine or ten years old, and while my half-brothers and half-sister posed for a photo, I stood close by and watched. Nobody invited me to come into the picture.

I was the oldest of the seven children and always considered my half-sister and brothers my family. My sister has been especially supportive of me and we have shared a special bond over the years. But I longed to escape, weary of trying to gain my stepmother's approval and earn her love.

At sixteen, I got pregnant by a boy I hardly knew and found myself married to a domineering, macho, womanizing bully. To be fair, he was only eighteen years old and didn't want to be married or responsible any more than I did. With three children by age twenty, I had no maternal instincts, no education, and no hope.

I spent twelve years with my ex-husband. He had numerous affairs, fathered a child by another woman, and was extremely jealous and suspicious of me. He would frequently come home drunk late at night and, if I said anything to him about where he'd been, he would fly into a rage. We never had many "family" times together. His interests were hunting, fishing and going to bars. I suffered busted lips, black eyes, a fractured back, and verbal abuse. For too many years I let myself be pushed, slapped, kicked and punched. I didn't dare speak up.

My biggest shame was that I too became a bully by taking out my pain and frustration on my young children—mentally, physically, and verbally. I knew how horrible it was and the guilt became overwhelming. I gathered up the courage and left several times but was lured back by my husband's promises to change.

Finally, in 1976, desperate, mentally exhausted, fearing for my life at times, doubting my sanity, and tired of ducking at sudden hand movements, I fled 3,000 miles from Florida to my brother's house in California, leaving my children in order to save myself.

For the first time in my life, I sat alone with only my thoughts, relieved to be free from fear, wondering what to do next, on a

California beach thousands of miles from home. Being alone helped me to be aware of myself, helped me to relax, to breathe easier and to let my mind rest.

The guilt of leaving my children never left me and I returned to Florida after three months, determined to begin a different life for both my children and myself.

I started working full-time, took some courses at our community college, and felt free to be myself. My daughter and youngest son came to live with me but my oldest son never forgave me. After all the conflict and anger of his childhood, he was unhappy and bitter. Who could blame him? He married and was an amazing father to his children, but he was not an easy person to get along with. He had several failed relationships. On Valentine's Day in 2008, he took his own life after being diagnosed with bipolar disorder.

Only after meeting my husband Philip in 1978, and being shown love while learning patience and acceptance of myself, was I able to deal with my oldest son's death and form closer bonds with my youngest son and daughter.

In spite of a childhood marked by pain, confusion, and nightmarish scenes no child should ever have to experience, my children grew to be loving human beings. They are the true heroes of my story: my son, Kenny, whose wounds were too deep to heal, the pain too much to bear; my daughter, Karen, who loves deeply and embodies the word kindness, whose generosity of spirit and compassion knows no bounds, who is more of a mother to my family than I know how to be; and my youngest son Ricky, a man-child whose easy, charming ways have served him well so far.

My other hero is Philip. He has saved my life. When we first met, I was so afraid that love wouldn't last, that he would see the deeply flawed person I was, afraid our love was too good to be true. His infinite patience and gentle loving ways nurtured me and let me see my better self.

I forgave my stepmother and we grew to love and respect each other. She was a strong, determined, hardworking woman who, with no support from my father, raised my sister and five brothers.

It seems I've lived two different lives, and I believe the experiences in our lives help our true selves emerge, if we're lucky. What

I've learned is that love is extremely powerful and my mantra—to love and be loved—is what life is all about.

The Pretend Mother

By Emily Charles

At some point in my youth I was designated to take on a role that should never have been placed on me. One that I never clearly understood for many, many years. I was one of five children growing up in the New England outskirts of a fast-growing town. We were a big family. A typical family where the mother stayed at home and the father commuted to New York City for his job. His travels home each night were most often on the bar car, so he arrived home in a state we came to know well and accept as our norm.

My younger years were devoted to trying to make my parents and grandparents proud of my school accomplishments. I remained a quiet girl with a constant desire to please everyone—mostly teachers and adult family members. I was frequently looked to as the quiet, good child who rarely strayed from very specific tasks. Behaviors of this type rewarded me with a reasonably quiet, "under the radar" position in the family.

With this sort of approach to daily life, I find it interesting, looking back, that I somehow escaped much of what my siblings went through. I cannot define why my role ended up as it did, but at some point in my adult years I decided to remove myself from much of the interaction that keeps a family in certain patterns of behavior.

The blessing in my life was that I left home for college on the advice of our childhood pediatrician who apparently told my parents I would benefit from being away at school and experiencing family life at a distance. Was she aware of more within the family dynamic than I was? She felt it would be in my best interest. And so, with pinching pennies being a common way of life in our family, enough money was scraped together for me to leave home. In addition to going away to college, I married a man whose job would take us outside the country. In that way, I was able to discover strengths I never knew I had and forge relationships that had been difficult for me as a child and adolescent. You could say that I found out who I really was once I got out of the family nest and developed a persona I was much more comfortable with—one that allowed me to grow in independence and spirit.

After a number of years, we returned to my hometown to set up a new life with our own three children. My husband, like my father before, became a NYC commuter. Once back in the family scene, I began to feel suffocated and tormented by the family life I had escaped through school and marriage. Back in my hometown, suddenly I could not escape hearing stories from my siblings about their memories of being abused by our father. It started as weekly calls from my sister who had endured abuse over a long period of time. She did not want this shared with anyone else, but just wanted me to listen and support her. All I could think and feel was, "Why me?" She lived with my mother through the years and had many opportunities to talk with her and other family members, as well as look for the help she truly needed.

In time, the burden of carrying this news became overwhelming and I developed deep depression. I received almost weekly calls from my mother to come quickly to their house as my sister was talking about ending her life. This was not behavior that my mother had seen in her before.

I eventually shared my sister's confession with my mother. There was no question that on the outside my mother was in denial, but I believe deep inside she knew—and probably knew even as the abuse was happening. As this came out, my two other sisters shared that they were also abused. I was in disbelief. This had never happened to me in all my years at home, but I was frequently put in the position, by my mother, to try to talk my father out of his constant drinking. What a fourteen-year-old girl was going to do to stop a grown man from drinking was beyond me. But the job was designated mine. I was not successful at getting him to stop and probably suffered some feelings of guilt and disappointment at not being successful. I struggled with all of this until I left home for school and married life, only to return to the uncomfortable reality of my origins.

I wish I knew what was the actual turning point in my life and when I developed a voice that I finally realized was my true voice. It was most likely always there—just never uncovered until I reached a point of desperation when I realized that my family under my roof needed me more than the others who had come before them. Perhaps when rushing late on a Friday night, week after week, to keep a sister from attempting suicide, I came to grips with the fact that one of my own children might come into a troubled situation and I would not be mentally or physically available to help them as only a mother can.

I had to start thinking about the needs of my children and my husband—and therefore myself—and get the help and support I needed to release me from the unspoken contract that had been established in my name with my birth family decades before. I had to define my own emotional needs and goals and put them ahead of a lifetime of "others first." This was not an easy fix. I was always a giver, rarely a taker, and constantly looking for a quiet, predictable life. To begin rethinking how I wanted to continue, I had to admit I also had serious problems that needed to be addressed. I had trained in college as a nurse with a specialty focus in psychiatric nursing. I did not get to practice those skills very much as we continued to move about, but the knowledge and the fact that I identified that I needed help led me to reach out and go into therapy. Through a mixture of guilt, fear, and apprehension, I spent a number of years finding the voice I needed to express long-held feelings of anger and blame at having been neglected by those who were supposed to care for me and protect me. The voice has become stronger over time; it took a number of years for me to even take it to the level it needed to be in order for me to feel somewhat healed. To this day, I do not speak in any depth of those years of confusion and burden. I feel I learned as much as I could from what happened and the role that fate and family placed me in. To continue to dwell on it does not bring me any greater sense of peace so I prefer to place it in a "box" on a shelf. I know where it is. I can open it a bit if I feel the need to. But as the years have gone by, I feel there is nothing more to be learned from it.

Occasionally, one of my sisters will broach the topic with me but I prefer to let it lie where it is and not open up a discussion from which there will be no further growth for me. I can only feel this after all these years: it was a terrible experience within one family, an experience that continues to occur daily in other families everywhere. I cannot fix those situations. The only thing I can do is hope that my story can help others in this situation. If someone came to me and asked for guidance, I would tell them to first seek help so that you yourself are healed and healthy, and then strive to protect and keep those closest to you safe from such a family tragedy. We cannot heal everyone we know who has such a sickness and we should never be forced to make someone else whole; to be a "pretend mother" at the tender age of twelve or thirteen is an unforgivable position to place anyone in. We cannot do that. We can only suggest a healthy path for them and then it's in their hands.

These days, I can still speak to my children about the past and the years when they were young and vulnerable. I can pick out pieces of time when it is painfully obvious to me that I was not totally vested in my parenting role; times when I was being pulled away from them back to old family patterns. I feel guilty, but then I realize it could have been so much worse. I feel that I nearly reached the first steps of "failure to parent properly." But I managed to teeter, not fall. I took a step back and then another, and got the help I needed to find my own voice for myself and my husband and children. How very fortunate I am as I rediscover this backstory to my own life.

Head North

By Natalie Clark

I was born and raised in Glasgow, Scotland. Until a few years ago, that was where I had lived all my life. I grew up in an academic family with a history of professional career paths and I followed that expected route. On the path to a doctorate in Child Psychology, I began working as a schoolteacher. I found myself teaching for a few years, as I enjoyed it so much and had a great job in a lovely school. It was easier to live a comfortable, stable life than to listen to the real dreams that I had pushed aside, namely my passion for music and my calling to create it. But I kept having a recurring doubt that my otherwise satisfactory job was the wrong direction on my internal compass. True North was music. It was my dream, my destination to be following the music full-time. It was an inherited north: a love of music runs throughout my family. But I just never really let myself think it was a possibility as a career option.

It wasn't until the end of one summer, when I had spent my time off diving into writing and playing music, that I felt this incredible sadness at the thought of going back to my job. I knew I would have to switch off that passion and put it aside. It felt like I was about to put my dreams in a room, switch the light out, and close the door. Over dinner one evening, my brother Stephen suggested (as he had done for years) that I should just take the leap and pursue my real passion of music. In other words, just keep following your internal compass, your real purpose. He knew—and I knew—that the compass of my heart kept needling north, and I couldn't be content until I followed.

Despite being terrified of the unknown, I overcame my fears, quit my teaching job, and moved down to London to pursue my musical aspirations of gigging, writing, and performing. It was so exciting, but I quickly ran out of money. Pursuing my dream of becoming a musician—my life's calling, my version of True North—while living in one of the world's most expensive cities, had literally left me penniless.

I was pretty terrified. I wondered if I had pursued the wrong path. Even if music was north, being broke and struggling in London didn't feel like I was heading in the right direction.

But then, a miraculous thing happened.

I won tickets to a BBC Q&A session with Sir Richard Branson, the legendary Virgin mogul. It was to take place in my hometown of Glasgow, so I took this as a sign to conclude my London chapter and fly back home.

Out of the hundreds of people attending, I got to ask Branson a question. With my heart pounding, I asked him about being brave and starting new ventures. He turned the question right back on me. "What are your plans?" Sir Richard Branson asked ME.

"Actually, I've just quit a teaching career to pursue music as a singer/songwriter."

"Well, give us a song then!"

Before I knew it, I was lifted onto the stage and given a microphone. I think I was in actual shock but I just had to go for it! I had about ten seconds to overcome my nerves and decide what to do, so I started singing my own song, "Weakness."

In another life I'd be married now, I'd be settled down, like you.

I would hear the sound of my babies crying, I'd hold them tight the whole night through.

But this is my life and now I realize some things may never come true...

Branson—and the whole audience listened and applauded me when the song was over. And from that day forward, Branson has been so supportive, offering great feedback and words of encouragement, and even writing several articles about our encounter, sharing my story to offer encouragement to others, too, in finding their own true norths.

This magical experience came at the perfect time, when my faith in myself was low. It gave me the confidence to keep going on this new path. It ticked the needle on the compass a little closer to North, where my heart and my dreams and the music lay.

One of these dreams was to go to America. Fresh from the excitement of recent events, I bought a plane ticket and just went for it. I flew out with only my suitcase and guitar. I didn't know anyone or have a specific plan—I just knew it was what I was meant to do. I was following my compass.

After a short while, some exciting things started happening. I was contacted by a producer from The Voice and appeared on the show. I was asked to do a Mercedes campaign for KTLA Channel 5 as one of their featured artists. It all felt like I was in a dream.

Although these incredible opportunities fueled my excitement, reality was also kicking in. There's an irony to the fact that when I moved from Scotland to Hollywood—the epicenter of film—I discovered that the reality of "living your dream" isn't the way it's portrayed in the movies.

Life isn't a movie. Living your dream, or at least the pursuit of it, is hard, sometimes terrifying, and sometimes downright ugly. Moving from the rain and grey of Scotland, part of me bathed in the excitement, the sunshine, the electricity of a city that is directly associated with the collective pursuit of people's dreams. But it turned out that despite the warmth and promise of a place of perpetual sunshine, one still has to face the everyday challenges and torment of being a human.

I needed to earn a proper living if I was going to stay in L.A. After struggling for a while, I started cat sitting, house sitting, dog sitting and couch surfing—anything to stay in L.A. I felt it was where I was meant to be, being surrounded by incredible musicians, people in the industry, and people making their real dreams come true—from professional songwriters, performers, and entertainers of all sorts working on their craft full-time. It helped me see what was possible, if I could just stick it out.

It was during this time when I had to cultivate that "grit" I had heard people talk about. When the adrenaline and excitement of making that first big move starts to fade away and reality kicks in, things get uncomfortable, challenging and uncertain. One day you're feeling confident and motivated, the next day you're questioning your purpose in life and not sure where you'll sleep the following week.

It felt like a constant fight to keep the passion and creativity alive. It's hard to stay motivated and driven when the comforts and assurance have been removed. I was trying to stay positive and hopeful but felt the weight of this huge question mark hanging over my head. Some days I had the confidence to know I was on the right path; other days I had a voice in my head saying, "Just give up and go home! Are you crazy? Who do you think you are trying to be a musician out here?!" I also felt guilt from receiving people's help and kindness during this time. So many people offered assistance, guidance and resources when I needed it and, without this, I'm not sure where I'd be. But at the time, I felt bad for leaning on that help and there were days when I longed to be independent and thriving again. I wanted to be the one offering support to others, not feeling like I was just taking all the time.

During this period, I also faced some serious learning curves about being in the music industry and trusting my instinct when it came to business and personal relationships. During one of these experiences, I found myself back in Scotland for a while trying to figure out the next step. My instinct told me I was only just getting started in the States, but my fear allowed me to question everything and doubt whether I would ever truly be a professional musician in America.

And that is when the idea of the North, which had led me from the day I quit my secure job and embarked on this journey, really kicked in. Each night of doubt, I had to remind myself: 'Head North'. Just keep going, keep moving forward, keep writing songs! So, that's what I did. I turned to the music. I picked up my guitar and played in the early hours of the morning. I sat at the keyboard and tinkered around and let the music flow and swirl around my soul, reconnecting with my purpose and briefly forgetting about the question marks and uncertainties of the future. I just made music. I sang, I cried, I played piano.

While back in Scotland, I began tuning into the work ethic and hustle I had experienced in L.A—the reality of being a freelance musician, of continually pursuing opportunities, of not waiting for them to magically appear. I emailed, I called, I texted everyone—booking every gig and festival I could. The ball kept rolling. The music kept flowing. And I was writing again.

And, wouldn't you know, that was when "miracles" started showing up—a promising email here, an unexpected phone call there. Before I knew it, I was back in L.A as a working musician ready for the next chapter.

So that's where I am now. I finally have a place, a car, and am a full-time professional musician here in the States. There are high and low days, but all days are part of the human experience. And here's the thing, I've come to learn: there's always a next chapter. There are always new opportunities and new challenges when you pursue your dreams, when you look to your own unique North, wherever or whatever it may be.

As Rich Roll beautifully put it, "We all have a unique song to sing here on earth, we have a unique blueprint, and our job is to discover what that is, and to work towards expressing that to the best of our ability." In other words, follow your own purpose, your own compass—head towards your own north. All I know is that I want to express the unique blueprint I've been given. I want to sing my own unique song. I want to keep pushing onward, and upwards, and encouraging others to do the same. I will keep HEADING NORTH.

Doubt

By Darla Eden

The most difficult obstacle in an emotionally abusive relationship is doubt. It's the weapon most effectively used by the abuser, and the main reason those being subjected don't leave. I was so mired in my own self-doubt that I couldn't see the abuse that was right in front of me. I didn't fully understand that emotional abuse was something that could happen to me. After all, I was smart, educated, and grew up in a fairly affluent community. This kind of thing happened to other people. He didn't physically harm me, and that was enough to prove that there was no abuse. I was so stuck in the perfect facade that I had crafted for myself that even as I listened to other women telling their abuse histories (I was a crisis counselor at the time), I couldn't see the same patterns of behavior happening in my own household. He latched onto and increased any self-doubt I harbored, while simultaneously increasing my faith in him. His manipulation was subtle and my blinders were large; the only thing I didn't doubt was him.

I met my husband when I was twenty-three years old. I had recently graduated college and left my first fiancé because he was physically abusive. Little did I know, I would be married to this new man in four short months. He swept me off my feet. He had a caustic sense of humor and his laugh was terrifying, but he took me places I'd never been and gave me things I didn't even know I wanted. He wasn't the type of guy who would bring me flowers—he wasn't romantic in that sense—but he made every moment of my life exciting. I couldn't get enough of him.

I was reeling from my prior relationship, having left in the middle of the night with everything I could pack into my Toyota because I was scared that man was going to kill me. This new guy removed all doubt from my mind. He wanted what I wanted: he wanted to be married forever. I wanted a bunch of kids and he already had three. I was sure at the time that I could never have kids on my own, so I welcomed them into my life and into my heart.

My parents had what you could call a tumultuous relationship. Neither was abusive to my sister or me, but they did have very violent arguments with each other. Then they had this habit of taking off their clothes. I guess one of them had heard at one point that you couldn't fight naked. It turns out you can, but fighting naked apparently leads to sex. I saw a lot of inappropriate things when I was a kid. Add to this my father's intermittent drug use and inability to keep a job, and you have my happy childhood. Don't get me wrong, I do remember being happy, more often than not. I didn't know any different. My parents were affectionate and did everything they could for us. We might have been poor, but we still had our basic needs met, access to good schools, and toys to play with. They finally broke up when I was twelve.

I always idolized my grandparents' relationships. Both sets of grandparents had met and married very young, had children, and celebrated milestone anniversary dates (fifty and sixty-five years) before death parted them. I was determined to stay married, unlike my own parents, but I didn't have any idea how to make that happen. I somehow got it into my head that it was more about determination than anything else. I was determined that my life would be different.

Of course, I'd heard the old adage about marrying someone like your father, but I didn't fully realize at the time that it meant that my relationship with my father was going to be my model for all future relationships with men. My dad, in addition to his drug problem, is also mentally ill. He is one of the many Vietnam vets who came back and never sought treatment. He told me once that he didn't want to share with the doctors that he was hearing voices, because he didn't want to be given the label of schizophrenic. This means that my model for all future relationships with men was a person around whom no matter how hard I tried, I would never, ever be enough.

Sometimes, my dad would show up on birthdays. Then he would be gone again. My mom tried her very best to cover it up by saying he was working late again, when the truth was he rarely had a job. I'll never forget the night when I was about five when he came into my bedroom at night and instead of telling the usual bedtime story, he said, "I am sick in the head. Your mom says I need to go away for a while." He said this with tears in his eyes and a catch in his throat. His announcement had the desired effect; he and I both blamed Mom for his going away.

I had grown up thinking my parents were honest and straightforward. Later in life, I realized that my dad was manipulative, selfish, and possibly a narcissist. This is the kind of doubt an abuser uses to control the victim. My dad was an excellent storyteller. In fact, he told us all kinds of things, which I believed to be the truth. Some of these "truths" I brought into adulthood and only realized by the smirking faces of the people I was speaking to that what I was saying was pure bullshit. This caused me to doubt myself and what I believed to be my world. I was the perfect target for an abusive narcissist. I was primed and ready to doubt myself and believe in him.

My husband and my father did not get along. Partially because they hadn't even met before my wedding day (we had unexpectedly eloped on a weekend trip to Vegas). I had thought that was because they were too much alike, and maybe they were. Perhaps because my dad was so similar to my husband, my dad saw through all of my husband's facades. The heavy drinking and drug use (by all parties in my life then) only added fuel to the fire.

My husband insisted I drink with him and try to keep up with him. He didn't like to drink alone, nor did he trust anybody who was sober. I blacked out often, and he used these opportunities to plant doubt in my mind. He would wake me up and tell me that I had embarrassed him the night before; I had said or done something in front of an audience that was so abysmal that he couldn't speak to me. Having no memory of the incident, I would try to make amends. My husband was a master at gaslighting. I had trusted him and told him so many of my secrets. He knew just how to draw out the angry beast inside me. Sometimes I lashed out at him. The more mistakes I made, the more indebted I felt to him. I had grown up unable to please my father, unable to make him stay. Here I was falling into the same pattern in my marriage.

Sure, there were red flags. They were all over the place. But when I found them, I buried them. I told no one of the slightest conflict. I didn't even complain that he left his socks on the floor and snored—partially, because I didn't want to see the larger problems in our relationship. It was also because he had forbidden me from speaking of our marriage problems to my friends. He claimed it was too embarrassing if people knew "our private life." Consequently, they only knew the positive aspects of my relationship with him. They might have viewed him as an asshole, loud and inappropriate, but they were also certain that I was happy. I was determined to stay married, whatever that took. So in my mind I created a world in which I had a perfect marriage. I wouldn't let doubt sully that veneer. But I did doubt the intentions of my friends. If anyone stood up to my husband, or told me anything negative about him, I would begin to doubt their allegiance to me. He would tell me they were just jealous and single, and what did they know of married life?

I tried to leave him twice before I finally was able to break away for good. The first time, I packed a suitcase and went to my mom's for a week. He took me out on a date—our first one, five years into our marriage. We had a wonderful time. I know now this behavior is called "love bombing," but at the time it felt like things were back to normal. He made a lot of promises—if I would just come back and live with him. Instead of waiting for these promises to come to fruition, I moved back in.

Of course, the promises he made evaporated immediately. Yet, I stayed. I was already back to our usual routine. I didn't want our marriage to fail, and that desire took precedence over any creeping doubt I had about what our marriage actually was. The second time I tried to leave, he actually laughed at me. That was in year eight of our marriage. At this point, he had taken me away from everyone I loved and moved me from all of my friends and family in California to the middle of nowhere in rural Arizona. After he laughed at me, he told me that I would get nothing in the divorce because he made me what I am and I would be nothing without him. He punched holes in my plan, telling me exactly how and why it wouldn't work. The worst part was that I believed him. I made a pact with him and myself that day. I promised I would never again try to leave him. That promise lasted for another six years.

On January 1st, 2015, he became physically violent for the first time. We were living in Australia at the time, as my mother and sister had followed us to Arizona and he needed to further isolate me. I had realized that he was gaslighting me (although, at the time I didn't have a term for it) and I was trying to record our arguments with my cell phone. He refused to talk to me "on the record" and took my phone from me. During the struggle, I not only lost an earring but I also lost consciousness as he closed his fist around my throat. Three times he choked me to blackout and relaxed his grip before he finally let me go. I grabbed my carry-on by the door and went to the police. I had planned to leave soon for a trip back to the United States to visit a friend who was dying.

I wish I could say that was the last time I saw him.

I had a return ticket, so I went back. He was love bombing me, and again, I was falling for it. I thought we could work out our differences. I thought we could get past it. I didn't want to throw away fourteen years of marriage because we couldn't communicate. He agreed to go to counseling for the first time—although it wasn't the first time I had asked him. He went in with a caveat: I was not to bring up the abuse. If I did, he would no longer participate. We talked about basic communication, each of our wants and needs in the relationship. This would have been a fine exchange had we been in an egalitarian relationship, but this was an abusive relationship, and neither I nor the counselor was able to see it. He was so charming, so cool and collected. I was hysterical. I sounded whiny, my needs childish. I tried self-help books, complete with couples' activities that we could do to discover the good in our relationship. He took that opportunity to point out all the things that I was doing wrong, according to the book, while taking responsibility for nothing.

I can pinpoint the exact moment I knew I had to leave. He was justifying the incident in which he had put his hands around my neck and strangled me to blackout, insisting he was doing what any normal person in his situation would do. No, it is not normal to control your spouse with force. He genuinely believed he had every right to harm me in that way. I realized it would only ever get worse. He had controlled me with guilt, fear, and doubt for fourteen years and now he had another tool in his toolbox. He was going to be violent again. I realized I didn't want to be around for that. This was one outcome in which I had no doubt.

I was all alone when I left him. He had made a point of destroying all the relationships I had built in Australia, and I had no one but him. I was able to sneak out to the library one day and use the free wifi to purchase a plane ticket back to LA. He was furious when he found out about the ticket, but he was aware I had gone to the police when he assaulted me earlier that year and he didn't try anything stupid in retaliation. I returned home in the summer of 2015. I was finally divorced on November 18, 2016—fifteen years and ten months from the day we were married. I was finally free, but now the true journey had begun.

The last three years were the hardest of my life. There were many times I imagined going back, only because the devil I knew was far less scary than all this independence, loneliness, and PTSD. My former husband drained our joint bank accounts the day I moved my belongings out of our home. I had no job and no money to hire a lawyer. I knew I had rights, but most of our net worth he kept in cash, so he denied it existed. He refused to buy me out of the property, and I soon realized that even if I received a settlement, he would have never paid it. I left with nothing, despite being the sole breadwinner for over ten of the fifteen years we were together.

I had family I could stay with while I got my feet on the ground. Although I had been working as a licensed counselor for the past five years, I was not stable enough in my mental health to carry on that career path. I went back to substitute teaching and enrolled in Medi-Cal so I could get some therapy. My first therapist was a great deal younger than me and most likely an intern, but she helped me so much. At this point, I was still binge drinking and blacking out about half the time. I wasn't ready to address my own substance abuse, so I pretended it wasn't happening. I had been a functional drunk for many years and I knew the routine.

After a while, a long-term sub position turned into a permanent job with medical insurance and I was able to afford to engage a licensed therapist. She helped me realize the depth and breadth of the emotional abuse I had suffered, as well as the origin of my abuse cycle with my own father. I learned a lot of new words to describe my sometimes-inappropriate reactions, like "codependent" and "PTSD." I learned that I was experiencing panic attacks and suffering from anxiety and depression. My PTSD is considered "complex" because I have had dissociative flashbacks. But I haven't had one for a while now, and the anxiety has definitely decreased. I'm also happy to say I don't drink like that anymore. All of this takes work. It's a lot of work, but I see now that recovery is possible.

Yes, I still experience doubt. I still hear his negative messages in my head. I'm still sad sometimes that I didn't take the time to get to know him before we married, that I didn't choose a more appropriate partner. I'm older and wiser now and I didn't have the tools then. I'm not sure I have the tools now, but I'm also not seeking a partner (I have a cat). I'm living on my own for the first time in my entire life. I have a well-paying job, I own my own home, I have a bank account with some savings, I have retirement accounts, I lease a brand-new car, and I buy shoes and clothes whenever I want. I also get to continue having a relationship with my three stepdaughters. Yes, it's terrifying sometimes, and I get triggered and backslide in my recovery. I make poor decisions. I still get depressed, but I no longer doubt myself. I trust my gut, because there is nobody to convince me I'm nobody. I finally have faith in someone who loves me and believes in my worth: me.

Resurrection

By Alane Ferguson

To live, die and then live again makes me an unnatural creature of this world, yet I feel that is what I am. Long ago a riptide of tragedy dragged my soul into the depths to drown, after which only the physical remained: body alive, soul gone. Now, years later, restored and whole, I wonder if the process of a spiritual death and resurrection happens to all who suffer. One thing I learned is that coming back to life is not the trick. Discovering how to be alive again is the true triumph.

The beginning of this soul-death came via something as mundane as a phone call. A stilted voice informed me that my best friend had been beaten, raped. A savage blow had cracked her skull before the coup de grace: strangulation with a brown leather belt. Savannah's body, naked and already ripened by the California heat, had been posed on her bed, legs apart, her face forever muted by a thick pillow. Blood soaked her mattress. I was told of defensive wounds and broken nails that proved how hard she had tried to fend off the blows.

"She was a *fighter!*" said the voice. I remember that word precisely, because that is the moment my legs buckled. And then I thought, *I don't give a damn if she fought or not, because she's dead she's dead she's dead.*

Savannah and I had been Yin and Yang, Split-Aparts, Soul Sisters. The two of us, friends since high school, had laughed, plotted, fought, teased, dared, pushed one another into trouble, saved each other. How could she be gone? No, I corrected myself, stolen! The only answer was it was a mistake—surely they had the wrong body. And so, confident in my denial, I dialed her childhood home number and heard the strangely calm voice of her father, Al Anderson.

I stammered that I'd been told something about Savannah.

"What did you hear?" he asked.

"That—that she's been killed." My words embarrassed me because of their cruelty. I waited an eternity for his answer, but the moment expanded into space. Over the phone, I could almost hear him lick his dry lips.

Finally, Al cleared his throat. "Savannah's been murdered. I'm making arrangements with the police right now in order to get her body released. I have to go." A click, and then silence.

The memorial flowers made the air at Savannah's funeral thick and syrupy. It had taken more than a week to hold her service because the pathologist insisted on picking though her body for clues. That is the first way a murder is different than a natural death. Savannah's remains had been turned into an object, and there is no privacy given to objects. Before the funeral Savannah's mother, Maxine, had called me, hysterical because someone had cut off her daughter's blonde hair—actually shaved Savannah bald—in order to record the blow marks on her scalp. "And the detectives clipped off her nails—her beautiful hands and face are ruined for eternity."

I, too, cried at this loss.

It's strange, now, to think how I mourned her physical destruction. Savannah's material self was destined for decay, so what difference did it really make? But it did.

Sitting there on that hard, wooden pew, I mechanically counted enormous bouquets, appeared to listen to church singers whose voices never reached me, pressed my fingernails roughly into my wrist, anything to numb myself from the agony of burying a friend who was barely twenty-three. Later, at the cemetery, I threw a rose onto her coffin lid. It gave a feeble bounce before slipping off the top, and I thought, *She will be laughing at me because I messed it up.* Her fiancé, Bill, threw a rose, too, but his was a proper toss and it stayed in place. Afterward, Bill gave me a valuable cherry wood clock that sits on my dresser today. This, too: when the murderer was finally caught, Bill called to tell me he was moving away. At that point I lost the clock's windup key and I decided never to look for it.

There is a hidden riptide that runs through murder. The waters around it are dark and cold, and if you stay too long in those currents you will freeze from within. Al and Maxine's grief overwhelmed me—what does one say to a parent who no longer has a child? I watched others drift away from them and their tragedy, so when Savannah's mother called, I came.

For a long time, the murder remained unsolved, which meant during that time of not knowing, Maxine obsessively reported the minutia of the case straight to me. She said that the police explained the killer had hidden in Savannah's bedroom closet—blood splatters told the story—and that Savannah had been dragged into her bathroom and washed like a mannequin. At night, I began to search my closet before going to sleep. Bathroom curtains became sinister, all men possible monsters.

Her mother's calls became more frequent and I honored my vow to never refuse Maxine. Eventually I became a kind of opaque presence in their home, gently sifting through Savannah's clothing or diligently working with Maxine on a grand tombstone that was never completed. I said very little during those times. Savannah's childhood home was a sacred space, and I felt that I was there to memorialize her. I began to believe that the more alive I was, the more dead she became. It's crazy how thoughts like that became normalized; I was sinking into them, drowning, dying.

One day I realized I had stopped feeling anything at all. It could have been the culmination of many factors—my husband had left me by then, and I was suddenly a single mother forced to move back home with a daughter in tow while pregnant with a second child. (I told no one but Savannah.) After Savannah was murdered, I lost the baby. In my own childhood kitchen, all alone, I hemorrhaged a tide of crimson that spread across the linoleum—it seemed to me a bloody crime scene of my own making. At that point, I was so dead inside I cleaned up my own mess while my daughter Kristin slept in her crib.

On my knees, too numb to cry, I used up rolls of paper towels, swirling my own blood like huge red petals that I then stuffed into garbage bags.

I remember how I felt a tug of separation. It was almost as if I could look down at myself from my parents' ceiling—from that odd vantage point I could see my skeletal arms moving of their own accord and the soles of my feet caked in blood. My physical being could function but it felt as though my lungs were filled with water and I could not breathe. It occurred to me that I wasn't sure I even wanted to. I understood that I could lean into this emptiness, let go so that I could float beneath the waves forever.

At that exact, pivotal moment, I heard a sound coming from a back room. My daughter had awakened and she was crying for me. At first, I did not move. I was too exhausted, too defeated, too dead inside. My white cotton nightgown was soaked and there were stains that reached my elbows like gashes. I knew I must look grotesque. Surely I would scare my daughter if she saw me. Frozen, I waited for her to fall back to sleep.

"Mamma mamma mamma."

Her cry reached me like a single, golden thread.

"Mamma mamma mamma."

I roused myself from the floor and washed myself as best I could.

"Mamma mamma mamma." Kristin was crying hard now, and I stoically made my way to her crib. Fat tears rolled down her cheeks. Her hair, blonde like Savannah's, made a halo in her nightlight. Her two-year-old arms reached up for me as I stared at her huge, blue eyes, searching for a way back. I found it. Through my daughter. Who needed me and whom, I realized, I needed more than life itself.

To this day, I don't know what would have happened without my daughter's intervention that night. I've thought a lot about how close to the letting go I came. When I heaved her out of the crib and into my arms I knew it was not my time to join the dead—it was time for me to return to the living. Kristin became the strand that knit together my disparate parts, and I've told her many times throughout the years that she saved my life.

The healing did not come all at once, but stitch by stitch. The first thing I had to allow myself to do was put a small distance between

Maxine and myself. I still visited her home, but I decided to bring my daughter with me. Because Kristin looked like Savannah, I think my toddler became a touchstone for Maxine as well. There was finally room in our conversations for the future, and Kristin's innocent love was a balm. Since I had dark hair and dark eyes, it was a tiny bit of grace that Maxine could see a shadow of her own child in mine.

Second, and I know how strange this will sound to most, I apologized to Savannah for living. It didn't seem fair that I, one of five daughters, was not the victim while Savannah, an only child, had been marked for death. I truly struggled with that—I felt as though the Universe had chosen the wrong friend. And yet...I had to accept that perceived injustice. In the end, I had not killed her. Robert Lloyd Sellers, the security guard at her apartment complex, was the one who chose to end her life.

The third path I took was to become an author. Writing is cathartic, and being able to at last control the outcome allowed me to excise my pain. In book after book, I saved my novel characters when I could not save Savannah. I changed the story. I wrote my own ending. And I made Savannah, through my newest protagonist in a series I am writing, live again. She is safe in my hands.

I am an unnatural creature. I resurfaced from those treacherous waters to live the life that was given me, through pain and joy. In reality, I have lived for two. And I plan to tell Savannah all about it, someday, when we meet again.

Keep on Keeping on

By Lauren Flores

Grief. A five-letter word with five stages. An endless road with no direction. That's how I felt sitting on the cold concrete steps of my apartment on the morning of March 8, 2018.

Struggling to fight back my tears, I looked over at my grief-stricken parents, searching for a reason why my twenty-four-year-old brother committed suicide. I will never forget the feeling of sudden loss and helplessness that consumed my body. Until that day, I had never experienced the devastating effects of suicide and that's why I'm choosing to share this story.

The night before I found him, I had come home from a long day of work and gone straight to my room. I showered and then walked into our kitchen to heat up some food for dinner. Typically, I would see Zach on our living room couch watching TV, unless he was out with friends. As the night grew later, I realized that his bedroom doors were both shut. I didn't think much of it since we both slept with our doors shut and I often closed mine when I would leave for work. Around 10 p.m. I still hadn't heard from him and began to worry. I called my mom to ask if she had heard from him—she hadn't. I knocked on his bedroom door. Still no answer.

I fell asleep later that night but then woke up suddenly at 3:30 a.m.—still no word from Zach. I began to really panic and knocked on his door again. At this point, I figured that he must not have come home. His bedroom doors were locked. As I think back to this traumatic day, I wish I had seen more signs from him. It wasn't like him to just disappear and not respond.

The next morning, I had to feed his cat Zoey. He kept her food in his bathroom. We lived in an older apartment with older locks that you could pry open with a hanger. I decided to just break in there. Once I did, I could see his bed from the bathroom and I sighed in relief. He wasn't home, I thought. His nightstand light was on. Turning the corner to grab Zoey's food bowl, I realized that our dining room chair was in front of his closet. As I walked around the chair I saw his lifeless body hanging from his bedroom closet. I didn't know what to do. I never expected to see my brother dead and there was nothing that I could do to bring him back. I immediately experienced head-to-toe chills and I ran out of the room for my cell phone. Within minutes, I heard sirens heading in my direction. Then I called my mom. I told her in an urgent tone to please come to our apartment. She asked what was wrong and I told her that I had found him but I just couldn't say the word "dead." I will never forget the screeching sound that came from our mother's mouth.

Zach and I were raised in a loving family by a single mother in Victoria, Texas, and had different fathers—both of whom had left. As we grew up, we moved schools and migrated through different apartments with our mom until we had the opportunity to start a new life. We moved to Austin, Texas when I was eight years old and adapted to each challenge that life presented us. We were the "three amigos," as my mom often called us.

Zach and I were two years apart in age and three grades apart in school. It was nice to have a little brother to go to school with and a sibling there for me each time we moved. Looking back, we overcame many adverse times in our lives—we were both navigating growing up without our biological fathers.

Throughout our childhood, I can remember going to the zoo, playing on the school playgrounds, and watching Zach play baseball, from tee-ball through select as he got older. He was a natural at sports and when we got to high school he lettered in wrestling as a freshman. We were adopted by an awesome step-dad and finally lived a "normal" life. After going our separate ways for college, we had the opportunity to live together again when I got my dream job at Google. He was working at a local digital marketing agency.

As I began my new job, I adapted to living with my brother again. We shared many laughs, hugs, and good food during the year. Zach was a great cook and always told me, "No carbs after 9pm." He always wanted the best for me and encouraged me to be healthier and kinder to people. I still hold many of his phrases close to my heart. Zach lived his life as a social butterfly, something I always admired about him. He always had friends over or was out and about in Austin. I never would have associated suicide with how he lived his life every day.

If he were sitting here today, I imagine he would want me to describe him as a handsome, tall young man with "great hair" and a charming personality. He loved being at home with his cat Zoey. "Be the person your cat thinks you are," he would say—another of his phrases. He radiated positivity towards others and had a beaming smile. He met people where they were in life and gave great advice. He had a big heart, yet he rarely showed his inner emotions.

The hardest part about losing him was that he never told his family or close friends about the darkness that was trapped in his mind. I wish that I could have been able to help him but it seems he was more in his element when listening and guiding others, rather than sharing his innermost thoughts. Our family would have done anything to help him get better. He had so much more life to live. Unfortunately, many victims of suicide don't show any warning signs or leave notes to their loved ones—and so their loved ones cannot ever fully understand why.

In this new phase of life, I decided to share Zach's story to encourage others to promote suicide awareness. As I sit here and think back on the way my life has unfolded over the last year, I am so grateful for the twenty-four years that I was able to spend with my brother, Zachary Ryan Flores. The biggest challenge was returning to work and holding back tears as countless strangers swarmed my desk, extending condolences. I started the Zachary Ryan Flores Foundation as an outlet to spread suicide awareness. I pour my heart into sharing Zach's story and will continue to do so for the rest of my life. My favorite of all Zach's phrases is to just "keep on keeping on"—a mantra I strive to follow in times of adversity. I try to keep his legacy alive through promoting the hashtag #LivingForZachFlores through social media. My hope is that my passion for mental health and suicide prevention awareness, something I came to care about because of him, will encourage more people to share their personal stories of struggle and find a safe place within their community.

By writing this today, my hope is that the readers who stumble upon my story will advocate for mental health so that we can all stand together one day against the tragedies of suicide. I hope that both my and Zach's stories can help save someone's life. You, whoever you are, are not alone. You are beautiful and have a purpose, even if some days you struggle to believe it. Never give up. You are so much stronger than you think.

Note: *Zachary Ryan Flores Foundation (https://www.facebook.com/ pages/category/Nonprofit-Organization/Zachary-Ryan-Flores-Foundation- 439642056469911/)*

Rescue

By Kerry Garvin

If you're a loner, you've got a drug that both soothes your desire for solitude while sparking your social synapses, allowing you to immerse yourself in the treacherous collective known as humanity.

Drugs come in many forms. For some, it's the smell of gasoline permeating fresh air and the rumble of a Harley across an open road. For others, it's donning a suit of armor and cosplaying. Or, like me, perhaps it's a dog that welcomes you to the world each morning, reminding you that unconditional love and loyalty do exist, and that there is still purity in what might feel like a wasteland of a world.

But when you're a loner and you wreck your motorcycle, or crash your computer, or your dog dies—you realize what hell it is to be truly alone and off your drug. We're all just scared. Or perhaps we've just been scared off—by others, by our pasts, by ourselves, by the fears between our temples. Yet, the desire for human connection, especially during turbulent times, is palpable.

The morning Manhattan sun splayed across my face around six. Instinctively, I rolled over and dangled my fingers, only to stroke the hardwood floor. My eyes stung upon opening them to the stark realization that the floor was bare where a chocolate lab named Max used to lie. My once bubbling motivation to rise and meet the day with a languid stroll through Riverside Park had been popped. The covers felt like concrete blocks. So I buried myself further beneath the rubble, searching for sleep, searching for a darkness that offered reprieve to the stark reminders of his sudden death.

Less than ten days ago I'd found my best friend suffocating. I was on a summer retreat with my parents at our family's cabins, blanketed by the wide leaves of long-standing trees, nestled into the Great Smoky Mountains of Western North Carolina. The mountains move like waves, rising in the morning haze that gives rise to their name, falling beneath pink-streaked sunsets in the evening. These mountains have been my constant, my unmovable peace since I was a child.

Max wandered outside of the cabin, gagging, struggling for breath, his legs shaking before he collapsed on the ground at my feet. His amber-flecked brown eyes pierced mine with a helpless look, one that told me he had surrendered, yet trusted I would save him, that I would find him breath. My parents searched for the nearest veterinary ER on their phones—the closest one being a mountainous and rolling forty-minute drive through the Southern Appalachians.

Convinced he was choking, never guessing cancer had swamped both of his lungs, I tried to make him throw up. In the back of my dad's Subaru Outback, I stuck my hand down his throat but nothing came up. He continued to suffocate. I did this time and time again on the drive to the vet, between whispering "I love you" and "I'm not losing you" over and over again into his ear.

"Here's your dog," said the vet three hours later as he calmly motioned me into a room where Max was lying on a stainless-steel table. Max looked up at me with bright eyes, wagging his tail beneath a white blanket they had placed over him. He had an IV in his left leg. And he was no longer choking.

I knelt down to be eye level with him. He offered me a rare kiss, slopping up the tears from my cheek. Max wasn't a kisser. And I wasn't a human who liked being licked or having my space invaded. Max enjoyed his space—sleeping in his own bed and showing affection on his terms. We were a perfect fit.

He had been kept in a cage for the first several months of his life before I rescued him. I presumed that was where his claustrophobia came from, or his repulsion at being cuddled too much. But here he was, licking salty tears from my face. It was a first. I imagined that in that moment, it was his way of telling me everything was going to be okay. His breathing had returned to a normal cadence and he seemed full of life.

The vet knelt on the floor next to me, in front of a computer screen that displayed x-rays of Max's chest and abdomen. I rubbed behind Max's ears as the doctor went on to say that there appeared to be a massive tumor behind Max's intestine that had metastasized into his lungs. Additionally, the tumor behind his intestine had pushed all of his organs towards his lungs, creating an immense amount of pressure.

I was in disbelief—I had just taken him to the vet ten days earlier for a check-up. But the vet explained that cancer in dogs works much more quickly than in humans. Still believing that I had more time with Max, or more options, I asked the vet what he thought I should do.

Just then, I heard a choke, and looked up to see my dad's face flinch in pain, tears streaming down his cheeks. His 6'1", 250-pound frame fled the doorway. I had never seen my dad cry. Never. This southern, alpha male could not stand in the doorway any longer.

I was in denial. Max was going to die. And it was all too much for my dad. He fled the scene but returned a few minutes later.

"I can't really tell you what to do. I can just give you this information. But when the IV wears off in about twenty minutes, he's going to be back in the same shape he was when you brought him in." The vet's eyes were wide with compassion.

It wasn't the answer I wanted. I wanted to be told what to do. This was a decision I had hoped I would never have to make. I'd hoped that Max would grow older and grayer—beyond his already old and gray thirteen years—and that his health and quality of living would gradually deteriorate. Perhaps he'd pass peacefully in his sleep. Or perhaps he would suffer a stroke and the decision would be easier. But this—this was sudden, dizzying, stabbing.

"I don't know what to do," I said through tears.

It was a lie. I knew the answer. I knew the decision that was before me, that I had to make—for Max. I couldn't let him suffocate to death.

My mom stayed strong throughout everything. She loved Max no less than I did. Her job throughout my childhood—between the turbulence of moving every year-and-a-half to keeping a blended family of five kids together—was to stay strong. She had this.

In the few days that followed, I sensed that my parents had conjured up a plan to be stoic and supportive, to offer platitudes to soften my tears. But I'd lost my support, my best friend, my drug that helped me cope with pain. So I drowned my grief in wine.

I wanted to fall apart, to isolate, to descend into darkness. The only way I knew how to emotionally process things was to be alone. Maybe that made me a loner. Maybe I was more emotionally porous than others. Or maybe I was weak. And scared. And distrustful.

I'd always chalked up my need for solitude to lonerdom. But that's too easy.

I hibernated in my apartment to avoid the crush of 4.25-million New Yorkers on my left side and 4.25-million New Yorkers on my right side. Back in my Upper West Side apartment, the loss was piercing. I numbed my porous and pained self with Oxycodone and Valium— leftovers lining the shelves of my medicine cabinet. Opening the door, without being greeted by a warm floor where Max had been waiting with a wagging tail, was a moment I dreaded each time I climbed a tread of stairs up to apartment 2B.

To be or not to be—that is the question.

With Max gone, I lived alone. I never considered myself to be living alone when I shared my one bedroom, one bath with Max. But I was alone—in my head, in my space. Nietzsche would be proud. Nihilism never felt so palpable. No man is an island, but this woman sure as hell felt like one.

The cruel trick of this life is that we enter it with a warm life-bearing force, but are doomed to die alone, to close our eyes to blackness, nothingness, breathlessness. Even cults can't quell the coldness of it. There's no solidarity in death. Death is a solitary experience, be it through shattered windshields, or a lost mind over time, or tumors spread out like webs hanging from soft tissues, or a field full of bodies bloated with cyanide. Loners know: prepare in life for what is inevitable in death. Max was gone. And so I fixated upon death.

Prods singed my side. I felt their nudges. It was time to come out of my hollow.

"Just get up out of bed right away and go for a run," said my mom.

"Force yourself to go meet a friend for a drink," said my best in London.

And the worst of all, "Get a new dog."

I stopped responding to texts, e-mails and phone calls. What hell it must be for a loner who is mourning in one of those cultures where you have to open your door for a week and people just drop by unexpectedly to visit. I liked my human interactions to be calculated. My excuses for leaving parties early were always plotted out in advance, with a reason why I had to be up early. If not, an Irish exit always did the trick.

Ten days after Max's death, I pried my laptop open and Googled "New York City rescue dogs." The first site I saw was RescueMe.org. I was surprised my photograph wasn't rotating through the sad slides of abandoned and stray animals in need of a "Forever Home." My long hair hadn't been brushed in god-knows-how-many days and my green eyes had a zombie-like outline of pink encircling them. I'd descended into dire cynicism, as my mind reminded me that nothing lasted forever, not even a "Forever Home." In that moment, I couldn't see beauty in the impermanence and fragility of life. Only death.

I searched the site by breed. Lab or Lab Mix. I wanted my Max back.

"Max can never be replaced," said so many friends and family members. Another burn, charring my skin.

The first dog I saw was a puppy with fluffy chocolate fur and light green eyes. I clicked on his name: "Saban." He was a male, eight to nine-weeks-old. I clicked on his photograph to enlarge it. Staring into his eyes, I saw uncertainty. He was sitting up, posed, looking straight at the camera. I recognized that look from my days starting out as a model in New York City, in a foreign land, where every heterosexual man felt like a predator and almost everyone else treated me like an object to be poked and prodded.

I wrote an e-mail asking if he was still available, explaining how I'd just lost my best friend of thirteen years. I was hoping "Saban" wouldn't be available, that he'd found his "Forever Home" filled with Frisbees, and frolicking children, and loving parents out in the free space of Connecticut or upstate New York. And he wouldn't be confined to his Forever Home with me, the Angel of Death, resembling a cave-dwelling zombie, in Manhattan. I pressed send anyway.

Days passed and nothing. I presumed "Saban" was adopted. Or maybe my depressive missive put RescueMe.org off. In feeling the first bit of warm light creak through the concrete covers, I made my first phone call in several days, telling my mom that I'd been thinking more seriously about adopting a new dog, and that I might've sent an e-mail inquiring about a dog. She gushed over the screenshot I texted her of the fluffy chocolate pup with sad eyes.

Back under the covers I crawled, burying myself further, beneath the books of poetry and fiction I held in my arms, feeble from the lack of any food. The fight was over. I'd surrendered to depression and suicidal ideation, frequent houseguests between my two temples, kept at bay for the last few years, rearing up to cause a racket in my space.

The loners of the world—the misanthropes, the introverts, the isolationists, the traumatized, the abused—have a secret crawl space to their darkness and an escape hatch from humanity. The depressive wants a reason to get out of bed. The misanthrope wants a creature aside from a human for connection. The traumatized and the abused want to learn to trust again. The introvert wants someone to share a small space with in solitude. If you're one of the above, or a bit of all of the above—like me—try rescuing a dog. They'll rescue you back.

Weekends during the summer in the city were hot, humid, and minus Manhattanites. I imagined them off gallivanting and eating overpriced lobster rolls, dripping mayonnaise onto their pink, popped-collar Polos in the Hamptons; or lounging poolside in a chaise with colorfully pedicured toenails at their summer homes in upstate New York. When the cars began to pry away from littered curbs, leaving long sought-after spaces void—the weekend was upon New York City.

And a loner like me could wander more freely without fear of being bumped into by or strangers on flooded sidewalks and subway cars—or worse, being bumped into by an acquaintance.

An acquaintance is truly the worst kind of relationship that exists—the sarcastic small talk of a neighbor, the super in the building next door who had been unsuccessfully trying to chat me up for the past three-and-a-half years, the hairdresser you dread seeing every few months. Desultory conversation is destructive to my psyche. I suspect they may think the same of me, and perhaps consider darting across the street when they spot my silhouette on the sidewalk ahead, just as my instincts urge me to do. Avoid small talk at all costs—even if it means being hit by a taxi.

Perhaps being a loner isn't truly a distaste for humanity, but rather despising the uneasy masks one has to wear while blindly, clumsily dancing with another human being, trying not to fall into them, never touching hands, just scratching around each other like an itchy wool coat. Perhaps being a loner is an act of rebellion against bullshit. Perhaps being a loner is taking a stand for truth and sincerity and authenticity. Perhaps being a loner is a load of self-absorbed, self-loathing, pretentious bullshit.

It's a sparse Sunday in the city on July 3. Flitting on my screen between research papers and writing, an e-mail pops up from RescueMe.org. The Oliver Twist of chocolate lab mix puppies is still awaiting his Forever Home. He was rescued with his sisters from a high-kill shelter in Alabama and flown to New York where he and his sisters resided in a foster home. A thump rattled my deadened heart.

His sad story, set against those sad eyes, made my heart feel something for the first time since Max died. Blood pulsed through my veins as I imagined an "Al A. Bama" engraved on his name tag, or perhaps hollering "Bam" from my lips in Riverside Park, beckoning him to return a Frisbee. I planned to meet with his foster mom, Denise, the next day, somewhere up in Westchester County. In case I fell in love, because I know I'd fall in love, I hit the bright lights of a Citibank ATM and withdraw the $350 adoption fee.

For the first time in weeks, the dark wood furniture and floors were spotless in my apartment. The place smelled of April Fresh as my laundry was folded and hung, instead of overflowing like a heap of lava spewing from my volcanic hamper. I brought Max's bed out from behind the leather sofa that had been acting as barrier to hide his things. Sinking to the floor, I smelled his dander. I couldn't bring myself to wash the brown faux fur blanket he'd routinely slept on in my car during our road trips. The blanket I buried my head in and cried into on the two-hour flight from Atlanta to New York City after losing him—as if it were his fur that I'd dampened with my tears throughout the years.

No, I couldn't wash his blanket. And I couldn't bring myself to gift his favorite Lamb Chop toy to another dog. But I'd prop the door open for another dog to wander into my home. Perhaps he'd usher out my glum houseguests of late.

The puppy fell asleep in my lap, amid the jarring but almost rhythmic potholes of the pathways that feed into Manhattan from upstate New York. Louis Armstrong's "Dear Old Southland" crooned from the speakers of the car. "Saban" grunted once, then fell asleep, snoring, his little puppy body vibrating along, added percussion to Louis' croons. His warm breath on the inside of my arm was a welcome contrast to the cool A/C, a reminder of a lifeform other than my own, frozen in grief.

I thought, it was July 4, and Louis Armstrong had always guessed he was born on July 4. He guessed, because he never had a birth certificate, and his mother couldn't remember the exact day he was born. And, in that moment, little Louis Armstrong Garvin was christened amidst the cries of the Louis Armstrong's brass. He was sweet and soulful and from the Southland, like myself. His puppy heart beat rapidly against my arm. And melted my own.

Little Louis Armstrong Garvin couldn't help but wag his tail at every passerby on the sidewalks of the city. And no passerby could help but stop, stoop, pet, and baby talk to his eager-for-attention-eyes. He killed my game—I couldn't tighten my shoulders and shrivel up into Cruella de Vil as people passed me. I had to stop. And I had to answer their questions. "How old is he?" "What's his name?" "Where'd you get him?" I answered all of their questions about Louis but then offered up a tidbit of information about myself.

"I just lost my best friend of thirteen years a couple weeks ago—a chocolate lab named Max."

 Not one face rebounded with a head tilt and nauseating platitude. Not one voice attempted to hush the harsh reality of loss. Not one pair of legs attempted to skip away from the mourner in black, with tangled hair, set against a sunny day.

"I hate to tell you, but it's a pain that will never go away. It just gets more dulled with time," said a man walking his dog that lived a block over. I must have crossed paths with him dozens of times in the three-and-a-half years I'd lived in my brownstone-lined neighborhood on the Upper West Side. His dog was white, fluffy and old. I felt like an ass, not having stopped and spoken to him in all the days of all of the years prior. He said he remembered seeing me walking Max. But I didn't remember him or his dog. I probably kept my head down, like a good loner, but more than that I wore the camouflage that most women wear for maneuvering the misogyny and harassments of New York City stress —sunglasses on, earbuds beating softly into my ears, baggy clothes hiding the bumps and curves that made me a woman. But this man wasn't a misogynist—he was a dog lover who empathized with my pain.

"I lost my best friend eight years ago and haven't been able to come around to getting a new dog," said the impeccably made-up older woman decked out in a St. John suit, who lived in the building next door—the woman I'd always avoided eye contact with since I was usually dressed in gym clothes, sans make-up, and insecure to the core in her presence.

"I hope you don't mind me saying, but if Max was ever reincarnated—which, I don't believe in reincarnation—but, I swear he's this puppy. Mellow, happy, in love with you," said the girl who managed the doggie daycare business conveniently run out of the apartment beneath mine. I always thought she said just enough to be friendly to me, as a customer, but never really cared.

"There's not one dog I've ever really gotten over or stopped missing after they died, even my childhood dogs," said the tanned and toned man named Roberto. He invited me to drop by his and his husband's home—the, ohhh, probably ten-million-dollar townhome on the corner, with the ornate gate and blooming garden in front, that I'd lusted over thousands of times, walking past it over the years. He wanted to introduce Louis to his rescue dog, Luna. He wasn't a heartless yuppie after all.

Damn it, more of my misanthropic bullshit was being cracked.

"This guy will rescue you as much as you rescued him," said the well-to-do blonde woman carrying a $5,000 Hermes Birkin bag who asked if she could hold him. His nails scratched at the delicate leather. She didn't care.

"A dog's love can really save you. It saved me after my husband died last year. My dog was there every night and every morning, and it helped that I had to take care of someone else besides myself."

One should never judge a woman by her Hermes handbag, I realized.

Pessimism had pointed its crooked finger at me, a proud and self-proclaimed loner (or, what was feeling more like a euphemism for "pretentious asshole") as those moments recurred on only our first walk together.

I rounded the corner to my apartment across from Riverside Park. The super who'd harassed me into saying "hello" to him for three-and-a-half years was resting against a car in front of the lobby to the building he maintained. His t-shirt was drenched in sweat, sticking to his beer belly spilling over his cargo shorts. I considered crossing the street, as I always did when I saw him. But I thought, "fuck it." I put my brave, big girl face on and walked toward him, toward home, Louis by my side.

"Hello."

I had no inclination of breaking my stride and caving to say "hello" to him.

"Can I pet your puppy?"

I considered ignoring him as I always did. But I didn't. I stopped and faced him. "Sure."

He knelt down at my feet, where little Louis Armstrong was hopping up and down in place, eager for attention. "What's his name?"

"Louis."

Out of nowhere, I spoke. Rather, I confessed to the super—to the man I've jumped in front of cars to avoid, the man who inspired letters in my head to the building's co-op board about feeling harassed by him, the man whose swagger down a sidewalk gave rise to a loathsome bubbling in my veins. "My thirteen-year-old chocolate lab just passed away," I said. "You've seen him."

"Oh man, I'm so sorry."

I pulled on Louis's leash, beckoning him to keep walking. Louis was quick on my heels, leaving the super kneeling on the sidewalk alone.

"Thanks for stopping."

I turned and smiled as I strode back to my apartment less than twenty feet from him. He might have been part of the reason I'd succumbed to what I'd always thought of as lonerdom. But in that moment, I was relieved—not necessarily because all of those people were something other than what I'd conjured them to be (which was, of course, horrible). Rather, maybe I was something other than what I thought I was all along.

Maybe I was strong enough to get through the loss of my best friend. Maybe I would survive because I told my story, because I entrusted others with my pain, and on the other end was an echo, a collective of people who'd been through that same pain, who'd survived, but who hadn't stopped feeling or remembering, because to feel, to remember, and to share our stories of struggle with others is what helps us heal.

The Silence After Bad Nights

By Sarah Graalman

When I was twenty-five, I had a bad night with a man I'd just met. I referred to it as a "one-night stand, but not a good one." That was all I ever said about that night for nearly a decade. No one ever questioned me—not even myself.

Years later, I was being pressed by friends as to why I was so picky when it came to dating. Why did I fall for those mostly unavailable? Why didn't I really try? I repeated my usual, "You know, I had that bad one night stand," which was a sentence I'd been running with for years. Why was it so difficult to be vulnerable? Why did intimacy seem foreign to me? My mind would always churn, wondering if I had deliberately shut myself off, like someone nonchalantly turning off the sprinkler in the lawn, "Why, I'll just shut this down for a bit, none of that healthy love for me this decade."

Friends pushed gingerly on the vagueness of my statement and what actually happened. I had a bad night—meaning, I'd met a guy in a bar, we flirted and had some drinks, then he asked me to go home with him and listen to records. He was expecting more. I wasn't. The night devolved from there. As I told them the real story, their eyes widened. "Holy shit, Sarah—you were raped," a friend stated. I nodded, and said the words aloud for the first time: I had been raped that night, a decade earlier. Saying it felt perverse. It felt strange, and even perversely funny to say. It felt like freedom. I then promptly fell apart for over a year, as I began the curious and difficult process of rebuilding.

I instantly began to reflect on that morning-after so many years ago. I remember walking into my apartment where I promptly froze: I couldn't get off of my couch, couldn't get food, couldn't talk without crying. All of the classic "something bad happened" moves. The only positive thing I could do for myself was find the closest Planned Parenthood so I could get the morning after pill. I made bucket-change working a makeup counter, so I had no money and no doctor I trusted. However, I'd always known that if something bad happened to me, I could go to Planned Parenthood. If I needed birth control or a wellness check, I could go to Planned Parenthood. If I was raped, I could go to Planned Parenthood. Someone there would help me.

I have known this fact since I was fourteen, long before I'd ever had sex: Planned Parenthood was where you went if something bad happened. (My mind still recoils at the knowledge that I was ever in that kind of trouble.) So there I went. I didn't give specific details to the nurse, as though I'd forgotten them myself. I just told her I'd had a "dumb" night, which was a soft-lobbed truth. I was cold already to the severity of the event—my psyche was only able to give me the strength to take care of myself, one tiny step at a time. The nurse gave me a pregnancy test and wrote me a prescription for the morning after pill, just to be safe. She told me if I ever needed to talk to anyone, I could always come back and talk to one of the social workers they provided. I've so often wondered if she knew, or how she knew, I'd been raped. I didn't realize it myself, until years later. In that moment, I felt safe and grateful for her compassion.

My life moved on around the incident, like scar tissue forming around that dark night and the darker days that followed. Instead of falling apart, I grew into a strong woman, successful and surrounded by loyal friends. Though, in my silence, a blank space grew where a romantic life should have been as I remained unable to express romantic or intimate vulnerability. I made up excuses such as, oh I'm just so picky, or I'm too opinionated, or my life is too busy. I'd do anything I could to shoot myself down while also protecting myself. I realized while confessing to my friends that night, ten years later, that I had to speak, or I'd lose the opportunity to experience romantic love.

I found a wonderful therapist, and after a few years of hard work, I became comfortable with my history. It's necessary, because it happens to so many of us. Hell—it's my duty as a survivor. I've mostly dropped the shame and embarrassment I was so affected by. Shame is a dense coat that never goes out of style and never loses a button. It clings to you, hoping to keep you company as though you need its unnecessary weight to survive or to remain protected. Frankly, I'd become exhausted by the weight of wearing it.

So I removed it, almost blindly. After nearly fifteen years it fell off my shoulders, hitting the ground with a thud, left in the dirt behind me. I'm not sure how it happened. I'm sure it was a combination of therapy, the passage of time, and the new awareness and outspokenness of society that let me know I'm surrounded by other survivors. There's safety in that. I'll now talk to anyone about my past. If I see them flinch I say, "It's okay, it happens to a lot of us, let's make conversation around the issue 'normal'." I listen to other survivors with empathy and without shock, encouraging them to say anything that comes to mind. I understand if they decide to stop talking.

Being raped or sexually assaulted is more common than someone getting a graduate degree, buying a new home, or traveling to Mexico on holiday. As often as I can now, I reference it in terms of the "stages of life" I went through. Hi, my name is Sarah. I grew up, went to college, moved to New York, was raped, became a makeup artist, then figured out how to be a person, put my trauma in my past, and moved forward. I place it right in there next to receiving my college degree— it was more impactful than my four years at a university. It was more impactful than being born with an hourglass figure and hazel eyes. It is part of my identity. I'm not grateful for the assault. But I'm grateful for who and what I am, and I'm a survivor.

Somewhere, between the mendacity of Trump's White House and the Brett Kavanaugh hearings, I'd seen enough, hurt enough, and remained quiet long enough that being shy or ashamed seemed the silliest (yes, silliest) thing I could do. If Kavanaugh can yell and cry about beer and his esteemed career being taken from him, then those held down against their will should express their own rage. I've become comfortable with my rage. It's appropriate. It's the correct emotion to feel. There's a lot to be angry at. It's the silence that's deafening and defeating us from sharing our stories. My rage has comfortably turned towards societal and governmental relationships towards women and our bodies.

Women's bodies have been talked about and treated as though they specifically aren't ours throughout history—as though we need some overlords to decide what is correct for us, even though we are dealt a hand the majority of men will never be forced to grapple with. Our government will continue to barter over our bodies when we are the only ones protecting them. I fantasize about standing in front of politicians, many of whom lack female reproductive organs, and ask, "Since your governance over my body is so personal, I'm curious—was your body was violated? If so, where did you go? Who did you turn to? How did you heal? How heavy has your shame been? Does it wake you in the middle of the night? Does it follow you, whispering in your ear that you're not worthy?"

In this fantasy, each congressman, judge, politician, or lawmaker must answer. No one gets time to create spin or pass their response onto someone else. The seconds of their silence tick by slowly, as they grapple with their answers. I need to have these questions asked of them. Maybe they'll surprise themselves with their answers, finding some deeply hidden well of empathy they assumed didn't exist. Or maybe they will acknowledge an inner fear that leads to their dismissal of women that has plagued them their entire lives.

There is value in asking hard questions of our leaders. There was value in my friends asking me difficult questions. Had my friends not questioned me, I might have remained mute on the issue forever, safely tucked away behind my own silence. We are powerful in our ability to hide difficult truths, even from ourselves, until we are able to deal with them. I am grateful to those friends who saw the flicker in my eyes that signaled I was ready to move beyond the past of that night.

My Crown, My Fire

By Janelle Gray

Growing up, my parents told me stories of how I descended from African royalty, from people who possessed great tenacity and pride, and that I should always carry myself with my head held high. My crown was a weight placed upon me but not a burden. Thanks to my family, to my ancestors, I've always felt conscious of my worth in this world—a contrast to growing up in the United States and a society that marginalizes Black women.

Some things are given to you, like a birthright, a crown. Some things are found along the way, things that ignite passion inside of you and give you purpose, a path forward that serves something greater than your self. I was given a crown by my ancestors and knew I was of value, of worth, in this world. But finding the fire, a passion, was up to me.

One weekend, while staying with friends in a rented house in Melgar, Colombia, far from my family in Texas, with nothing but green mountains all around, I had a chance encounter with fire.

Months earlier, I'd left my life—a safe, comfortable life, far more privileged than most. After seven years of promotions and good money, the 401k and benefits and corporate perks, I hadn't recognized that what passion I may have been building was being extinguished by a nice apartment, bi-weekly massages, spa trips, and financial freedom. I couldn't understand how, even in the midst of such privilege, I was going through one of the longest bouts of depression I'd ever experienced.

The lack of passion in my life caused my crown to slip, and it was then that it became a burden. But it was my family that reminded me I was built to carry that weight. I just needed to do something different, something drastic.

The last text I received before powering down my phone on that flight to Bogotá in 2015 was from my uncle. "May you find something transformative, lose something that held you captive, and may those things lead you to be a better citizen of the world."

And with those words, I left. I left my job and my country, and I moved to Bogotá to become a teacher.

Months later, in Melgar, I awoke early, after a night of drinking with friends, and stumbled to the kitchen table. The cook hummed an unfamiliar song as she cooked *arepas, huevos,* and *papas.* Her daughter, a girl of maybe fourteen, offered me a Tinto and told me to take it outside. *"La mananas acá son distintas que en Bogotá."* And she was right: Mornings in Melgar were really different. Quiet. Peaceful.

Sitting on the swing by the pool, I noticed singed plants in the garden. I asked the cook why the plants were burned, and she said there had been a small fire. I lamented the loss, assuming that the vegetation was their livelihood. The cook smiled and picked up a small seed, holding it in the palm of her hand.

She explained that she wasn't worried because some plants need fire to grow. *"El fuego calienta el suelo, haciendo que se rompan las semillas, provocando la germinacion, forzando el crecimiento."*

She told me that the fire heated up the soil, and it was the warmth of the soil that ignited something in the seed that caused it break wide open, triggering germination and ultimately growth. I have no green thumb, so this explanation was new to me. But it was applicable to my life. I was so focused on how fire adversely affected the plant that I could not conceive of how it helped.

Her words were a revelation. I had spent my life thinking that fire destroyed things, that fire was to be feared. But sometimes fire is necessary.

That moment with the cook was a small lesson I had stored along with other life lessons from my time abroad—a lesson I nearly forgot until recently.

Now that I'm back home in the United States, it feels like the world is on fire as I write this in 2020. The coronavirus surges, racism and hate thrive, and—for both reasons—people continue to die.

In the last year, I have lost thirteen people who mattered to me. Some were family. Some were friends. And some I hadn't seen in years, or even decades, but their deaths shook me.

Our culture glorifies working hard, staying strong, and keeping your head up—sometimes at a detriment to the individual, as if there's a one-size-fits-all standard of success. I'd lacked something greater, a purpose beyond myself, a fire that would evoke not only change in myself but in others' lives.

It was in Colombia that I learned to ride the waves of insecurity, of uncertainty, of self-doubt. I became baptized in the faith of my ancestors, from whom I had inherited my crown and the tenacity that my parents often spoke of. I filled many roles in my life abroad. I built a family of friends who are still some of my best. I became a university teacher and a private instructor. I became an author and started a social justice organization that features a blog and a podcast. I found my fire, my fulfillment. In Colombia, I learned *how* to be, not just *what* to be.

I'd be remiss if I didn't recognize the economic and nationality privilege I had there—something I had never really experienced. Despite my skin color and the racism I experienced in Colombia, I still lived a charmed life, ups and downs and all. And perhaps that was part of what drove me back to the U.S.

Having both studied deeply and written about the civil rights movement in the United States, I felt called home to action by the deaths of Philando Castille and Alton Sterling. Even in a place I'd called home for three years, a place where I grew into the person I loved being, I felt uneasy. I felt that my tenacity, my hard-earned self were needed in my country.

I had found my fire in Colombia but it was my return home to the United States that would force me to right my crown and put my fire into action.

The United States has undergone its own transformation in 2020. The coronavirus has brought the world we knew to an abrupt halt. Lives of those we love have been both threatened and lost due to the virus. And what's more, there's a new civil rights movement happening as the calls for Black Lives Matter grow.

As I was writing the first rough draft of this essay, I received a call from a firefighter friend who told me that the fifth Black man in two weeks was found hanging from a tree—less than a week after the decision not to prosecute for the death of Breonna Taylor. In the past eight years, we've called the murders of Freddie Gray, Rekia Boyd, and Botham Jean modern-day lynchings. In the past year, we've also called the murders of Ahmaud Arbery and George Floyd modern-day lynchings. There's an activation for action in my DNA that happened when my country sanctioned the murder of my people. My fire has not only been ignited, it is constantly being incited and stoked by all of the injustices to my people.

Before my move abroad, a family friend, Dr. Janice Franklin, told me that when thinking forward through the generations, our ancestors would have imagined me—a woman unencumbered by the chains of cannot, should not, or will not. That thought keeps me in the U.S., working for a better world. I am their child. I am happy. I am free.

And I cannot forget what it felt like to be passionless, to have a weighted crown that no one—not even myself—recognized as regal, as powerful. It is this feeling juxtaposed with the lesson on the little finca in Melgar that keeps me fighting for equity and freedom.

As the world burns, even as tears of anguish and fear and pain for my brothers and sisters fall down my cheeks, even as my heart drops as the coronavirus death toll rises, I stand firm and face the flames. Despite feeling battle-weary, I also feel strong, baptized in the waves of faith, forged in fire. Because I know, that fire yields growth.

Rescuing Jeff and David

By Kristiana Gregory

In the spring of 2016, in the courtyard of an Italian restaurant, the noise of New York City softened. We sat by a fountain under a trellis of sparkly white lights, a most tranquil oasis for our meeting. The head of Scholastic's Trade paperbacks, Craig Walker, said, "Kristi, we'd like you to come up with a series for middle-grade readers. Six books to start, many more to follow." Though a recent cancer survivor, Craig was ebullient with boyish good humor. His passion for children's literature was contagious.

Oh wow, I kept thinking. As a California beach girl and former newspaper reporter, my dream had been to write children's stories for traditional publishers. And so far, so good! After three historical novels with Harcourt and a dozen for Scholastic, I was happy to set aside research and just daydream. That patio lunch was wild. With other editors at our table, ideas raced. By the time dessert arrived, we had agreed on the setting of a mountain town in the West, called Cabin Creek. Stories would be based on mysteries I told my boys when they were little, featuring the young sleuths Jeff, David, and their cousin Claire. "This'll fill the sweet spot missing from kids' books," Craig told me. "A good clean adventure series." He mused on memories of his boyhood, and loved the idea of my adult son Cody drawing "David's Map" for the front of each mystery.

Our editorial team included my beloved, long-time editor Ann Reit. Already we had worked on fourteen books together. She had written and edited many of the Boxcar Children Mysteries, so she offered motherly advice: "Make sure the cousins have a good lunch and are kind to each other." Craig agreed. "Also, let the kids get muddy and into mischief," he insisted.

No problem! This would be fun. I modeled the characters and mishaps after those of my sons and redheaded niece. These good-natured stories meant a lot to me. They emphasized care for the environment and community, respect for elders and, as such, would be a legacy for our small family.

The joy of publication fizzled, however.

Craig's cancer returned. He died before being able to read the delightful letters coming in. He would have been thrilled to know *The Secret of Robber's Cave* and *The Clue at the Bottom of the Lake* had found an eager audience: reluctant readers, boys especially. Teachers and parents were rooting for more of these easy-to-read adventures. Momentum swelled. Excited and encouraged, I forged ahead, writing from my home in Boise, Idaho.

But the next summer my black desk phone rang, bringing cold news from the president of Scholastic. *Cabin Creek* had been cancelled, she told me. "Sales are not up to expectations. Book Fairs have dropped the series."

"Already?" I asked, my voice tight. "So soon? Number three isn't even out yet."

"A sign of the times," she said. Scholastic would fulfill my contract and publish the next four mysteries, but would not promote them in schools as planned. I understood the stiff competition of Harry Potter and other fantasies, but had thought there'd be room enough for all of us.

I managed a courteous good-bye and hung up. Head on my desk, feeling defeated and sorry for myself, I wept. I ached for another visit with Ann in her Upper West Side apartment where she was now bedridden with cancer, as Craig had been a few months earlier. She would understand my disappointment and tears, but I didn't want to upset her with that phone call.

She died three days later.

"These things happen, dear," I could hear her say. "Move on."

I mourned the loss of Ann and Craig and *Cabin Creek.* My previous four-book series, *Prairie River,* had also been cancelled. The letters "OP" began appearing on my other royalty statements.

Out-of-Print is heartbreaking to an author. It means the publisher has given up on selling, promoting, and caring for a title despite vigorous fan mail. It always comes down to sales. I grieved this loss deeply, noting in my journal, "I wrote these stories to be read, not just to collect an advance." For several weeks, I wrote nothing, not even in my journal. Wandering through a bookstore, seeing all the young adult novels and mysteries in print—not OP—put a lump in my throat.

Soon, however, a surprise. My sons Gregory and Cody, both entrepreneurs, told me about a new possibility: Amazon was offering authors a dignified way to design and publish books as paperbacks and for e-readers. With my husband's encouragement, the boys urged me to give it a go. Though somewhat terrified by the mechanics of self-publishing, I decided to try.

I began asking my publishers to revert the rights of my OP books. This took many months with many refusals, but I persisted.

When Holiday House returned *My Darlin' Clementine,* my family and I got to work. Set in the lawless Idaho Territory of 1866, we wanted to give it fresh visibility. We registered a new ISBN number and reti-tled it *Nugget: The Wildest, Most Heartbreakin'est Mining Town in the West.* Full of fresh hope, we launched it with a new cover and twenty of Cody's illustrations to capture the adventure. With an updated Author Note, we published it on Amazon.

Success—one OP back in print!

The rescues continued.

Next was *Bronte's Book Club.* A coming of age story, so close to my heart and set in a town by the sea—Gray's Beach—now has another chance to be read. Next was *Orphan Runaways.* A title I had never liked but the publisher demanded, has returned to its original—*Madame Mustache and the Boys of Bodie*—and I made sure to include the missing glossary and photo. Then *Jimmy Spoon and the Pony Express, Prairie River #1-4,* and *Hope's Revolutionary War Diaries #1-3.*

One by one, my formerly OP books were coming back to life, in a new form I could feel proud of. Soon came two of my *Royal Diaries* with Scholastic: *Catherine: The Great Journey, Russia 1743* and *Eleanor: Crown Jewel of Aquitaine, France 1136*.

Though the list was growing, I still couldn't get the rights for *Cabin Creek*. For five years I tried. Then, one random day in 2014, the contracts department at Scholastic emailed. They finally gave the thumbs up and even sent the digital files to save me typing and scanning. As soon as we launched these titles on Amazon with fresh illustrations by Cody, sales jumped. Not enough to land an Oprah interview, but floods of mail have encouraged me to create more adventures. Now I'm free to do so.

My family and I have had a blast brainstorming four more *Cabin Creeks,* the most recent, *#10: The Shadow at Shark Cove.* Its new setting of Gray's Beach connects Jeff, David, and Claire to their California cousin, Bronte. We've sprinkled in Cody's drawings to make each book friendly for young readers, and have redesigned the covers with beautiful artwork. I smile at this serendipity. The young detective David, who draws clues in his sketchbook to help solve each mystery, is modeled after my artist son who now illustrates the very tales he heard as a child.

This solo journey is exhilarating, but I miss my editors, their camaraderie and wisdom. The teamwork was such fun. I miss lunches at Italian restaurants and chauffeured rides to the airport. I miss the whirlwind tours and spotting my titles in far-flung bookstores. But despite all that, I'm deeply grateful to my former publishers—they put my books into the hands of so many children all around the world, in many different languages—and now many of those children are 'grown-ups' reading to their own sons and daughters.

Now I can reach readers quickly and keep prices reasonable. To publish with a click of a computer key reminds me of my days writing for a newspaper.

Instant gratification.

Also, I'm happy to report that rejections don't sting as sharply when you have an option.

All In

By Gillian Hill

My firstborn just turned seven. He's a little short for his age, but not by much. There he is running around the playground with his friends, laughing and chasing one another. He's a healthy weight. We only see the doctor for his annual check-up. He loves his teacher and he loves to learn. He writes books and reads voraciously—like his mama. He tells the funniest jokes.

I see all this vitality and health as my boy mingles with all the other children. I can barely spot him amongst the mass of first graders. But I also see the waves of his past radiate around him—an aura of spiky panic and caught breaths.

After a series of miscarriages, too many to count, I was finally pregnant, and it was sticking. Once I was into the second trimester I felt the fear of being pregnant after loss—you can't define what you're scared of, because it makes no sense. I was past the point where I'd lost previous pregnancies, so there was nothing to worry about, right? That's what everyone else thought, sometimes even said. It didn't calm me; the fear gnawed at my insides, and I tried my best to keep it away from the fragile life growing inside me. I had my hand permanently on my belly, cradling the growing bump, feeling a need for even more protection than my feeble blood and skin could provide. We didn't buy anything for this baby. We struggled to pick a name. Whenever a relative sent a piece of clothing in the mail, my insides would curl as I opened it. I was barely able to look. I could not and did not want to imagine a baby inside the tiny onesie, and when my brain tried to conjure up that image, my eyes blinked and shut it down.

As I approached the third trimester, I started to feel calmer. I just needed to get past that final hurdle, and then I could really believe in my pregnancy and this baby. Up until this point, the unreality of the situation had stared me in the face every day as I looked in the mirror. My outward appearance, lacking any noticeable bump, matched my inner feeling of being a fraud. I wasn't a mum yet, and I didn't know how I was going to become one. They say that the nine months of pregnancy allow you to prepare mentally for what's to come. I had frittered away the best part of six months refusing to believe what was growing inside me, unable or unwilling to connect and bond with the cells and tissues forming. I would jump this final hurdle, I told myself, and then I would commit, and I would be ALL IN.

And then, at a routine OB visit at 27 weeks pregnant, I was examined. The OB looked at me oddly and asked if I was feeling any contractions, any pain. I shook my head. I didn't feel much of anything, except the itchy fear that broke every thought, every sentence, from a complete whole into a jagged mess. It turned out I was dilated, and those slight pains in my belly were contractions. "We can fix this," the OB said calmly, "let's get you into the hospital and we'll put you on drugs to stop the process."

Ironically, at this point, with all my fears coming true, I became pretty confident. There was no way I was having the baby right now, it was too early, plus it was still 'the baby' to me. I hadn't hit that third trimester mark, I hadn't gone all in yet. So the baby couldn't be coming.

And yet, come he did. I stayed in hospital a few days as they put me on magnesium sulfate (or "mag") in an attempt to stop labor. Mag is a bitch of a drug, causing hot flashes, itchiness, and an awful weak buzzing across your whole body, as if you just consumed a triple espresso after running a marathon. My body was writhing and fighting itself as labor continued despite the doctors' efforts to stop it. My mind, however, was surprisingly calm. I was in the hospital, hooked up to monitors charting the baby's heartbeat and mine. I could look over and see our dual spiky lines threading across the computer paper as it slowly spewed out of the printer.

I realized that one of my biggest fears up until that point was that I didn't know what was happening inside my body, and I wouldn't know if I lost the baby, just as I hadn't with all those miscarriages. Now, while I was in a very bad place, I felt comfort that I could look up at any time and know with certainty what was happening inside me. Even if that something wasn't good. And so far, while it wasn't good, it also wasn't the worst-case scenario. This baby was still there. My body was rebelling, as it always seemed to do, but the straps across my belly that caught the heart rate were holding my body in place, forcing it to give up its secrets.

I went on and off the mag three times during my ten-day stay. Each time I came off it, labor would start up again. After the second attempt, they put me in an ambulance and moved me to a hospital with a neonatal intensive care unit (NICU) that could take a baby born at 28 weeks.

From that point on, my mind balanced this amazing sense of calm with a terror that was finally being realized in front of me. I am not normally one to stay in control under pressure; I panic, and can feel the cortisol rushing through my body as I flap about. This time, when it came down to life or death, I found myself feeling deathly calm. I called to cancel my birthing classes from the labor and delivery ward. When we realized there was no stopping the labor, and the doctors decided this was the day my baby was going to be born, I lay there, unsure what to do. My contractions had become worse during the night, but I had barely noticed, putting it down to gas pains.

Once again, my body was failing me, masking what it was doing, disconnecting and hiding its experience from me. I remember leaning forward so the nurse could give me the epidural and her laughing with surprise that I was so flexible. I didn't say that the thing that made her job so easy, my tiny bump, was because this baby was not supposed to be coming out today. Maybe saying that would have pierced the veil of calmness, forcing us both to see the horror that was lying so close underneath. Maybe I understood that once I ripped that veil open there would be no turning back, and that's why I didn't confront her.

The hospital staff had prepared me for the fact that when my baby was born, I wouldn't get to touch him. I probably wouldn't even get to see him. "He won't be breathing," they said matter-of-factly, "so we'll need to get him on oxygen and up to the NICU immediately." I pushed him out, but I did it in an operating room with an extra team of nurses and doctors just for him. I don't remember how many people were in the room—maybe ten? Having never given birth before, never even having made it to birthing classes, I had no idea what was normal, but I was pretty certain this wasn't it.

While I was on the mag, they had given me steroids to mature his lungs, just in case labor continued and I had to give birth. As a result, after very little pushing, this tiny 2lb 9oz mass of blue skin and red hair came out crying, and therefore breathing. It was the tiniest noise I have ever heard, and I never want to hear such a noise again. It was delightful and horrific and astounding, and it broke my heart. They laid him on my chest for a few seconds; I'm not sure I could even really see him, because he was up high on my breast, and he was so small, and before I knew it he was gone again, and my husband and the team of nurses and doctors left to take him on a cart to the NICU.

I gave birth at 8 p.m. I didn't get to see him until 1 or 2 the next morning. I remember being told to eat, and waiting impatiently for the food to arrive. I didn't care about any of it. I just wanted to see him. We didn't get to hold him for four days. They had to check that he was stable first. They had to take scans of his brain to check for hemorrhaging to assess the risk of even picking him up out of the bed. We could only touch him through the portholes in the clear Perspex box he was encased in. Even now that he was born, the disconnect between us was there.

After six months of fear and panic and refusing to think about this baby, while doing nothing but think about this baby, I was suddenly a mum. My husband and I learnt to parent in the NICU, surrounded by monitors, feeding tubes, alarms, and those tiny mews that only very premature babies can make. I clung fiercely to my boy once they let me hold him, and it's been hard to let go. He's seven and we've only just removed the baby monitor from his room. I remember when he was first home and we hooked up that monitor and a special plate that lay beneath the crib mattress that tracked his breathing. I would wake up in a sweat every hour and stare at that monitor, despite the fact he was in the room with me, and my heart would be in my throat until I heard the beep that confirmed everything was as it should be.

I am thankful that I am the only one who sees the aura of his birth story. It isn't his aura, anyway, it is mine. The first moment I could hold him, I anchored onto him and left this imprint. He is unaware, thankfully, and no one else can see it, which is as it should be. But I see that trauma resonating out from the day he first burst into the world. The scorched burn marks, as I was born again through his birth. Born as a mother who was decidedly ALL IN.

Don't Call It a Comeback, I've Been Here for Years

By Diane Hughes

Why do people so often describe a downward trajectory as a spiral? Mine was straight as an arrow—swift and disorienting.

"It's everywhere," were the words that broke the silence.

The result: a cancer diagnosis so resolute that it left no room for wondering. This was the exact moment my charmed life went straight to hell. And while my demise was swift, my recovery would take more time, but not before another cancer diagnosis was doled out—a grueling eighteen years after the first.

I grew up in an idyllic suburban neighborhood in the southwest corner of Baltimore—the mile between our house and the city a sufficient buffer from the city's rough reputation. My parents raised my sister and me with love and stability on the corner of a cul-de-sac filled with neighbors as coveted to us as family. A kindergarten teacher and a college professor, our parents were the bookends of formal education, as well as the parentheses that held our every happiness together.

If I allow myself to flip through the pages of my childhood, I see the four of us sitting at the round, butcher block table in the kitchen that always gave a little under the weight of my dad's elbows despite its thick pedestal. Most nights my mom would serve up a home-cooked meal on that table and my sister and I would inevitably start giggling—seemingly about anything, or nothing at all—until milk trickled out of my sister's nose, only making us laugh harder.

As we got older, friends would join us around that table, sometimes for the food, but more often seeking my mom's generous help or my dad's sage advice. Everyone was always welcome at that table. Looking back, it felt like the incubator for all the best ideas, the most exciting plans, the biggest revelations, and the greatest love. It was the security of that table—anchored by our parents—that allowed us all to ride out the waves of self-discovery without getting lost.

Graduating from high school filled me with more apprehension than eagerness. At seventeen years old, I chose to go to college within forty-five minutes of home and the comfort of my close-knit family. Always hesitant in unfamiliar situations, I liked being able to return home on the weekends until I felt settled in my new surroundings.

Another graduation four years later filled me with even more trepidation—for the first time, my path had no predetermined next steps. While I longed for security, it felt like the road led straight off the map. I stumbled around until I found my way with a string of dead-end jobs and roommates with yearlong leases. Then, the monotony was broken by a phone call. My mom wanted to know if I'd accompany her to the hospital the next week.

Huh?

It seemed my dad was having some discomfort after eating and all of the tests so far had come back negative. Numerous labs, scopes, and scans—from the top down and the bottom up—all told them nothing. This left no other option except exploratory surgery.

As my mind raced through the logistics of a day off from work and some time spent at the hospital where my sister was born, my heart flinched only slightly. My mom reassured me that she just needed some company throughout the long day. Without feeling much alarm at her request, I agreed to drive the half hour and join her.

Looking back on that sunny day at the hospital, my memory is more snapshots than rolling video. I couldn't tell you when we got there or even which car we took. I have absolutely no recollection of bidding my dad farewell or kissing him before he was rolled down the sterile hallway. Cruelly, my very first memory from that day is boredom. As I see it now—some twenty-two years later—it was my stalwart privilege that spawned that boredom. A privilege so ingrained that I didn't know it existed despite its constant comfort.

There was a nurse who updated us on functional details throughout the morning, but it wasn't until the surgeon surfaced that afternoon that we got any meaningful information. He did not preface it and there was no sugarcoating.

"It's everywhere." And, for emphasis, "He's black inside."

Freefalling is the best way I can describe the state-of-being that resulted from that one-way conversation. When I realized he was talking about cancer, my mind went straight to death and that wasn't something I had ever considered being an option. I wouldn't have thought it possible to yank a foundation straight out from under a home, but that is precisely what happened that day with those words.

The instability and discomfort that ensued were all-consuming. And I was totally ignorant to their effects. I started feeling trapped: by the traffic that confined my car on the highway, by the hours that chained me to my desk at work, by the silence that consumed the house at night. These anxiety attacks—though unnamed at the time—started to control my life. I stayed home as much as I could and cautiously ventured out only to familiar places and only with people around whom I felt safe. I started to lose sleep, weight, and confidence as I watched my dad carefully through the corner of my eye, not knowing what every wince meant in the larger scheme of his prognosis. He rarely acknowledged the tenuousness of the situation, choosing instead to focus on his work in cancer research—ironic, I know.

For eight-and-a-half years, we lived through periods of relative stability punctuated by episodes of acute medical intervention until my dad's body finally gave out two days after Valentine's Day. It was 2006. He had just turned sixty, and I, thirty-one.

Walking out of the hospital that final time, I was surprised by the relief I felt. I silently rejoiced in the demise of the cancer and the freedom that came from finally knowing how it would all end. My dad's silence about what he was experiencing left me constantly worried and gripped by fear. It had steadily run me ragged for years.

Unfortunately, my relief was short-lived. Leaving cancer purgatory dropped me into a new realm of hell—the one where I had to deal with never seeing my dad again. That is the crux of death after all. That solitary fact tainted everything in my life—most importantly, my relationships. I avoided my family, lashed out at my fiancé, and resented any friend I viewed as happy.

For nine years I moved with the awkwardness of a zombie. The more I ignored my grief and focused on surviving, the larger my grief loomed. I did not look at pictures of my dad and I did not talk about him with anyone. Those years included a picturesque, beachfront wedding, buying our first house, having two healthy baby girls, and adopting numerous dogs, but it is hard to recall a moment of unfettered happiness.

Fast-forward to the summer of 2015. Our girls are four and six. The sun is shining on a warm August morning and my husband has already left for work. My phone rings.

"Unfortunately, the biopsies show cancer: invasive ductal carcinoma."

Again. Straight as an arrow—swift and disorienting. This time, my own cancer diagnosis.

I am forty years old.

When my husband rushed home and found me hiding, I told him in no uncertain terms, "I do not want to get back on that cancer rollercoaster. I don't want it for the girls!"

I thought I had been down this road before—the one with the blind curves. And I can tell you with 100% certainty that the fear is in the not knowing. Not knowing what is going to happen, what you will have to endure, what you will have to give up, and what will simply be ripped out of your control. The weeks following a cancer diagnosis are filled with more questions than answers—more *not knowing* than knowing.

In addition to the doctors and the appointments and the tests and the scans, there are people you have to tell. You have to say the words over and over again—*I have breast cancer*—and it's exhausting. Each time I said the words, images would flash in my mind of vomiting, misery, and the final scene of my dad's corpse lying in the hospital bed as I walked out. My every experience with cancer told me the same thing: it was horrible.

When you become everyone's worst nightmare, news spreads quickly. I started to feel the sideways glances when I arrived at school pick-up. I grew paranoid about the conversations that stopped abruptly as I walked by. With my self-consciousness mounting and my first surgery looming, one afternoon it hit me: everyone was looking to me for an indication of what to do—just as I had looked to my dad. The problem is that in the absence of any guidance, people will take it upon themselves to imagine the worst—because if you aren't talking about it, it must be bad. I'm sure my sweet, stoic Daddy was just trying to protect my sister, mother, and me with his silence, but in all reality the not knowing only fueled my fear.

What initially felt like pressure, I realized, was actually power. *I* was in the driver's seat and *I* could dictate how this was going to go. So, I wondered what would happen if I made a joke. Would people laugh with me instead of pitying me? Would that laughter ease my fear? Could I turn this whole situation on its head?!

I started with a little profanity because no one can blame a cancer patient for throwing around an F-bomb or two. And who would dare scold a sick person for talking about losing her hair *down there* to chemo before the hair on her head? No one! Then there was the purple wig, the (temporary) neck tattoo that everyone thought was real, the Charlie Brown curlicue drawn on my bald head, and—last, but *certainly* not least—me flipping the bird at my final chemo infusion.

As the weeks wore on and the treatments wore me out, I told my husband that I kept expecting to get depressed, but I just wasn't. To which he simply replied, "Babe, this is your true spirit coming out."

My honesty involved tears and setbacks, as well as laughter and triumphs—this is a cancer story after all, and its realities were ever present. But it all felt like freedom.

Occasionally, throughout the seven months of my treatments—including two surgeries and six rounds of chemo—I had inklings of déjà vu. There were times when people would say the wrong things, make assumptions, or inadvertently make me feel bad. More than once though, I realized I had done or said those same things to my dad. I winced, acknowledging my ignorance, yet smiled, realizing his silent forgiveness of me. In those moments, I felt connected to my dad for the first time in years, and that connection allowed me to forgive as well—myself and others.

One of the greatest gifts of my cancer journey has been the under-standing of what my dad never said about his. Yet deciding to blaze my own trail with blatant honesty is what finally set me free.

It has now been almost four years since my cancer diagnosis and I rock my short hair proudly, knowing there is nothing to hide. There really never was. Our girls will talk to anyone who will listen about their mom's breast cancer—how I only have one nipple, how the medicine made me lose my hair, and how they helped take care of me when I was sick. And they'll say it all openly—without fear—like it was just something that happened to us once.

I still occasionally long for those carefree days of my childhood before fear took hold of me. But I wouldn't trade the solace that I carry, knowing I faced that fear and freed myself once and for all.

From Homeless to Healthy

By Elizabeth Hunter

Christmas has always been my favorite time of year. People travel from far away to be together. But in December of 2009, I hit a new kind of crazy that I had never experienced.

I was so happy—a new level of high, of "mania" I would later learn. I bounced from conversation to conversation, enthusiastically helping my family and volunteering to rake my uncle's leaves just so I could play and fall back into them. However, by late January or early February of 2010, there was a change in my behavior.

During the week of Valentine's Day, I had my first manic episode. I was twenty-nine years old. I had gone to hang out with some friends and arrived home late. Earlier that day, I had visited my mom, aunt, and cousin. I remember driving back and forth several times before ending up at a friend's house. But when I got home I was extremely disoriented. I felt afraid of my father and his girlfriend and thought that aliens had intercepted their bodies and were communicating through my father's voice. It was my dad, but it wasn't. My feelings and delusions felt very real. So real, in fact, that I stopped talking to my dad altogether.

He felt he had no choice but to call the fire department to assess me. I was then escorted to the hospital where they ran a series of tests and determined I had THC in my system, nothing more. This was insignificant, as I normally smoked weed when I hung out with these friends. I remember thinking I didn't trust the ER doctor because he was wearing a New York Yankees emblem on his scrubs top.

The doctor then referred me to Hillmont Psychiatric Hospital. My father loaded me into the car. Surprisingly, he and his girlfriend remained calm during the drive. When we walked into the hospital, we three were left in a room with bright Fluorescent lighting and a paisley-print carpet. I hadn't slept in over a day, so the floor looked like it was moving. I remember getting up to pretend to read the Arabic characters on the wall of a HIPAA notice that had multiple languages on it.

The intake nurse asked me a few questions, but I was clearly agitated at this point. The admitting staff put me on what I would later learn was a "5150"—an involuntary 72-hour hold. They determined that I was incapable of taking care of myself and so I was labeled a gravely disabled adult. The staff walked me down a long corridor and made me take out the laces in my shoes. I couldn't wear my belt or my hoodie—because it had a string. I spent three days in that hospital in a complete haze.

For the first time in my life, I was administered psychotropic drugs: Depakote, Klonopin, and Cogentin. I immediately proceeded to sleep for the next day and a half. I woke up the next day, just in time for dinner. Every four hours the staff would take my vitals, blood pressure, and, if needed, administer more drugs. Most of the time I didn't even remember when they came in, but I know they were required to do this because they didn't know how I would respond to the drugs.

On my third day at Hillmont, my dad came to visit, and all I wanted to do was cry. I didn't know why I was there, or why he told me to tell the doctors everything, or why I couldn't leave until I had. By 4 p.m. on that third day, I was given a packet of information about my prescription, pick-up instructions, and a follow-up appointment time with a psychiatrist outside of the hospital. I, at that moment, was free to go about being myself again, without ever having to think about staying in a mental hospital again.

On the drive home, my dad stressed the importance of taking my medications, going to the follow-up appointment, and not smoking weed. I wasn't able to focus or listen because I was still tripping on the new medications. I felt weird and not myself, like a shell of a person. I had an abundance of restless energy that wouldn't allow me to sit still long enough to enjoy a meal.

My doctor's appointment came and went. When my dad found out that I had missed my appointment, he became angry—angrier than I could ever remember. I felt like it wasn't that big of a deal that I missed my appointment—I would just reschedule. Well, that wasn't good enough. So, later in the day, as I was busy dancing at home in my room—as dancing was my only way to cope with all the excess energy I had—my dad gave me $40 dollars and forty minutes to pack up my belongings. He kicked me out of his house. He said he couldn't watch me ruin my life if I wasn't going to get the help I needed. He said he had already dealt with destructive mental health behaviors with my sister, who had been diagnosed with schizoaffective disorder at age thirteen. This time around, my dad thought the best approach in dealing with my disorder was "tough love." He hoped it would be the catalyst to snap me back from my manic episode. He didn't want to watch me go through the struggles he had seen my sister go through.

I felt as though my father had sucked the air out of my lungs. What a devastating blow. First, I just had this crazy mental breakdown experience, and now my safety net had kicked me out, making me instantly homeless with no other options or places I could stay. I asked my dad if I could leave my car at home, so I wouldn't lose it or end up with it stolen. I certainly couldn't afford to put gas in it. My dad agreed. I then asked him for a ride to Ventura.

He dropped me off at a local shelter. There I got an emergency couch for the night, but I would have to find alternate arrangements the next night. It was explained to me that, in order to keep women safe from any "funny business," there could not be a man on one emergency couch and a woman on the other emergency couch (only two couches were available); yet, only a partition separated the emergency couches from the women's beds. To make matters worse, the shelter had seven beds designated for men and only three beds designated for women. In any case, that first night, sleeping on the couch, I could hear music playing and I thought that there must be a movie being filmed. Ventura was known for all the movies that have been filmed there. So, I got up, got dressed and started to leave. The gentleman at the desk told me that I couldn't leave, and that if I did, I couldn't return that night.

At the time I didn't understand why he was so angry with me for wanting to leave in the middle of the night. It was 3 a.m. but I thought it was more like 10 p.m., and he didn't correct me when I said so, he just let me leave. He was true to his word and when I returned, he didn't let me back in. When I discovered there was no more music and the bars were closed down, I wandered the streets all night, afraid to sleep by myself in the dark.

The next day, I went back for my bag of clothes and personal belongings, but the shelter said they threw my bag away when no one had claimed it in the morning. I cried for a good five minutes and then left with nothing. I trespassed mostly, because I didn't have a care in the world—all my stuff was gone. I wandered into churches, spoke confessions to priests, and was offered food to eat and a floor to sleep on. I trespassed in other places and anytime I got caught and a cop picked me up, instead of going to jail, I went to the hospital on a 5150 charge. There at the hospital I had a bed to sleep in, three meals a day plus snacks, free time to color and listen to music, an hour to talk to the doctor, and time to go outside and play basketball or just enjoy fresh air. I mostly kept to myself, but every time I was in there, there was always a cute, famous person there, and that person would always gravitate toward me. I could never figure out why, but I guess it was because I seemed the sanest of all the patients.

On one particular stay at Hillmont, I was asked to meet with a woman who ran a group home for people with mental health disorders. I was only allowed to go if I didn't mind doing things as a "group" or being involved with "group" activities. I said that sounded fine by me and so I was escorted across the street to a mental health rehabilitation center. They gave me my own soap, shampoo, conditioner, toothbrush, toothpaste, hairbrush, comb, scrubby sponge—the works. They asked me how I was feeling my first night there, and I said, "I feel like I won the lottery." They laughed and said I would do great there.

This facility is one of several throughout the States that house lower-functioning individuals, providing 24-hour nursing care. There is an on-hand psychiatrist, therapist, and case manager, as well as group leaders and nurses. There are also cameras in all the hallways and therapy rooms. It is really a marvelously structured environment for people with mental disorders and disabilities. And to the people who work in this field, God bless them.

My nine-month stay became really torturous toward the end, when I seemed to be getting better and coming out of the fog. I had gained over forty pounds on the drugs I was prescribed, as they made me want to stuff my face all the time. The carb cravings were out-of-this-world crazy. I would eat a meal, only to be hungry for some sugary snack thirty minutes later.

When I was homeless I had met a guy who invited me to stay at his house for two weeks. I asked him to be my boyfriend the first night I met him. Later, at the facility, I found him on Facebook, because in the height of my delirium, I could remember everything he ever said to me. It played like a record in my mind over and over until I finally reconnected with him. When I went to visit him the first time, I asked for and received a pass to leave the facility. I agreed to come back later in the day. The first thing he said to me was, "What up, thickness?" He had clearly noticed that I had gained weight. I was so hurt by that question, yet still so excited to see someone who knew me before all the months of what felt like brainwashing from the pharmaceutical drugs.

We smoked weed together that evening and then I caught my bus back to the center. When I got back, they smelled the weed on me and gave me a drug test. Part of the condition of staying at the mental rehab center was that I wasn't allowed to do drugs of any kind. My passes were revoked and all of the staff watched me carefully for the duration of my stay. After three months of applying for disability benefits, I finally received them. As soon as I did, I wanted to leave. The caretakers urged me not to leave but I did anyway. I moved in with the guy whom I had met during my crazy homeless life.

Life was pretty rough with him because he had his own mess of mental issues: he was bipolar with PTSD and anger control issues. He hit me once in the four years we were together but it was the emotional abuse that really took a toll on me. Before I was with him, when I was living at the mental rehab center, I had started attending Alcoholics Anonymous (AA) and Narcotics Anonymous (NA) meetings. I initially went to get out of the facility, but I found that the more I went, the more of an education I got about my own family's history. It was therapeutic to listen to strangers talk about their drinking days, because I was able to forgive these people for their indiscretions while also symbolically forgiving my family for their own stupid shit. After I had begun dating this toxic guy, I decided to go back to AA. Also, I had been attending women's meetings three times a week and had met enough strong women who were able to help me move into a cleaner, safer environment and lifestyle, and away from those lost years of sitting in hospitals, taking all kinds of drugs that made everything worse, and being with a guy who preferred me sick because that way he could control me better.

Nowadays, I have adopted a healthy lifestyle that includes healthy eating and several forms of fitness that bring joy to my life such as dancing, hiking, yoga, and jogging. I have been struggling to get the weight off ever since I was in the facility and on the prescribed medications. I have learned that the added weight I carry now has to do with feeling safe. When I'm bigger, people in general tend to leave me alone. When I was skinny and crazy, men took advantage of me and most women seemed to hate me. I'm a lot smaller than I was when I was on the prescribed drugs, but I'm a work in progress.

Eventually, I returned to my pre-breakdown career as a licensed massage therapist, caring for others' well-being after I was fully able to move on from my breakdown. I had taken a five-year hiatus from working after the mental breakdown, diagnosis, and road to recovery. As a massage practitioner, one must be of sound mind and body to perform the work without transferring emotional or physical harm to the client. I take my oath as a licensed practitioner seriously. It has been seven years since my last manic episode. And I haven't had a psychotic break since then. Instead, I have a thriving business, a wonderful and stable husband, and a home. I also have coping tools and tricks to help keep me grounded and balanced.

I will never allow myself to forget what happens when I don't face my fears or emotions. I am still not precisely sure what caused my breakdown, but I do know that shortly before it I had gotten a divorce, been laid off from my dream job, and lost my home to a foreclosure because my ex-husband didn't want to pay the bill anymore since his name wasn't on the deed. Combine all of that with little to no sleep, and my mind just couldn't take it. It took a vacation from sanity.

In AA you can count your sober days and track your progress that way. But with mental illness, how do you count your healthy days? By how many days without another breakdown? For me, it's been seven years, and I hope to keep that going. I exercise, write, read, and do things for me, so I hope I won't ever have to go down that road again.

The Kestrel

By Natalie Komlos-Zeiler

I hear her strike, her fall.
like her I'm
crawling, clawing
an exposed fetus
scrambling for inner safety
for forgiveness
for certainty that phoenix stories are real
for this to be a story about rising
hook-like
in my stomach
deeper than guts
deeper than feeling's birthplace
on her feathered back panting
toweling her
wading through my eyes
a kestrel
our guests. our ghosts. our guides.
dying at my door?
a fetus myself, I only knew to swaddle her

and shush and shush and shush
and shush
shush
a settling
she rights herself
silently from hands to concrete earth
calling hollow-boned spirits to save her
a rustling
she saves herself to a needle-covered tower
and waits.
are you coming?

The Event

By Kristine Hope Kowalski

The fire started near my belly button.

Prickling hot and lightning fast, the powerful heat turned to numbness as it traveled up to my sternum. A dull ache I'd been feeling behind my ribs for ages suddenly ignited into intolerable pain which began shooting down my arms. Like needles, like knives. In its path, the pain left behind more heavy numbness.

I was driving slowly, less than a mile from my house, when I was forced to pull over down a dark, unfamiliar street. As I tried to shift gears into park, I realized that my hands had become paralyzed, balled up into fists after anxiously clutching the steering wheel. I tried to use a wrist to uncurl the fingers of my other hand, but the great effort made me dizzy. I felt the dim light bulb of consciousness flickering out, but remained alert enough to panic about freezing to death in the January snowbanks on the side of the road. Should I call my mother, or an ambulance? I reached for my phone, but the clenched fists offered no grip.

"Okay Google! Call home!" I tried to shout.

My tongue felt swollen, too big for my mouth. I sounded garbled, strained. Like I was whispering through cheeks stuffed with marshmallows.

"Call home! Call home!"

The phone voice assistant didn't register my voice as anything human. It almost made me chuckle: I sounded like E.T. The technology couldn't detect anything wrong either.

Somehow, I unlocked my screen and dialed one number with my knuckle. Speed dial connected me quickly to my mom. I knew I was near the house, but suddenly I couldn't describe where. It still felt like I was shouting when I slurred out, "By the highway! By the hill! By the trailer park!" Was I having a stroke? Was my mom going to find me? Since when was there a trailer park in my urban town?

Instead of hanging up the phone, I curled up as small as I could and lay down across the driver and passenger seats. Still constrained by my seatbelt, I felt trapped but secure. I closed my eyes and let the numbness take over.

As consciousness crackled back to my brain, I saw my parents pull up next to my car. I sat up easily, and looked out of my frosted-over window.

Later, a doctor in ill-fitting trousers who knows me by my first name would try his best to get to the bottom of what triggered the trauma. He furrowed his brow and wondered aloud, "What could it be this time?" He'd learn that the fire that started in my body in the car that day ignited on the drive home from a childhood friend's funeral.

Her heart gave out on New Year's Eve.

It happened out of nowhere, fast and unexpected, one month after her twenty-seventh birthday. In the new year ahead, she was supposed to be getting married, starting a new life. She was happy and, as far as any of us knew, the picture of health.

So why, ten years after we graduated high school together, were my old friends gathering for a reunion in front of her casket? It was too tragic, too unfair.

Then, my doctor would adjust his glasses like he'd solved the case. He'd ask how sad I was about it all, on a scale of one to ten. When was the last time I'd seen my friend alive? Am I sure the grief didn't cause the "event"? More questions I couldn't answer.

He would call this episode a non-epileptic seizure. Or if I prefer, he'd unhelpfully suggest, an "event."

My whole life, I had thought of events as weddings and birthday parties, not going temporarily paralyzed on the side of the road after an old friend's funeral. But over the next few weeks, the calendar's series of events included bloodwork, heart monitoring, and several trips to the imaging center.

The only bit of relaxation I got was during my brain MRI. A technician would come by to stuff me into a cozy, towel-padded helmet, and ask me for a preference on the music playlist she'd pump through the scanning machine. I'd distractedly say something like "whatever," and later break out in a full chuckle when she decided upon thirty uninterrupted minutes of Demi Lovato's greatest hits.

"Stay still, please," she said as she pronounced my name wrong.

For torturous days, I'd wait for test results: not feeling any better, but not getting any answers either. It would be a blessing, but a trip right back to square one to get the news: my heart was healthy, my brain was fine. It was a relief, but there really wasn't anything to be done about it. Sometimes things just happen out of nowhere.

It's not the first time I'd been delivered unsatisfying results.

Since I was about ten years old, I have had a series of chronic, invisible illnesses that didn't quite feel urgent to anyone but me. Not big and bold and capital-"I"-Important illnesses like a sudden heart attack. The quietly erosive kind that seep in slowly and challenge your livelihood by making everyday actions a struggle.

At first, it was a goiter: a swollen, underactive thyroid that was stunting my growth and causing me to gain weight out of nowhere. Then came the awareness of that weight, and my obsession with doing something about it. I'd be shuffled from pediatrician to specialist for years, given one pill or another, and told that the blood tests returned from the labs normal. Fifteen years later, another specialist would call it Hashimoto's thyroiditis and I'd cry because it sounded like an answer. But in the moment, I'd suddenly grow taller than any woman in my family had ever been, and the weight would spread itself out over lithe limbs.

In my teens, I'd go in to a clinic worried about a thyroid ultrasound and walk out baffled by the so-called compliments of an overly impressed technician. As she glided a camera over my swollen neck, she'd say she never seen such a thin woman with such a sluggish thyroid. There would be disbelief in her tone. Then she'd say she wished she had a body like mine. I'd join school sports teams just to stay fit, but soon compete in varsity instead. I'd struggle to keep up the energy required to perform well. I'd eat ravenously, unable to get my fill, and later not eat much of anything at all. I'd faint during a track meet, sprain both my arms when hitting the burnt orange AstroTurf, come to, and cross the finish line with stars in my eyes.

In my twenties, I'd feel dizzy all the time, and faint more often. I'd see emergency rooms more than specialists, but return home without concrete diagnoses every time. I would tear the knees out of good pants, falling when my strength sometimes gave out. All a medical fluke.

Then I'd have a seizure on the way home from my friend's funeral, feel level-10 sad, and find myself meeting new specialists: like one with fancy designer eyeglasses who cared deeply and wholeheartedly about what he could bill to my insurance. He'd hypothesize that my acid reflux, caused by years of eating No Things or The Wrong Things, was aggravating something called a vagus nerve, thus triggering anxiety and strange brain activity like those non-epileptic seizure "events." He'd say it was all connected, years of feeling wrong. He'd then run invasive tests, stick an endoscopy camera down my throat, and compliment me on my unwanted weight loss. He'd send me off with a placebo drug. And file a claim.

I felt sorry for myself for years. But when I picked up a $3 prescription for a fake pill I'd never take, I realized I never wanted to look sick. Or go into cardiac arrest on New Year's Eve. Of course not, nobody does. I never wanted sympathy or special treatment. I didn't want my old high school friends gathered around my hospital bed, weeping. Or flowers delivered when I fainted at work.

I wanted to be taken seriously. I wanted to be believed.

After nearly a lifetime of having big concerns diminished, lightly medicated, and brushed aside, I already knew that I had to become my own wellness advocate. I just didn't know how to do it. Studies show that women's health concerns are too commonly downplayed by healthcare professionals, written off as melodramatic hysterics. Many strong, resilient women can even talk themselves out of seeking help for the most extraordinary of pains. Even the big ones, like early warning signs for heart attacks. Would they be believed? Had they already survived worse? Sometimes the consequences are deadly.

I wasn't an expert at fighting for extra tests and second opinions in my own health journey. It took a life-altering roadside emergency to realize it wasn't just that my illnesses were invisible to others, but that my worries about them were too. No longer was I getting pushed out of doctor's offices for "complaining about childhood growing pains," when recalling symptoms of an autoimmune disease. My most visible, traumatic health struggle had also been reduced to an "event."

I thought my complaints had been persistent, messy. But I had camouflaged them too well.

Through the years, I'd crave a name for whatever was happening to me. No matter how grim, or how terrible, a thing with a name seemed fightable. Undiagnosed, unresearched, and unnamed always made me shiver, and felt too scary to face. Answers would still be wonderful, but even without them, I want to move forward.

The fire that started in my chest that day wasn't just acid reflux, or grief about the sudden loss of a friend, or some other undiagnosed, unnamed ailment. There is an additional pain that comes with not being seen, like a tax on what already ails. It sits with you, nags, and weighs heavily. It makes you wonder if you're worth the extra look.

But sometimes, it bubbles up like anger, and it helps you find your voice. It's worth listening to.

How Disney Brought Me to Life

By Amber Paige Lee

I will never forget the excitement I felt on January 12, 2009, as my family drove me down from Georgia and onto Disney property in central Florida. After months of waiting, I was here to start my six-month internship with the Disney College Program. At eighteen years old, I knew this was where my life would finally begin. Looking back on that day, I remember the nervousness I felt at being on my own, the excitement of being at the place where dreams come true, and all of the expectations of being a part of the magic, surrounded by beloved characters. Everyone knows that Disney brings a smile to people's faces. But for me, it became so much more than love-able characters and memorable songs. It was about my discovery of self-love.

In the summer of 2008, I applied to the Walt Disney World College Program. My whole life I had clung to Disney fairy tales, and my heart longed to experience that type of magic. Playing pretend, my mind would constantly drift away to thoughts of magic carpets, white horses, glass slippers, undersea kingdoms, and enchanted roses. Growing up in a small town in Georgia, I was sheltered from most of the world. I always knew my family was too good for that place, and no one in my family thought the same way as the people there. Everyone in our town looked the same, acted the same, and believed the same things. The fact that I was starting college in the fall was questionable for some people. The fact that I was moving to Orlando, Florida to work at a theme park was absolutely unheard of.

At the time, I had no idea that there were such a variety of people living beyond my small town—people who thought completely differently and did not judge others for their differences. At that point in my life, I had no idea who I was or how I should feel. My town felt trapping, and it made me feel as if something were wrong with me because I was the only one who did not seem content. I felt as if I were suffocating, frantically gasping for air that did not exist there. I felt lost and unsure, which in turn caused me to have low self-esteem. I battled an eating disorder in secret when I was sixteen. When I looked at myself in the mirror, my eyes would fixate on what I thought were flaws. This person I saw in the mirror was nothing like the princesses of my childhood. Why would she deserve a fairy tale? But maybe, if I lost enough weight, Prince Charming would show up and make things all better. These villainous thoughts poisoned my mind and cast a spell of doubt over me. By eighteen I still did not know who Amber was—but I was desperate to find out. I could not express why, but I knew that Disney held the answers I was searching for.

Driving under the giant purple banner that read "Disney College Program," I felt my heart pounding in my ears. I could feel heat rising on my neck in anticipation of this adventure. My legs were heavy and my hands were shaking as I walked through the check-in process, waiting to hear where my work location would be. Finally, the cast member at the last station told me where I was selected to work: The Magic Kingdom. Relief and excitement washed over my whole body, and a smile widened on my face. I was going to be working at the most magical part of Disney. I could not believe my luck. Saying goodbye to my family that day was hard—they would be leaving me in a completely different state for an entire six months—but knowing that I would be at the Magic Kingdom gave me courage that this would be worth it.

Walking into the Magic Kingdom on January 14, 2009 felt unlike any other time I had been there. Stepping into the park was like walking into an enchanted castle where all of the objects came to life. The lights danced on the buildings, the smells from the bakery spread down the street, the music suggested that everyone should dance, and the vibrant colors of the park turned the ordinary world into a Fantasyland—the most magical area on property. I had walked into the park many times in my eighteen years, but to walk in as a Disney Cast Member—an official employee of the Place Where Dreams Come True—made me feel like I really was a princess walking through her own kingdom. My heart soared as I glided down Main Street U.S.A. By the end of the day, my cheeks were numb from grinning. I could not help but question how someone like me could even think of comparing herself to a princess. Yet, with each passing day, no one called me a fraud. I started to feel that maybe I did belong here. What if every girl really did deserve to feel like a princess, and not just for pretend?

Knowing that I was a small part of spreading and preserving the magic that Walt Disney had established so many years before me made me glow. I started to feel significant, as if I had value. This thought, no matter how trivial it sounds, gave me a new, powerful confidence. I had the power to create magic for our guests and help them celebrate meaningful moments in their lives. I started to feel my own self-worth, because for the first time, I felt that I was needed and doing something good. I learned that confidence is not necessarily just about feeling good about something as superficial as your outward appearance, but it is something that comes from within you, when you know you have helped others and lived up to your full potential. Making other people feel special, and creating magic in someone else's life for no other reason than to spread cheer, created a glow inside me that I could not help but release. To me, that is what it meant to be a "Disney Princess."

The people I worked with became like family. Being immersed in a place that houses cast members from all over the world, I was able to interact with people from all of the Earth's corners. Learning about their different cultures and backgrounds opened my eyes up to the world beyond my town. Working in a culturally diverse environment saved me from growing up to be an unsympathetic person. These people loved me for who I was, supported me, and encouraged me—things that I never knew friends were supposed to do. They accepted me, and pushed me to be my best, for no personal reason at all, but simply because they were my friends. They spoke life into me and helped me see myself as an equal to anyone, even the fictional Disney princesses I had admired my whole life. This in turn helped me start to love myself, just the way I was.

After the semester, I could not part from the magic of Disney. I remained a seasonal cast member so I could still attend college in Georgia but return to Disney each summer and throughout the year. Disney was there for me through college, continuously teaching me more about myself, reminding me how the small things I did truly could impact the world. After Disney, my family members were inspired to move away from that small town and create their own kingdoms in new lands as well. Of all the things Disney taught me, self-love was the greatest lesson. I did not need to starve myself and hate my natural features in order to look a certain way. If I truly appreciated myself the way Disney inspired me to do, and I always made sure I was trying to bring magic into people's lives, then happiness and confidence would follow, and I would feel like a princess. Cinderella does not even wear a crown, so I did not need a crown to be a true princess either.

Through Disney, my fellow cast members showed me that I actually had it in me all along. That is what I miss most now—not the characters, shows, or magic—but the people. My Disney family. They showed me that the magic lives inside us all, and we carry it with us wherever we go. Like a princess under a sleeping spell who gets awakened, Disney brought me to life. Only instead of Prince Charming waking me up, I awakened my own soul. Now that I know what self-love is, the clock never strikes midnight on my adventure.

Once I realized that I felt happier with life, and about myself, confidence started to permeate through me for the first time, and it still continues to do so today. In my story, I was the one who could save myself.

Now I Know

By Rochelle Lierz

I met Robert when I was twenty-three. Our experiences of death were from two universes. His family was in a tragic car wreck that ended his mother's life when he was four. I, on the other hand, grew up in a hearts-lightly-broken bubble, fraught only with puppy love. Before Robert, I only glanced at graveyards as I drove past.

On a working Tuesday, twenty-six years later, I carved out the morning to be Robert's ride from his first colonoscopy. His doctor had added an endoscopy as well due to his complaints about not being able to swallow normally. My mind was in a haze of busy, so the possible endings of this day were lost on me.

The time in the waiting room went quickly before I was called back to his recovery bed. The young doctor swept in to give us the routine aftercare instructions. Then he landed on the last item. He stepped closer to me, nearly to my nose, and spoke in a hushed tone to almost shut Robert out of the conversation.

He wanted to talk to me with his eyes. The words that came out of his mouth were that he didn't like what he saw during the endoscopy. The message that came out of his eyes was that I had a flinch of time left with my husband of twenty-five years. At once, my eyes told him that I accepted responsibility as a caregiver, but I denied my husband's impending death.

On our ride home, I said, "So...are you calling your therapist, or am I?" Robert didn't respond. Our different universes showed up in how we confronted problems. Robert had a deliberate, take-no-chances approach, while I approached problems by experimenting with risk until achieving the desired result. Like any partnership, it took us a long time to find a way that gave both of us, as well as those around us, peace. The tension between us confronting various issues was like the breakthrough our brains needed in order to find the best solution. We weren't comfortable to be around sometimes—according to our sons, parents, and siblings—but it was one of our best features. We survived and thrived because we made this tension work.

My hands were tense on the wheel as I turned the corner and waited for his answer. I was holding back a dam of tears. A bedrock of our success was complete transparency. I could feel steel enter my body as I created a new normal. I raised a wall between what I was thinking and feeling, and what I shared with him. If he was to die, I didn't want him to see how my heart and soul might collapse; how the strong foundation we'd built for our family may turn to ash. I had decided it was time to separate my thoughts from his. After we had been home for a bit, he found me behind the wheel of the parked car in the garage—where I had stayed back to wail the first of many animal cries—to tell me that his therapy appointment was scheduled.

During the first three months of our journey, I was a stubborn and, probably, horrible wife to him. I wanted to climb into his mind and drive his human vehicle. I wanted him to say no to chemotherapy. I wanted him to talk about his prognosis in facts and figures like the analytical man he was. I wanted him to tell me what he wanted me to do after he was gone. He had none of it. He wanted to drive his mind, make his own decisions. He knew if he abdicated steering to another soul, his dignity and his reason for living would vanish.

Three months into treatment, Robert began his third chemo round, and I stumbled onto the threshold of his universe by falling onto the floor of the chemo suite. The nurse saw the struggle on my face as I held back tears at his bedside. She asked me if I would like her to find the social worker for me. I nodded quickly. Robert's eyes bulged with concern. He watched as his wife and caregiver was ushered quickly and quietly away.

In a dark and quiet room, the social worker encouraged my tears, asked me questions, and reminded me gently that I needed to only carry what was mine to carry. I did not need to carry anyone else's decisions, survival, or grief. Just my own. I needed to ensure that I was taking care of me. The energy that was left over could then be divided between Robert and our sons, in that order. As I left the chemo ward that day, my caretaking attention turned to me. I spent the rest of the week accepting life's essential lesson: death comes, no matter what you do.

A few days later, my good friend Stacey came over to spend a few hours with Robert and sniff out my own well-being. When she left, I walked her out. I hadn't seen her since the social worker rescued me. Once away from Robert's view, I broke down. She listened with compassion for a few minutes, then switched gears to problem solving: "How will you move beyond this?" I rambled off a list of ideas. She nodded a stern affirmation, and then said, "I'll give you a week, and then I'm calling in reinforcements." A hug later, she headed out of the driveway, and I was left with my work ahead.

My therapy-soaked life began. I saw as many, or more, wellness professionals in a week as Robert did. I learned how to breathe better, how to face grief better, how to stay safe as a caregiver and how to talk about the end-of-life process better. I asked for more help. I took people up on their "tell me what I can help with" offers. I separated my soul from his choices, ensuring his comfort and that his moments were spent as he wished. I managed our life like a business project, my best survival skill.

My substitute caregivers often told me that he asked, "Where's Rochelle?" That question injected guilt into my heart because I felt like I should always be there. Then I would stop myself and remember the caregiver statistics, which told me that many caregivers shave years off their lives while caring and can die before their charges due to the added stress burden. I was now living not only for me, but for our sons. The bossy "don't orphan your kids, Rochelle" voice paved the road for me to stay alive.

Two months before Robert's death, he and his growing cancer lay sleeping while Stacey told me that she was engaged. She said she'd been waiting to tell me because it didn't feel right to share her happy news with me. Love had entered her life and grown into the kind of relationship that she had longed for, while my love's body was dying. She said, "This isn't fair. Why can't we all grow old together?" I vehemently typed, "I'll never do this again. I won't put my heart out there again." We both knew my words were a protective lie. She said, "Oh Ro, your heart is so big and you have so much to share. I hope in time you'll reconsider."

As his cancer spread, my vibrancy lessened alongside Robert's, as much from my frantic caregiving as from my spreading sorrow. My ability to second-guess his likely decisions evaporated—I had nothing left to give. I could no longer pretend that his vitality was there, or that he was my partner. The decisions became mine.

The day he died was a holy day for this non-religious family because we seemed to float on air that day. Angels felt near. He died at 5:15 p.m. and the funeral home took his body away at 11 p.m. One of the legs on our chairs had broken so we wobbled and fell into each other. The night he died, my sons and I piled into the bed he had suffered in, but it was cozy to us, we felt close to him, close to each other. We lay there resting on each other's weary bodies.

Within days of Robert's life ending, I began to collect shrine objects so I could make it through my daylight hours without him. While they were only inanimate objects, when I held one of them, it was my own version of a virtual reality. Holding the rock he carried in his pocket—the one that his six-year-old son gave him—created a hologram of him as a father. Each object held a different hologram, each object kept me in the past.

Work had become a chore for the first time in my life. I had worked for pay since I was ten so I couldn't remember a time when I was not going to work each week. Yet, that familiar and beloved pastime felt unreachable. I only cared about Robert: his life, his grave, his voice, his face, his mind, his opinions. It reminded me of when you fall in love and can't get your lover off your mind, but the only reciprocation is in your imagination.

Occasionally and with growing interest, I was able to break

through and see three things that mattered. My two sons' movement away from their grief and toward their futures, and my own wellness. "Dear God," I would say to myself when I would fall, "what if I am one of the caregivers who gave too much and dies soon after her mate's death? You've got to get it together for the sake of your boys." Because I had experienced the purest kind of love in lockstep with Robert, I felt complete about my run at life. The abyss's voice was tempting me: "Your life has been good. You can let go now." The voice came a lot, as I felt my sorrow and stumbled through widowhood.

Along the way, I released my original reason for recovery, the one about recovering for the sake of my kids. That isn't my kind of a well-lived life. What I learned in the chemo unit on that day in July—about caring for me first and foremost—is the thought that manifested my own recovery. I could see that my future life was worth the effort.

How did I turn the corner in my grief recovery? A billion things—I tried it all—anything to help me find a speck of life, to build new memories, to make a new path forward: jigsaw puzzles, eating food I loved, turning away from alcohol as a soother, asking a trainer to teach me to move again. I became aware of my professional-grade co-dependence and began my journey to recovery from that. I learned about the grief process, what I do and what others do. I focused on sorrow, often waking up in the middle of the night to wail. I scheduled "grieving Sundays" so that I could park my grief work for a specific day, rather than race past it or have it interrupt my life's flow. I asked for help when I did the hard things, like deposit life insurance checks, pack Robert's stuff away, or go to visit his grave. When I became so tired from sleepless, grief-filled nights, I took a sleeping pill to get some solid rest. I got my nails done and had massages. I worked hard at finding things that reminded me that my one life was worth the effort.

Prior to Robert's cancer diagnosis, I was holding a veil between my version of life and embracing death as a part of a well-loved life. "Everything comes to an end" was only a sentimental fantasy to me. I hadn't ingested the plainest part of the message. Now I know.

Only a narrow slice of the human tribe knows what walking each other toward death really means day-to-day. Only a few take heed of that reality. They know that each sunrise brings a new opportunity to love. They know that heartbreak is part of the deal. They know that choosing to love again is the way through the pain. They know that misunderstandings disconnect people, and love glues them back together. They know that the fear that rises when you think about loving means that you are heading toward the light. They know that every act of love is the fuel that makes life worth it. And mostly, they know that no matter how deep the heartbreak cuts, it is always worth doing it again.

I didn't know when I met Robert, the grown-up little boy who had a deep scar on his heart, that he was a part of that tribe. He knew. He knew how he and I would end up in heartbreak, having thrown it all in, all of the love we had to offer. In his death, he invited me into the tribe, pulling me forward with his steady pace and not-so-gentle nudges, just like an ellipsis.

"Now you know...keep going...that's it...love again...and again."

Essay on Resilience, Take 38,474

By Bethanie MacDonald

I'm sitting on my back porch wondering how I got here—a bucolic garden with ivy-laden paths leading to woods behind my old, white Cape Cod in the Sandhills of North Carolina. Cardinals fly in between the camellia bushes that bloom with bright pink and red flowers in winter. I'm happier than I've ever been—though, I haven't always been here.

Seven years ago I lived in noisy Fayetteville, North Carolina. It's where Greg and I worked while stationed at Fort Bragg, home of the Special Operation Command. He was a soldier in the 3rd Special Forces Group. I was a Department of Defense civilian working for a unit nearby. We had a daughter, a few dogs, and a daily routine. Our lives were busy, loud, crammed with tasks, crisis, war, and homework. It was mundane, but satisfying. We were making a difference in people's lives, but not in a conventional way. We specialized in unconventional warfare and resources for their families.

Greg knew that his chances of surviving war weren't the best. I knew it, too. How could I not? He deployed seven times over nine years. It would be ignorant and irresponsible not to acknowledge and prepare for his death. Every time he left for a deployment we planned his funeral, arranged all the necessary paperwork, updated our wills, living wills, and powers of attorney, then hoped for the best. But hope is a dangerous thing.

In the summer of 2012, Greg's luck ran out in the Helmand Province of Afghanistan. There, in the arid dessert, he was shot in the head on a dismounted patrol. A medic at his side intubated him on the battlefield, keeping him alive in a coma from which he would never wake. He survived over a week, never recovering, actively dying, eventually being transferred to Walter Reed Army Medical Center in Bethesda, Maryland.

It was a humid morning at 0200 when I met the ambulance carrying my husband home from the battlefield hospital. Men standing around me told me I'd not want to see him in the condition he was in. I looked at them strangely: how could I not be there to hold my husband's hand as he was taken off the ambulance bringing him home one last time? When Greg was alive, he could barely handle having a cold. Now, as he lay dying, how could I not be there? How did I manage all of those years of war, unsupervised, with a career, a family, pets and plants that I didn't kill and a mortgage that I kept paid on time? I almost wanted to check the date on my watch to make sure we were not in 1812.

I always had heroes growing up. My childhood playroom was littered with dolls in the images of Wonder Woman, Amelia Earhart, and Clara Barton—women who were brave in the face of fear and adversity. As I grew up, my playroom became an office, and my heroes became women like the legendary Molly Pitcher, or the wives of Sparta. Women who faced death and bravely moved forward, heads held high, to rebuild their lives and their countries.

I had long kept an excerpt from Steven Pressfield's *The Warrior Ethos* in my desk at work. It detailed aspects of the battle of Thermopylae. Spartans were raised to be warriors. They were expected to be brave. More than that, the king carefully chose "specific warriors for the strength of their wives and mothers to bear up under their loss." He knew they weren't coming back from battle. Those women would rebuild Sparta. I kept that excerpt, I held onto it, as if these women were real and I knew them.

Greg was an organ donor. While I was prepared for everything else, I wasn't prepared to choose his extubation date. Choosing the date that your husband is going to die bears great sorrow, responsibility, and so much doubt. How do you know you're doing the right thing? What if he wakes up? What if he could actually survive? What if he could actually recover? You can never be prepared for all the feelings and questions that swell in your head when you bear the burden of making that call. I didn't make the decision to "pull the plug." Greg did. I had to oversee his living will. I had to do what he asked me to—the horrible thing he trusted me to do. I wasn't prepared to be so angry with him for asking me to repeat the words "remove all life sustaining efforts," or asking me to watch him die. But having been married for twelve years, I figured I'd been mad at him for less, so this was at least a very good reason to be mad.

For the week that Greg survived, I had to wake up every day and do something I didn't want to do. I trudged through every day, trying to make it from beginning to end, praying for something that would never happen. I depended on the comforts of science.

Science is pretty definitive. Faith is sketchy. You have to lean forward in faith and hope in the end it all works out. Doctors ran tests that showed us that Greg was brain-dead. He was having strokes, his organs would fail soon, and he had two heart attacks. He was not going to survive this catastrophic injury to his brain. To abide Greg's living will was the right thing to do. And that gave me comfort. But still, letting go of hope, and loving Greg enough to let go, was the most desperate leap of faith I ever took. Every story you hear on the news of some miraculous recovery is the story you want to be your own—like winning the lottery. For every day and every choice I made during that week, I prayed there would be a different outcome. But there wasn't a different outcome. God doesn't work like that.

Greg took his final breath in my hands in the early morning hours of August 8th of 2012. He wanted it that way. I didn't. I didn't realize it until I had to watch him die, silently screaming in my head, in a roomful of people. I had no control. I couldn't change the outcome. Death isn't as romantic as it is on TV. It's horrific. It's desperate. My insides felt like a raging explosion. Outwardly, I felt like I had to appear dignified. I refused to look like a crazy person, screaming and begging for one last chance for something that wouldn't happen.

I had always heard you shouldn't make any big changes the first year after a crisis. I knew my brain was rewired. I knew I was fragile. I was going through a mental checklist of things I should do to avoid the "crazy train."

I saw a psychologist and I dutifully took our daughter to one. I maintained a regular schedule. I did everything I was supposed to do. Our daughter, Gwen, turned nine the month after Greg died. I had a small party for her despite the grief we both felt. I celebrated holidays through tears. It wasn't the first time we were alone for a Thanksgiving or Christmas. It was just the first time Greg wouldn't ever come home for one. It was the beginning of how we would always be from here on out.

Then, right before Christmas, just a few months after Greg died, four unrelated life-changing events hit me like a pile of bricks. My car joined him and left this mortal world. Two of my friends died within days of each other. And I was notified that the Department of Defense would not be further funding my position. So much for not making any major changes.

I heard Greg's voice in the back of my head, "Get up. Move." Where to? What now? I had to do something. I bought the same car I had before. I thought that was smart. Don't make any major changes. I didn't want to learn a new car's buttons and features. I bought it in a color I wanted though. Greg had picked out the last one and I hated it. It was black with a black leather interior. I told him at the time he was crazy and I would burst into flames in the North Carolina heat with that kind of car. I bought a red car with tan leather interior. I felt dangerous.

I began talking with Mason, the widower of my good friend who had died right before Christmas. Bobbi and I had become friends in Vicenza, Italy when our families were stationed there in 2002. For years, our lives were intertwined by war for the men, and the daily hum of daily life for those back home. Bobbi hosted Gwen's baby's shower, our families met for dinner for when they visited, and we all supported each other as our careers and lives moved forward with each passing milestone. Her husband, Mason, was someone that Greg loved and admired for his broad wisdom, humor, and integrity. Right before Gwen was born, Greg asked Mason to be her godfather. Now, we were both in the same boat—widowed young, each with a child, and treading water in a world alone. Our friends were slowly backing away from us, not knowing what to say. For example, a friend had said "good morning" to me in passing, then immediately followed it with more apologies than if we'd gotten into a car accident, which was then followed by telling me I'd never have a good morning again. That shocked me. I *did* want to have a good morning. I *did* want to have good days. It was in my inherent nature to search them out. Even on the days when I woke up doing the awful things I didn't want to do, I just tried to muddle through my days, but I certainly never tried to make them worse. I was just waiting for them to get better.

Mason and I would have long talks about what to do next. We helped each other through the endless paperwork of death, finalizing estates, spellchecking headstones, and figuring out how to help the kids through their grief. We became best friends in the absence of our old friends.

Without a job I decided to go back to school. I had always chosen safe schools, ones that were easy to navigate. This time I chose the Harvard Extension School. I thought it was a long shot but I got accepted. Mason encouraged me. He cheered me on.

When it was time to make another decision, this time about homeschooling Gwen, he helped me do research. Gwen had wanted to be homeschooled for years. I had long told her she was safer in the public school system because I was not smarter than a fifth grader. I couldn't use that excuse anymore. With careful planning, I began homeschooling her the next year.

By the summer of 2013, Mason and I had been exhausted by grief, the process of death, and dumb things people say with good intentions. On a whim, he said we should take the kids to Mexico for vacation, half-joking. I agreed. What did we have to lose? We'd already lost so much. We left in July.

That vacation was the beginning of so many more. We went to the Bahamas, the beach in South Carolina, New York City, and eventually Mason asked to be stationed in North Carolina. When he asked me to marry him I thought he was crazy. Why would we want to go through the pain of losing another spouse all over again?

It didn't take me a full five minutes to realize that it didn't matter if we were married or not. It was another brave step in the face of fear. I never expected him. He was wise, kind and funny—and it didn't hurt that he was tall and handsome. We trusted each other, we knew what that dark part of the soul looked like when you tried to hide it from the rest of the world. He, too, held his wife in his arms after she died. He knew my secrets. He knew my pain. I knew his.

More than that, our kids were bonding with us, with each other. We were all becoming closer through these tragedies. Our children shared the bond of losing a parent. I remembered how Bobbi loved her son Eli. I wanted to care for him, as she'd want me to, as she would have: as a mother. If I were gone, I'd want someone to love Gwen and mother her, nurture her, and guide her through life. Mason stepped in and loved Gwen as Greg would have wanted her to be loved. The day she was born, Greg cried, held her, and said, "Daddy's got you." Mason knew that story. He knew that love for his own child, and he extended his heart to include Gwen. We each knew the love that was lost, the cost of that on the soul, and we felt an immeasurable amount of love that words can't qualify to comfort those aches. We were becoming a family. Color was beginning to fill our black and white worlds.

In 2015, after we were married, we chose a new home in a small, quiet, postcard-perfect town. Mason was set to retire from the Army in a few years. We began planning what that would look like. We mapped out new goals: what would make us happy, what would be truly fulfilling?

It took years of struggle, mud, and mess that people don't always see because we keep those things private. Each struggle, each time we got knocked back down, we got up. We had to. We had to be the heroes for our children, not on pages told in stories that weren't real. But we had to show them how to survive, how to rebuild our own Sparta. Death is for the living to survive, to thrive after. You take it— the grief, the heartbreak—and mold it into a legacy to honor those who are gone. It's an opportunity that should never be wasted.

That's how I got here. I got back up. I built something better.

The Common Denominator

By Angela McCall

How did I get here?

The truth is, I dug this hole for nearly seven years.

Seven years.

That's how long it took me to reach the rocks at the bottom.

No one helped me.

I actively and knowingly participated in every bad decision that led me to where I am now.

I am the common denominator.

I am my own worst enemy.

How did I get here?

I once

Drunk drove, totaled my car, and fled the scene.

Had reconstructive facial surgery because my ex-boyfriend broke my eye socket.

Was addicted to painkillers for more than three years.

Drunk drove, totaled my car, and fled the scene again, this time on my mother's birthday.

Was abused by my father as a child.

Moved halfway across the country to escape myself and my past.
Cheated on my boyfriend, repeatedly.
Drunk drove, totaled my car, and fled the scene one more time.
Moved again to start fresh.
Was arrested for a DUI.
Spent a night in jail.

The illusion I had of myself, of being invincible, was shattered that night. The culminating destructive decisions reached their peak, and I finally reached the rocks that I so foolishly thought I'd discovered long ago.

It wasn't the DUI, the humiliation, or the disappointment. It was the realization that I couldn't weasel my way out of this one, the realization that I had to dig myself out of this hole alone, and the realization that no one would help me, even if they could.

I'd been the girl calling wolf so many times that no one felt sorry for me this time, not even myself.

The hardest part for me was realizing that *this is all my fault.*

I couldn't blame anyone else.

I remember thinking for the past seven years, convincing myself of the fact, that I could handle anything.

Pain pill addiction, reconstructive facial surgery, abusive father, drunk driving accidents...

I. Could. Handle. Anything.

Every time one of my destructive decisions dug me farther into this hole, I'd tell myself *you can only go up from here;* but then I'd hear a whisper from within saying *things can always be worse.*

It's funny how alcohol tricks your brain, gives you the illusion that every decision you're making is the best idea you've had in your entire life.

Once it plants the seed, it grows until its vines have reached every cortex, suffocating you, inhibiting your rational thinking until it gets its way. You become a slave to the (sweet) nectar, a puppet at the mercy of the poison.

My drinking habit had been building for some time now. I traded one "salvation" for another when I made myself get off the pills. I convinced myself how much money I would save, because being an alcoholic would be more cost-effective. I convinced myself that I was doing better because I wasn't using *my drug of choice.*

It's funny what alcohol does to your brain.

It will convince you that anything you want to believe is true; it becomes the voice of reason in your head when you can't trust your own thoughts anymore.

How did I get here?

Because I let myself.

Because I both unknowingly and knowingly chose to be here.

Some days are better than others;
some days I live my life (almost) normally,
as if nothing ever happened.
Some days I live with myself.
Some days I can't get out of bed.
Some days I forget to eat, forget to keep myself alive.
Some days I let myself cry,
and some days I can't feel anything at all.

I thought I could ignore my past, run from it, push it farther and farther down into the deepest, darkest crevice of my mind, body, and soul.

I thought I could blame anyone but myself, especially *him.*

I thought by keeping on and not thinking about it, it would eventually go away, life would go on, and I would eventually forget.

But forgetting wasn't what I needed.

Forgiveness was.

Expecting someone else to apologize dug me deeper and deeper and inhibited me from allowing myself to move on, to grow as a person, to find myself, and to love myself enough to say *enough. is. enough.*

The only comfort I found about hitting rock bottom is that I was finally able to start climbing the steep slope back up.

I had to give myself permission.

I had to tell myself that I deserved a journey along the road to happiness.

I had to forgive myself.

I might never reach the top of the mountain, but every day I choose to keep climbing regardless of the setbacks.

I choose to get out of bed in the morning,

to let the sunshine kiss my face,

to set my eyes on the beauty that California has to offer,

to eat breakfast,

to take our husky puppy, Kodah, on a walk,

to feed our Manx cat, Luna,

to feed myself,

to love my patient and supportive partner, Micah, to love and cherish him for who he is, what he has done for me, and what he continues to do for me,

But, most important of all, I choose to keep figuring out how to love myself.

Robber Face

By Elisabeth Sharp McKetta

When I was a child I read a fairy tale about a robber who wished
to marry a well-bred girl. He knew nobody would take him with
his robber's face, so he used stolen money to have a mask made—a
perfect face, virtuous and innocent and trustworthy. With his mask
he courted the girl and she fell for him. They wed. They bred. And
many years into their life together, he confessed his story. He was
only pretending to be good. He had a mask. "Take it off, then," his
wife said. He did—and the face below matched the mask exactly.

Growing up in a family of four kids, a lawyer dad who traveled, and a
PhD-ed and law-degreed mom who chose to stay home with her young,
I spent most of my time in the company of a crowd. The exception
were those days after school when I went over to my nana's apartment
and had a woman all to myself. My nana was partially deaf, a heavy
smoker and heavier drinker, and a reader who could float on her back
in a swimming pool while reading a book. We adored each other. We
cooked, read, talked, and she gave me boxes of her old sewing scraps,
corralled in a Cutty Sark Scotch Whisky box.

When she was dying of liver failure at age sixty-seven, everybody who came through her hospital room believed she would recover. Each time she disagreed—in her quiet reader's voice, laden, I imagine, with subtlety and symbolism—the room silenced for a moment and then all the well-meaning adult voices swelled up to interrupt her, to say, *stop talking doom, you will be fine, you will kick this liver thing.*

In the end, she chose me, age nine, as the one she trusted not to argue. The room had emptied for a brief time—the adults were in the hall—and I was alone with her, and she held hard onto my hands and peered hard into my eyes, squinting at the brightness outside the window: it was springtime in Texas. "Elisabeth," she said, drawing out each syllable in my name, "I am going to die."

I did not interrupt her as the adults had done. What I did was worse. I ran screaming down the hospital hallway looking for another adult. I was whisked away home; she was told by the adults once more than she would be just fine; and late that night, she died.

It was the first time a person I loved had trusted me and I had let her down. It would not be the last.

No matter what else the adults told me afterward, I knew the truth: my woman was alone at the end, grasping for connection—and if this could happen to her, then it seemed the human condition is to be alone and grasping for others. This knowledge panicked me. It isolated me too.

It is easy to say now that the fairy tales of religion, which my Episcopalian elementary school taught us each day in chapel, appealed to my imagination and to the writer I would become. But in the two and a half years following her death, I descended into a bizarre stage of religiosity. *He descended into hell...He ascended into heaven...* These prayers we said each morning were nonsense, as far as my heathen parents were concerned.

I was alive when the Challenger blew; I watched it on TV. I knew that humans went into the sky, somewhere, and I also knew that there was an alternative to flight, and that was fire. The death of my most treasured adult, the one I felt so possessive of and singularly heard by, even though I had failed to hear her, merged in my mind with heaven, hell, outer space, and the people who died there. I became, in a whirl of weeks, obsessed with the afterlife. Obsessed, specifically, with a terrible idea that I might go to heaven, where all the prayers promised believers like me a ticket, and that my parents, nonbelievers, would go to hell.

My choices: heaven alone, or hell with my family. Both alternatives frankly sucked. This paradox ran though my head day and night. It merged with the sort of OCD many kids have (don't step on a crack, you'll break your mother's back) and I found myself saying silently, *step on that crack, you'll go to heaven, step on that crack, hell.* Every single day of being alive was terrifying. But being dead wasn't any better, for then the theoretical choice would become actual.

Fifth and sixth grade were marked by this mania. I dared tell nobody, because somehow I felt sworn to secrecy, a heaven-hell-determining oath between myself and presumably God, or Nana, or whoever was waiting for me on the other side. But my family knew. They knew because they'd find me kneeling in prayer in the kitchen and doing other strange and unsanctioned things. But I refused to talk. Once they tried to get me to talk to the one believer in my family, my Catholic aunt; she told me her own stories of trying to do well by God, such as not looking in a mirror for a year.

This was well-meant but did not help. Everything I did, every wrong word, every wrong thought, every wrong action, every mischief—such as going to toilet-paper some cute boy's house with my elementary school friends—glowed in my mind as a sin. I spent my days heavy with the awareness of my death and all the loneliness that would follow it.

By the summer before seventh grade, I had worn myself out. I think some part of my brain dedicated to my survival told me that God or no, heaven or hell or only blessed earth, I had better let go of worrying about this stuff if I wanted to make it to adulthood. So I did.

I couldn't control what happened after I died—maybe I was good, maybe I wasn't, maybe none of us were, maybe goodness in general was simply a collective mask—but I could act on the loneliness front while I was alive. I knew this was, to some extent, a sham. I had seen first-hand that you could love someone completely and still run screaming from them as they lay dying. Death, it seemed, was the only story. All the other stuff in life, friendship, fun, toilet-papering

and whatnot, however lovely, would not last. Those were only temporary distractions from the eternal question. Still, needing that
distraction, I turned toward action. I decided to screw my energy to
the sticking point and be very, very kind to everybody. If somebody
needed a friend, I would include her. I put a great deal of energy into
this, and my way of doing so at age twelve was to be very goofy, very
giggly, very innocent-seeming, and very hyper. Look up hyper hypo
in the old Saturday Night Lives and you'll get something of an idea of
what I was like. My efforts worked and I was not lonely at school.

Yet my isolation stayed around me, like a ghost sheet. The true
self, with its knowledge and its fears—this I could not reveal to any
of my friends. But I had company and people who valued me, both
at school and at home, and this was something. Movies helped:
watching movies and entering another story alongside other people.
This bonded me to other lives. I thought less about heaven and hell—
except for those nights when we all went toilet papering, then I felt
reminded of my sinner's guilt.

The summer between seventh and eighth grade I learned another
way to leave your death awareness behind, briefly, and connect to
another person: kissing. My first kiss was a sordid affair, in a broom
closet at a condominium at the beach. My second kiss didn't count;
it was supposed to be from my boyfriend on my thirteenth birthday,
but instead ended up being a wet peck on the lips from his dad in
an exuberant embarrassing dad-swoop in front of both our families. Years later I wrote a poem about it called "The Wrong Kiss." My
real second kiss was finally this boyfriend, though a few weeks later.
My third kiss, post-boyfriend, was the best of all, but I couldn't tell
anyone. It happened at a family lake camp. The boy was not a boy at
all but a twenty-something man who taught waterskiing. My body had
matured beyond my age while his had not kept up, an illusion that
made us appear closer in age, though we both suspected a wide gap.
We kissed—and nothing more—in his Texas pickup truck. For the rest
of the night, I could not hide my rapturous smile, reflecting to me in
the mirror. Perhaps there was a second story, besides death: perhaps
love, even temporary love, was worthwhile.
I went back to school in September after this marvelous summer of

kisses. I had told nobody about any of them, but the boyfriend (by this point former boyfriend) spread the news of our kiss far and wide, and the story grew and grew. On my first day of eighth grade, I went from being the girl who was everybody's friend, formerly the girl who was afraid to step on hell-cracks, to the girl who the boys and even some girls called a "horny ho." Boys who I didn't know grabbed at my breasts in the hallway, stared at me licking their lips suggestively across the classroom, stuck fingers without invitation down my jean shorts. They called out at recess, *you are so ugly, you are so horny, you are just a ho.*

The old crisis began to swell again. There would not be salvation for me in prayer and belief and being as good as possible, nor would there be salvation in physical intimacy, at being a jolly sinner here on earth—one was too private, the other too public, and both horribly shameful. My friends were not much help: they too felt afraid of being left out, though I suspect their terror was about social groups, while mine was about the afterlife—but in the end, it didn't matter. One group of girls in my grade pushed me against a bathroom wall at a birthday party and demanded that I swear on the bible that I had not done all of these things I had been accused of. The religious fear lingered enough—I would not swear—and I survived eighth grade, tainted in this way.

I went to a different high school—went on, and focused on friends, though even with my closest friends I always kept one part of my heart private, unconnected, one part that nobody could see—a secret protection, like a layer of fat for the winter, or a candle at an altar. I never got into drugs, I think primarily because I was afraid of what my mind might reveal if I dug too deeply beneath its rational floorboards. I played sports and for the most part I enjoyed schoolwork—I did well in high school—I excelled in field hockey—I got into Harvard—and I went to college a virgin, because hell if anyone would have any reason ever again to call me horny ho.

As the years parted like water, I found people—slowly, and one at a time—with whom I could share my solitude. From age twenty onward, I claimed writing as something I enjoyed and was good at, and through it I slowly hauled myself above ground. I began to connect myself to the other selves in the world. I found a joy, a lightness, a grounding in the world of the living, on good days. Most days, eventually, grew to be good. Eventually, I wove a life around this forbidden knowledge, as muscle forms stronger around an injured ligament. Yet, underlying life there is loneliness, a grasping for connection.

But still.

But still, I could make my life about forging connections. I could become a writer to connect through words; a teacher to connect through ideas; a mother and a spouse to connect through biology and love.

I see this story now as a fumble of my efforts at human connection on a broad level, through spirituality, friendship, imagination, and intimacy. None of these would be the whole picture, though all would combine in my adult life—though the religious zealousness would go away and be replaced with intellectualism, a book-curiosity that would later propel me to earn a PhD and become a writer, toiling privately, monastically, and writing about the things of life: birth, love, and death, as I have known or imagined them. I would have children, I would eventually have sex (in reverse order); I would stop being so afraid of death, but I would still feel safer with actuals than theoreticals. I would disappoint more people, but I would also do well by others. I would be called beautiful. The taboos and terrors of my childhood would melt into adult routine.

I still surround myself with a quietness: mornings of solitude when I am alone, writing, while my husband and babies sleep like the dead. Sometimes I wonder if this is the right way, or if somehow my heart is too closed, and I need to find a way to wrench it open more to chaos, to mystery.

I would grow up to study fairy tales, and when my children, growing up in Idaho, which is about a third Latter Day Saints, would ask me about God, I would tell them about myths and fairy tales and even bible stories, to the extent that I remember them. I tell them stories about my childhood, about my nana too, and I try to offer them the depth of attention she gave me. It feels as if my babies are grounded in the real, much more so than I ever was. They are connected to each other, to their dad and to me and their friends, and they are not ashamed to talk about big things; they seem unafraid. We talk at home about birth, love, sex, death, and any question that they ask. This feels right.

And I have found, in adulthood, that there are other stories besides death. Two, to be specific. Birth and love. Those three stories—birth, love, and death—cycle through our lifespan in a thousand different ways, many unseen, many times in a single day. I could spend my adulthood recognizing this holy trinity, rather than only seeing death.

My young believe that I am good but not perfect. Once in a while, they sense a vulnerability in me, and they come, usually offering a stuffed animal like a holy gift, to offer comfort. There are days when I wonder whether the mask has become real after all these years. I am taken back to the original petrifying question: *am I good? Am I only pretending to be good?*

So the mask, it seemed, was a way to cover imperfect love with perfect love. Maybe this is what we all do, and in the way that green things grow toward the sun, perhaps our life's work is to grow toward the mask. To grow and grow, until finally our real face becomes our ideal face and the robber mask pops off and is gone.

The Legacy of my Great Grandmother's Diamond

By Isla McKetta

My grandmother, the beloved matriarch we all called Baba, passed away in late January of this year. In the hours before her February memorial service, my family gathered in her apartment in Austin while the women prepared to sort through and divide Baba's jewelry. It was a day my grandfather had orchestrated involving a hierarchy, rules and a stop watch. Four generations of McKetta women took turns visiting what had been my grandparents' bedroom and pawing through the jewels and plastic beads laid out across what had been their bed.

A few sentimental pieces were set aside in the weeks between Baba's death and the memorial service and my cousins and aunts were already wearing their bequests. Because I live so far away, my cousins and I had conversed over email about the awkwardness of the great jewelry grab and about the fact that it had been decided that as the eldest granddaughter, I should receive her wedding ring. All my life I had seen that ring and its accompanying diamond on her hand, but I had never coveted it. Perhaps I saw it as inseparable from her. But on that morning, no one could find the ring and my grandfather's anxiety about finding it was contagious.

Halfway through one of my turns in the bedroom, my grandfather entered. The morning had gone on so long that the solitary visits where we each selected five items were abandoned in favor of clusters of women who were supposed to take more and more on each visit. I think I was leafing through Baba's drawer full of gloves and handkerchiefs when my grandfather pulled on my elbow and led me to the kitchen. The three-room apartment was filled with masses of bellowing relatives, but I felt a moment of quiet when my grandfather held out a green cardboard jewelry box. His gnarled hand shook as he cupped its small brown lid. I don't remember the words he used, but I think he said he wanted me to have this. That she had wanted me to have it. He pulled from the box her ring—a yellow gold band soldered to a diamond solitaire.

"This," he said, pointing to the diamond, "was your great grandmother Smith's engagement ring. Grandad Smith bought it at Macy's in New York in 1916 for $1,000. There was no sales tax back then. Baba got it when Grandmom passed away in 1948. And this," he indicated the gold band, "is Baba's ring. It cost me $1 and my ring cost Baba $2. Price was not the determining factor."

My grandparents were married for sixty-seven years. When they met, a day he describes as when his whole life changed, she had $70 and he had $5. The story goes that they divided their later assets using the same 14-1 ratio. I always thought he, who grew up in the coal mines of Pennsylvania and to whom money was important like it can only be to someone who has been hungry, felt unworthy of her whose family had been in America since before The Revolution.

As I slipped Baba's ring onto my middle finger—even with the sizer it was too large—I cried and thanked my grandfather. I told him I was honored. I was. I was also a little lost. I played with the ring, slipping it on and off my finger, I twisted it, but mostly I gazed at my hand and that perfect diamond—and at the weight of sixty-seven years.

I never thought of myself as a diamond kind of girl. Early in my relationship with Clayton, I sketched out a marquise-cut emerald I thought I wanted. Later I cut pictures of silver floral rings and hunks of shadow-boxed carnelian from catalogues. But there on my finger was a diamond solitaire and a gold band. My grandfather's band.

On that day in February, my relationship with Clayton was in a rough patch after two years of my Master's program, the resulting depression, and the pool of grief after my Baba—the person most like me in the world—declined and slowly passed away. I had always wanted to marry Clayton—I truly thought I had found my life's partner, and despite two breakups and certain days I didn't think we were going to make it, he was the one. But I wanted to marry him, not just to be with him. Even though I found the difference ineffable.

Clayton and I also came from disparate backgrounds with very different expectations about money. The blend of those expectations found us in a house we would soon own but were struggling to afford. Generous gifts from my grandparents and parents had accumulated into the down payment on our home. Clayton had no home as a teen-ager. I knew if we did marry that any engagement ring he bought would put us both into hock. But I couldn't stop thinking about Baba's ring and the pride and love invested in it.

Like an heiress, I spent willy-nilly in the days following my grandmother's death. No price was too high to make me feel pretty and offer some consolation—though everything left me feeling flat. Those totals plus the last-minute plane tickets were all added to my staggering credit card debts. Clayton had already been working two jobs to get us into a better financial position. He spent evenings with a gorgeous series of linked Excel sheets tracking where the money came in and left, and I threw fits when it came to talking about our joint accounts and was unwilling to even open the statements on my separate accounts. But after I came home from the memorial, I started to see the debt as both tangible and my responsibility. I had never been hungry, but I was working my way toward it and I couldn't visit a food bank with that diamond ring on my hand any more than I could hock a century of family history—history that had survived the Great Depression—so I could buy something pretty. And I couldn't ask my grandfather, a man who had worked for every penny he ever had, to dole those pennies out to me. I was an adult, and my finances were my responsibility.

The months following the memorial were months of opening and learning to treat Clayton as a partner. Months of using the benefits of our divergent backgrounds. He made sure we were in the black every month and I made sure we took our first vacation in years—booked with coupons and for only two days—because we needed to sometimes look beyond the numbers. After fifteen years we were working together on shared goals. And I was getting impatient again to get married. We talked about marriage and our upcoming anniversary, but I didn't really think this year was any different than last or the year before that.

During those months, I looked often into that diamond, slightly clouded with the oils from my grandmother's skin. I transferred the ring from finger to finger as I lost or gained weight. Resizing the ring would have destroyed the engraving—the initials of my great-grandfather on one ring and the date of my grandparents' wedding on the other. The ring didn't yet fit, but I wanted it to.

In October when Clayton wanted to go to the beach, I hoped he was going to propose in the way the mantra in the back of my mind hoped every day he was going to propose. Among the mass of kids playing in the surf and the bellowing sea lions, we found a moment of quiet sitting on a driftwood log. When he asked me, "Baby, do you want to marry me?" I didn't believe I was hearing those words and I made him ask me over and over. I held his long fingers as he slipped my grandmother's ring from my middle to my ring finger. As we kissed, I slipped the ring back so it wouldn't fall off into the sand.

Though I am not an heiress, I spent willy-nilly on our wedding, but I recorded every expense in a spreadsheet. I discussed the totals with Clayton as we went along and we paid off any amount that went on the credit cards. My dress was from H&M, my trousseau was not. My wedding ring—the ring we bought together—is yellow gold inset with sixteen tiny diamonds—one for each year we have been together. My ring honors and complements my Baba's and great-grandmother's rings. It also keeps all three of those rings—generations of family history—tightly on my left ring finger where they belong. Maybe next year Clayton and I will take a honeymoon. Until then, we are building our future together.

Romancing Risk

By Mage McManus

Eleven screws, two plates, three nails. A modern vision of an ankle repaired.

The ankle breaking felt like nothing. A swift, sharp crack was heard only within my own body, followed by a deep breath, many concerned eyes staring at me, and what I now know as shock settling in. I believe a woman may have several rock bottom smashes followed by the inevitable piecing together. This was only my latest one.

Considering myself an independent woman is a nomenclature I've always met with trepidation. I've lived my life as an independent woman, and yet I've often known my own description of independence to keep me caged. I've long confused independence with closing myself off from others—resulting in loneliness. Independence never felt good. Independence felt like a punishment that I, the martyr, must endure forever. The martyrdom gave me freedom to indulge in and chase recklessness—I deserved to be a risk-taker, I earned the release.

For so many years I had been torn apart by loss. Each year, another friend or family member would call, relaying the news that someone

I loved was dead—typically by drugs, suicide or an aggressive attempt to solve the pain that they felt. I related to it every time and hated that I couldn't give them what they needed to hear, what they needed to feel. I spent years in hateful relationships, trying desperately to save boys who had lost faith in themselves.

It was my job to seek them out and lose my mind trying to show them that there was still so much to be grateful for in this life. I mirrored this by throwing myself out of airplanes thousands of times, scuba diving with no licensing or experienced guides, buying and riding motorcycles, and romancing risk as often as I could afford to do so.

Skydiving had been my obsession, my sublimation for five years, alongside my "rescued" lost boy of six years. I would run back and forth between them—mostly solitary, as my family hated both. The edges of my handles and the sweat lacing my palms before the leap were the details that I sewed myself to in a time of my deepest unhappiness. I felt lost and manic. I felt joy on the days I was able to spend in an extremely expensive fantasy of driving or flying to drop zones, meeting others who loved this bizarre sport, feeling competitive and youthful and insulated. I managed to stay with just enough space between others and myself—just enough space so that the guilt would not follow my inevitable departure.

I remember a girl in school laughing when she learned of my skydiving. She calmly looked at me and said, "I wonder what you'll be doing after you're done with that in a few years." It saws through me more when a stranger sees me more clearly than a parent or a sibling. It illustrated how faulty I was at wearing the disguise of a freefalling, independent woman.

But she was right. Eventually, skydiving began to lose its appeal. Somehow, jumping out of a plane, thousands of feet from the ground, became repetitive and monotonous. And, as my classmate had foreshadowed, I was off to find the next thing.

I hadn't been interested in rock climbing in the past, with the exception of an awkward first date at Brooklyn Boulders. I met a rock climber who was also my first intro into real dating after my agonizing and violent end with the lost boy. He invited me to a bouldering gym in Long Island City, a place where the "serious" climbers would show off for each other. It felt contagious. I scaled one section of the wall, without any ropes, over and over again throughout the day—failing to scale to the top, letting go and successfully falling down to the mats without injury.

Then, it happened. There's no way to know why I fell and it cracked that one time. I lay there stunned, while everyone rushed around me telling me with pale faces not to look at my leg. I felt no pain, just confused and scared and desperate to convince these people that they were wrong—I was in the best shape of my life, as my failed relationship had spurred me into the gym constantly. I finally was getting back to feeling a sense of normalcy. This was not the time to have my hard-fought momentum just die on this dirty, chalk-coated, deep blue plastic sheeting.

As the ambulance made its way to the hospital, the EMT tried to get my number. He remarked that I was handling the pain very well. I arrived at the ER trying to chat lightly with others and trying to be a good patient. The doctors and nurses kept asking me if I was in any pain, not understanding my negative responses. Then, I was shown an x-ray of my ankle. The image of my ankle in pieces made me sweat instantly. I called my parents and calmly told them not to worry, that I would have to be set in a cast and hospitalized on bed-rest with surgery in two days.

I went to the hospital alone. My dog was taken care of for the foreseeable future, my parents were out of the country, and my new beau was just a little too new for me to be asking for help. I had worked in operating rooms for several years. Knowing what was about to happen made everything worse. I've had a few surgeries in my life and, for some reason, when I'm about to go under anesthesia I begin to cry. I cry silently and pridefully, with stoic tears rolling into my hair. This was no different—I obediently listened. I felt the familiar warm wetness on my face, just before I went to wherever we go when the medicine is flushed through our veins.

I can handle pain. I have many tattoos. I have sustained many injuries over a long-lasting, athletically-inclined life, and I am a stubborn jerk who will always try to show how tough I am. But this was very different. This was a spectacular agony. My nurse for the week-long hospital stay was named "Hollywood"—her maiden name that became her affectionate nickname among the rest of the staff. She left a little smiley face under her name and was one of the kindest people I had ever met, with big bright eyes and a crocodile smile. I was told it would hurt; however, I was not told that it would hurt so much that I would need a little button that released an extremely strong pain medication every ten minutes and that those ten minutes were to be the longest of my life. Still, I hung on, not quite ready to succumb to the bottom that was there in plain sight.

Once I was home, things became even more difficult. My button was no more, I was discouraged from moving frequently, and I had to maneuver myself into hot bathtubs on one leg, keeping my injured one out of water. The baths were the only thing keeping me remotely sane. I spent hours on my sofa, never getting comfortable, never finding a sweet spot. I feared going to the bathroom, as the blood rushing down into my leg would almost make me pass out. I was alone.

There's a reason solitary confinement is one of the most brutal ways of punishing someone, of breaking their mind. In all fairness, I was far from being confined and had an option of how solitary I chose to be. I wonder now if there was a part of me that kept my recovery so intensely solitary in order to push myself where I needed to go. I was alone most days and wouldn't have my dog back for several weeks. I would go into the bath every other hour, lowering my aching body and crying. I cried about my lost boy, I cried about my dog being gone, I cried about the six years I spent trying to change someone else as well as myself. I cried about my losses, my friends. I cried for all of the things I never cried for, and I did it every day for six weeks. I looked red and ugly and puffy. My eyes were glassy. I could be ugly in my bathtub by myself, I could let my belly fill with air and push it out with involuntary heaves.

I would get out of the bathtub, slowly dry myself off, return to the sofa and watch garbage television, repeat the process throughout the day. Toward the end, before I got out the stitches from my first surgery, I felt depleted and exhausted. I spent months in physical therapy learning how to walk again. I certainly didn't feel like I was climbing up from the bottom.

My second surgery, six months later, was to remove the impressive amount of hardware that was causing me daily pain and stiffness.

This surgery was supposed to be different—I was allowed to go home that day, even told I could walk on the leg. But this prognosis turned out to be laughable. I was back to near-bottom again—back to the bathtubs, back to the crying. I couldn't believe there was more.

This time, I emerged with some form of mastery. I had learned what a little too much of feeling sorry for myself had resulted in. I wanted this time to be different. I wanted to change myself before the bathtubs ceased. I started asking for help from my friends—I worked out a system where my dog could spend the nights with me before I slowly returned to being able to walk him on my own. I told people how I was feeling and even cried with a few of them.

My parents have always taught me the value of a good cry and a good shower, or in my case, many good baths. My rock bottom came not because of me, not because I wanted it, but because the powers that be decided I needed it. I think this is often the case. I hope I don't break any more bones. At the very least, now I make choices to use the energy that I once spent hurling myself toward death instead hurling myself into open, loving relationships.

Eleven screws, two plates, three nails. I will not miss them, yet I'll always have a fond feeling whenever I'm in a hardware store.

The Van

By Breanna McPhillips

In writing this, it feels like I am telling someone else's story. And in some ways, I am. Eight years ago, on an evening that doesn't stand out for any particular reason, I stepped off the curb to cross the road—not in anticipation of getting to the other side, but to end my life. I wanted to be released from the pain and trauma that cut so deep and that I could find no peace from. Suicide was my only escape.

I stepped off the curb into the path of a fast-approaching white Ford van. The driver has been etched into my memory—a fairly handsome man in his thirties with a few days' stubble on his face and a slightly receding hairline. Even though he was quite a distance away, I cannot forget the look of shock mixed with dread etched on his face, as he realized what was happening, that he was part of my story.

He slammed on his brakes and veered the van violently to the right. I stood motionless where I was and waited for the inevitable conclusion, content that the pain would soon be over. I felt at last in control. I remember the noise of the squealing brakes and the screeching horn warning me of his approach. At the last moment, I felt as though there were a hand on my shoulder causing me to take a half step forward. The van brushed past me, stroking the hair on my arms and ever so lightly propelling me forward to safety.

A few hundred yards up the road, outside the Tower of London that was beautifully lit up, the man brought his vehicle to a stop. As I stood there, I saw him get of his van, stumbling onto the pavement. He sat down on the curb, utterly shaken. I was still alive but not relieved; in fact, quite the opposite—ashamed that I'd failed again. I could not imagine the pain and despair ever ending and the idea of the nothingness that accompanies death still seemed the only respite. I was not out of my mind—yes, I was in incredible pain, but this was a lucid, rational, measured choice.

I turned and started to walk away, going through the options of how I could end it all: jumping off a building, jumping into the river, an overdose of pills, a knife in the bath. I decided I needed help, that I needed to go to the hospital, as I wasn't in control. I couldn't think about getting through the next day, the next hour, the next minute. I was literally living in that second, merely trying to survive. I decided to check myself into a hospital. I stopped at a few pubs on the way and downed a few shots. I was broken, crying, shaking, and hitting myself uncontrollably.

Somewhere between the Tower of London and the Royal London Hospital, I gained some strength and the darkness inside lifted just a little as I started to inch my way back towards the light. Wisely or not, I decided to head home to bed instead of seeking help. Although I didn't know it, my life had changed forever, and I felt as though I had nothing left to lose. This is an accurate description of the events that night but it doesn't explain why—why I stepped off the curb intent on killing myself and what drove my pain and depression that night and the many nights before.

Well, I suppose I should introduce myself. I'm Breanna and I'm a trans woman and yes, I do feel like coming out is somewhat like being in Alcoholics Anonymous. These events were all pre-transition, when I was still trying to present an image to the world of what I thought it wanted me to be. To some, I suspect that's enough information to fill in the missing pieces of my story, as sadly my story is in no way unique within my community. In the U.K., where I'm from, around 48% of trans young people have attempted suicide and 85% have reported self-harming.[1] (In the U.S., 40% of transgender adults have attempted suicide while 92% of those adults reported attempting suicide for the first time before the age of twenty-five.[2])

To fully understand the event of that night, one must understand what it is to be "trans" and suffer from "gender dysphoria." The full explanation is highly complex but hopefully this brief explanation will aid one in understanding my story and the story of the many others like me.

In the womb, the brain develops before the genitals do. For most people, the brain's assignment of gender coincides with genital assignment. But, for trans people like me, a mismatch occurs. For instance, my brain has always been female but my body didn't match. Gender is the sociocultural expression of our sex and for trans people it is in conflict—we feel this mismatch intensely as we are expected to act differently and are treated by the world differently from how we feel inside. This feeling of incongruence causes incredible distress, intense pain, and depression that is called gender dysphoria. The only treatment for this is transitioning and fixing our bodies through hormones and surgery to match our brains.

I've always known that I was a girl but it didn't seem possible throughout most of my life that I could ever be me. Instead, I thought I had to simply learn to cope with gender dysphoria. Growing up, my parents discovered me dressing as a girl numerous times but they couldn't accept it—in fact, they told me this was wrong and that I'd never find happiness or any love on this path. As a teenager, I saw a counselor but that proved unhelpful, as the advice that was offered to me was effectively to "man up"—a phrase I've grown to hate.

I internalized all of the negativity in my life as well as the negativity towards trans people in society and the media. I grew up really hating myself. The feelings I had inside me, as hard as I tried, would not go away. I grew up before the Internet revolution. I did not have information on what trans was, nor did I have contact with other trans people. I felt confused and completely alone. As I grew up, I learned how to hide and suppress my feelings as best I could.

However, these feelings never disappeared and every now and again would explode in a glitter bomb of cheap supermarket eye shadow and polyester skater dresses. This relieved the pain and tension inside me momentarily but left me feeling ashamed and hating myself even more. I think most of us in some way or another put on masks, but the image I presented in no way reflected me. Inside I was crying and dying each day I was alive. I could not look at myself in the mirror without crying, as it wasn't me who I saw reflected back.

At eighteen, I decided I needed to transition. I had read the story of a James Bond girl and model (Caroline Cossey) who was also a trans woman and I identified completely with her. Reading her story, it was as if I'd written the words myself. Reading her book exposed to me the "real me"—the one below the mask, crying to be set free. Looking at this beautiful, brave, strong woman I felt I could be me and decided I needed to be me. I told my parents and friends (which didn't go well) and then went to the doctor to be referred to the gender clinic (which also didn't go well). It's a long sad story, but I didn't transition at that point due to lack of support from the medical professionals as well as from my parents. I returned to university but a dark curtain of depression descended on my life and I attempted to end my life for the first time.

I lost all hope of ever being me and I didn't know what to do. I returned to trying to suppress things, as it was the only thing I knew how to do. I consciously decided if I couldn't be me, I'd focus on other things: career, relationships and material gain. Okay, I understand, these are the same things most people on this planet focus on, but those things had never been my focus, or my dream. All I ever wanted was to be the woman that I was—I went to bed every night praying to god that he'd fix his (or her or their) mistake and that I'd wake up the next morning as a girl. I never prayed for these feelings to be gone, as I just wanted to be a girl.

My life became about coping with pain and dysphoria, getting through the next day, terrified that the mask might slip and people would see the real me—a weird pervert who was unlovable and destined to live a hard and sad life alone. The next decade of my life merges into a sea of nothingness. But somehow I managed to get a good job, marry an utterly amazing and beautiful woman whom I loved with all my heart, bought properties, gained material wealth and took at least two dream holidays per year.

From the outside, I had everything anyone could ever want. Life should have been perfect and I should have been happy. However, I wasn't. And I was in even greater pain and inner conflict than ever. The gender dysphoria worsened as I aged. My feelings hadn't disappeared—they'd intensified. Every day I looked in the mirror and saw a smartly dressed, short-haired, professionally successful male looking back at me. In return, I would feel a sea of sadness, emptiness and numbness. I felt absolutely zero connection to the person staring back at me and felt that I was moving further away from the woman I was inside. I feared I'd never get to be myself. I started pushing people away in my life because I could no longer force myself to smile, laugh or care about anything anymore.

Every day I was at work I would lock myself in a toilet stall and weep, washing away my tears with toilet paper while trying to remain silent so as to not be discovered. I felt trapped in my comfortable and secure life that I loved in many ways and I feared its loss. But the future laid out in front of me made me utterly despair.

The night of the van, I got home, broke down and told my wife everything. We stayed up all night talking. There was a lot of shouting, anger, pain and tears; but also love, empathy and support were expressed that night and over the following years. When I stepped off that curb, I didn't end my life. Rather, I unintentionally shed any illusion that I could carry on wearing the male mask. That evaporated. It's been a marathon becoming me but the first step was definitely the hardest, as the other steps fell somewhat like dominoes afterwards.

Accepting that I was a woman, and a trans woman at that, has been the greatest struggle of my life but what ultimately led to me finding happiness. In accepting that I was a woman, I have medically transitioned (a fight all its own) and that has given me great inner peace and a reduction in the body dysmorphia that I'd always felt. However, I found accepting the fact that I was a trans woman particularly difficult, as it seemed to me to be in conflict with me living my life authentically as a woman. Now, I draw strength from being me, in my community, and being open and owning who I am. That I am trans in no way diminishes the fact that I am a woman.

I have experienced many struggles on this journey: experiencing the loss of privilege from no longer being seen as a man, being now seen as a woman in a society wrought with misogyny, challenges in connecting to being trans, prejudice, pain, assaults, and the loss of friends and family. Our journeys—the journeys of trans women and men—are long and marked with many milestones that never really seem to end. Over the last few years, I've learned so much about the world around me as well as about myself. Being trans, our stories aren't simple, straightforward, or identical. Our stories of becoming ourselves are stories of self-acceptance, medical transitions, coming outs and losses in doing so. As a woman, I've learned to listen to other women's plights as bigotry and prejudice are intersectional. We do not all experience oppression to the same intensity or configuration, but by listening to one another we understand our sisters and find empathy, love and common bonds.

Unless one has experienced immense sadness, hopelessness and despair, then one often sees stories of suffering as something that happens to other people, to those weaker, less strong, with failings in themselves and mental illness. However, what I've learned is that the shadow of depression is closer to all of us than we'd like to admit. Mental health must be taken as seriously as physical health, and investments in community and support structures must be made. We must break down the stigmatization of mental health so that people can face their issues and get help. Being able to talk openly and honestly to people you love makes such a huge difference.

I have only ever shared this story with gender specialists and a handful of people whom I trust implicitly, as I feel the stigmatization and prejudice of society. My first two suicide attempts made me feel such shame that I didn't tell anyone and buried my issues rather than deal with them. The van that was supposed to end my life, instead, started it anew. There have been many struggles since then I have had to face: from the loss of friends and family, to verbal and physical assaults, to facing prejudice both in being a woman and being trans, to the loss of my marriage as our life paths eventually diverged. But now, when I wake up, I see me. I feel right and true to who I am. And although life is immeasurably harder, it's also immeasurably better—I feel strength in facing the day rather than pain from merely surviving it.

If one wants to improve the lives of trans people, then one only needs to listen to us, believe us, respect us and support us in

becoming ourselves. Recognizing the power of one's voice and standing up to transphobia is another way: prejudice is never "funny," "in
jest" or "good banter" when you are on the receiving end of it. Let
trans voices be heard—do not talk for us or over us. Never debate the
existence of trans people—I don't debate cis individuals' genders, so
don't debate mine as a trans woman. Do not sexualize or ask trans
people about their body parts as this is personal and complex. The
names we previously went by are irrelevant, so don't ask a trans
person what their name was before; or, if you knew a trans person
previously, don't call them by their former name, as it really hurts. Do
research. Remember, there isn't one universal trans experience and
Google exists to uncover more stories.

Above all, treat trans people as human beings and don't be afraid
of making mistakes—mistakes will happen, but trying means the
world!

[1] Nodin, N., Peel, E., Tyler, A., & Rivers, I. (2015). *The RaRE Research Report:
LGB&T Mental Health—Risk and Resilience Explored. Project Report.* PACE
(Project for Advocacy Counselling and Education), London.

[3] James, S.E., Herman, J.L., Rankin, S., Kiesling, M., Mottet, L., & Anafi,
M. (2016). *The Report of the 2015 U.S. Transgender Survey.* Washington D.C.:
National Center for Transgender Equality.

The Thread of All Sorrows

By Melanie Mendenhall

When I was young, still in elementary school, I used to have a recurring nightmare: my grandfather was dead, and I was sobbing so much that I couldn't stop. Eventually, the grownups in my dream would tell me that I needed to give it a rest—crying didn't help, it didn't change anything. But I could only stop crying only once I was awake and aware that it was just a dream.

At that time, my grandfather was alive and well, though he was a smoker. The pulmonary disease that would end his life still lingered in the future. He was live and wiry, with a spring to his step. Unlike many other grownups I knew, he had a mischievous grin, a flash to his dark eyes. He'd come over to our house in the winter and head straight for the thermostat. He'd turn up the heat to some ungodly number like 78 degrees—even though my parents liked to keep the house cool. They would tell me to put a sweater on, but Poppop—as we called him—could just waltz in and turn up the heat. I liked that about him. I wanted to be warm, too.

When my grandfather was alive, there was so much about his life I didn't know. So much I'll never know. However, I did know that he'd never been close to his own father, a man named Ben, who abandoned his family during the Great Depression. My grandmother once told me that Ben was a "hard man." When researching the Depression and Dust Bowl for ninth grade history class, I'd interviewed my grandparents. My grandfather had told me how, although his family didn't have any money, they'd kept a garden, grown their own food. They didn't have toys, but they made up their own games and fun. They'd been happy. Later, my grandmother told me that my grandfather had nearly starved during that time.

Years after Poppop died, a cousin of his shared other stories about my grandfather's childhood. They were not happy ones. Not only had Ben been a "hard man," but he had severely beaten my grandfather and his brother. His abuse was not only physical. On one occasion, Ben promised to take his sons to a visiting carnival. Not accustomed to such treats, the two boys waited—as prearranged—for Ben to meet them at the carnival's entrance with the tickets. Ben arrived late. He flashed the tickets before the boys, then turned, laughing, and gave the tickets away to some other children.

Learning those stories reawakened the grief I'd felt over losing Poppop. It was difficult knowing how he'd suffered as a child. But I was in awe of him—of his spirit and character. Like anyone, he had his flaws and had made mistakes. But he always demonstrated such an encompassing love for us—his family. All the time I was growing up, the love he gave me was nothing but accepting and unconditional.

The last time I saw Poppop, I was home on a holiday visit. He'd gone into the hospital; it seemed like the end. We all gathered to say goodbye. I can still hear his voice—ragged and broken—as I waited outside his hospital room. He was groaning and telling whoever was in the room how much it hurt to breathe. I dreaded going in to see him. I didn't want to see him struggling and so vulnerable.

By the time I did go in, morphine had calmed him. We looked at each other, and I took his shaky hand—his hands had started shaking all the time in recent years, a side effect of medication or just a general breaking down of his body, I didn't know. Everyone in our family joked about his shaky hands. He couldn't hold a camera steady enough to take a picture anymore. I hated the shaking and didn't find it funny. It broke my heart to see him unable to do simple things.

After that day, he stabilized somewhat and was eventually able to go home. Prior to his release, I went by the hospital again before flying back to my life. He seemed better. I felt hopeful. At the time, I was twenty-three and didn't fully understand that he was already there—in that liminal space between life and death. Three months later, he died. Of course, I was grateful he wasn't suffering anymore, but I wasn't ready for him to go. I wanted him to somehow beat the disease. Beat all of it. The coughing and struggling to breathe, the stupid oxygen canister he had to carry around, the oxygen tubes stuck up his nostrils, the medications that wrecked his body and bloated his face. I wanted him to emerge phoenix-like from the ashes of all those old cigarette stubs. At least, that's the story I would tell about his resilience, if I could.

Instead, the story I got was buying airplane tickets to go back home, going through the funeral's awkwardness, gathering at my grandparents' house afterward, combing through old photo albums with everyone and laughing at Poppop's funny captions. Then it was back to my job, back to everyday life. Yet, I felt thrown into an unknown world. How could everything continue as if nothing had changed? How could I look out the window of my tiny apartment, see the same sidewalk and trees and sky while this new and enormous rent existed in the world?

Many years after Poppop died, I received something like a message from him. I was in the midst of teaching a summer community college course when I learned that I was going to have a miscarriage. Though early in the pregnancy, I became distracted, distraught. I missed one class due to the physical pain. Although I'd found a substitute for that class, one student decided she'd had it with me and started sending abusive emails. She threatened to have me fired. I shared the emails with my supervisor, who took over the situation. The student did not pursue her threats, but I ended up stepping down because I dreaded returning to class. I dreaded seeing that angry student. I dreaded breaking down in front of everyone.

I felt grateful and relieved when my supervisor found another teacher, but I also felt enormously guilty. About breaking my contract. About putting my supervisor and another teacher in a bind. I felt overly thin-skinned, incapable of handling one challenging life experience. I couldn't understand why my body had failed at something that everyone around me seemed to have no trouble doing.

In some way, I connected the miscarriage to my own difficult birth. One of my lungs had collapsed as I was being born, and I'd nearly died. The OB/GYN told my parents that my survival was a miracle, but obviously it was the doctors, with their medical technologies, who had saved me. Now I started telling myself, "I wasn't even supposed to survive. I shouldn't try to bring another life into existence." Somehow this reasoning made sense.

That's when Poppop's words arrived—on a wave of sympathy cards and phone calls from my family (mobilized by my mom). One call came from my Uncle Ron. He told me that he'd been crying about what happened. He told me he was so sorry. He told me, "Remember what Poppop always said. Just stick your face out in the wind and keep fighting." I laughed at those words. I'd never heard Poppop say them, but they rang true to his voice. Ultimately, it was those words—along with support from my family and close friends—that worked as my scaffolding. Defective and thin-skinned as I felt, my grandfather's words, my uncle's call, the family and friends who cried with me, listened to me, sat with me, and never belittled by sadness—those were the things that brought me through that loss and failure. Unlike in my childhood dream, no one from my family told me that crying wouldn't help. Not one of them told me to stop feeling sad.

I would go back to teaching in the fall. I would get pregnant again, give birth to a healthy baby. But that loss has stayed with me. It's changed me—in the same way losing my grandfather did. Those losses have tied me, inextricably, to what I once thought of as a huge rent, or fissure, in the world. The poet Naomi Shihab Nye calls it "the thread of all sorrows." In her poem, "Kindness," she writes that when sorrow truly touches us, breaks us, that's when we realize kindness is the only thing "that makes sense anymore." Once we know kindness in that way, it follows us "everywhere / like a shadow or a friend."

Last year marked twenty years since Poppop died, and I made a kind of pilgrimage. My husband, daughter, and I visited the California redwood coast. As a child, Poppop had loved and briefly lived in this place. He told me about walking to school underneath the trees, amidst ferns and flowers and moss. He painted it as a calm, almost magical, place. The first night that we camped under those towering trees, it was raining. The wind shook the hidden treetops, but on the ground, we were safe and sheltered. I wish I could have visited with Poppop. I wish I could have even dreamed about him while I was there, but I don't dream about him anymore. I do think of him, nearly every day. The thoughts are warm, fleeting. They feel like his presence. In a sense, they are. He's encoded in my old memories, linking up to the new ones. He's present to me, like a shadow. Or a kind friend.

Mosaic Woman

By Kelly Mercer

I felt like my life had become the accident on the side of the freeway, the one that everyone assumes has casualties. But when people saw it, they were too afraid to stop and ask, "Is everything all right?" I hoped that sharing my story might help someone, someday. I prayed that one day all the pain I went through would empower someone else. The only thing I ever wanted to accomplish in my life was to help another human selflessly, which is why nursing was my calling.

I met my Jezebel in March and by the month of May, we were officially dating. Life with her was an adventure. She was a force to be reckoned with and made me feel like the luckiest woman in the world. I was head over heels and backwards in love. I had found my soulmate. Jezebel learned all of the intimate details about me that others never tried to discover. I opened up to her and shared things that I had never shared with anyone before. She told me, "Forever and always." It seemed like us against the world. I graduated from nursing school in September. By November of the following year, we wed. I kept telling her that the words "I love you" couldn't explain how much she meant to me and that I would travel to the ends of the Earth for her. We had a connection. The kind that your heart craves, that your heart starts and stops for. I felt on top of the world. I had my love, my life, my career, and my family.

But on April 22, 2017, I got the call that brought my world crashing down on top of me, the words that burned my euphoria to the ground. My younger brother "B," who never called, rang my phone. He was in a panic and asked me to come over to the house immediately. He lived with my father about twenty minutes from my wife and me.

"Dad had an accident," he said.

When we arrived at the house, there was blood on the sidewalk leading inside, blood spattered all over the tile floor. My dad sat there on the couch with a bandage on his head, bent over, barely breathing. I screamed at "B" and demanded he tell me what the hell had happened. Neither of them would give me a straight answer and, at the time, I was in no mood to argue.

I saw the condition my father was in and knew we needed to seek medical attention fast. My father refused to let me call 911 so I dragged him into my car and drove him to the hospital where I worked as a registered nurse. In the emergency room triage, the nurse asked what happened. I didn't know what to say; I just knew we had to get him assessed.

After a CT scan and X-rays, the diagnosis came back: multiple broken ribs, head trauma and a laceration to his spleen causing internal bleeding. We transported him to a trauma center where he ended up in emergency surgery and was placed in a medically-induced coma on life support. The surgery to repair his internal injuries resulted in the failing of his other vital organs. As a nurse, I knew what this meant. But as a daughter, I wasn't ready for that reality.

Over the next month, I split myself into so many roles as a nurse, a wife, and a daughter. I was exhausted making sure that everyone was okay, except for myself. I worked twelve-hour shifts at the hospital and then traveled southbound forty-five minutes to see my dad, hug him, and tell him I loved him. I came home late and tried to be a good wife, making sure that Jezebel was okay and knew that I loved her. My days off work I woke up, kissed her goodbye, and spent in the hospital by my father's side.

I fed him, helped bathe him, and comforted him when all he did was cry out to "go home." My father suffered every single day up until his last hours. The images of his agony haunted me every day and night and still do to this day. I lost sleep and precious hours of my own life reliving that heartbreak. What seemed to be the most horrific tragedy—the "accident"—was only worsened by the thirty-five days he endured while suffering in the hospital.

It took me too many conversations to figure out what happened that day, between my brother "B" and my father, but the truth finally came out. After years of arguing over money, school, and teaching "B" how to be an adult, my father and "B" finally had the fight that ended all fights. "B" brutally assaulted my father outside on the sidewalk that day and caused the injuries that ultimately took his life.

I remember the day before my dad died, I turned on the television in his hospice room and a re-run of a hometown baseball game played in the background. I sat in the chair next to his bed and reminisced about the times we would go watch games and eat hot dogs in the empty stadium. Tears streamed down my face as I told him how sorry I was for every time I hung up on him, for all the times I might not have been the best daughter, and sorry that no matter how hard I tried, I couldn't save his life. I told him I loved him very much and I would always be his "baby girl." I begged the nurse that night to please make sure he didn't suffer because he didn't deserve any more pain.

On May 27, 2017, my dad took his last breath at 6:20 a.m. When the call came in, my heart shattered into a million tiny pieces. I sat in shock and disbelief that my father was actually gone, that he had died. He would never be able to tell me he loved me ever again. He wouldn't be calling me that next day to wish me a happy birthday.

Then, the night before my father's funeral, Jezebel kicked me out of the house. She said in a text message that my father's death had "uncovered emotions that I had never dealt with" and now she was left to "deal with it all." She made it clear to me that she didn't sign up for this.

On May 5, 2018, days before our three-year anniversary and the one-year anniversary of my father's passing, my Jezebel told me she wanted a divorce. I lost my father in an unthinkable tragedy, I lost my younger brother to the judicial system, and now I was losing my wife. I begged and pleaded for her to stay, I told her that I needed her, that I wanted her, and didn't know how my love just wasn't enough. The pain running through my bloodstream was overwhelming and my heart literally ached.

I remember how the days became nights, dark and alone. Night was one of the scariest places I had ever been. I quickly learned that the monsters that used to live under my bed now resided in my head. I started calling out of work to a point that I was on the verge of losing my job—after I had worked so hard to accomplish being on an amazing career path, a profession my father was proud of. He used to brag to all his friends about his daughter, "the nurse."

I went to stay with friends who lovingly welcomed me into their home. As the first anniversary of my father's death and my birthday approached, I became quieter and even more trapped in my sadness. One night I told my friends to go have a nice dinner, enjoy their date night, and not to worry about me, that I just wanted to be alone. I cleaned the tub and drew myself a bath, grabbed a glass of wine and a scalpel. I knew how, and I knew why. But thankfully, I didn't.

The month of June rolled around and my younger brother was being prosecuted by the State of Florida for what might have been manslaughter charges. The State Attorney asked me what I thought about his sentencing, considering my dad's honor and what seemed appropriate. I had the fate of my twenty-year-old brother in my hands. All I kept asking myself was what would my dad want? He would want my brother to be a man: someone who, like my father and I, would give the shirts off our backs to a stranger in need; someone who makes people laugh and always has a great time.

But "B" wasn't like us. He felt like he didn't deserve punishment and it wasn't my job to punish him. I wanted "B" to be held account-able for his actions and to give back to others. I asked for him to be mandated to do community service, receive mental health counseling, and obtain his GED. It wouldn't bring my dad back, but maybe it would have made him proud.

On June 22, 2018, exactly fourteen months after the call that brought my world crashing down on top of me, I sat in the courtroom next to a victim's advocate, a stranger nonetheless, who held my hand as I sobbed. Without her there, I would have been alone. My father was a name on a desk, a case that had to be filed, and a memory—I missed him so much on that day and every day since. I heard his name, I heard his story being read out loud, and all I could do was cry. I wanted my brother to feel my pain, but he stood there, emotionless, and pled guilty to a crime and lack of punishment. I couldn't save my father, my brother, or my marriage. I felt alone.

One night in August of 2018, I never went to sleep. I watched the minutes on the clock tick until the sun started to rise through my bedroom window. I had finally hit rock bottom. I'd never felt so terrible in my life. I could no longer grasp what this life was even meant for. I didn't understand how someone who had been through so much could take punishment and loss over and over. I felt like I was a good person, I felt like I didn't deserve this. Suicide was never something I thought about, except for that single time at my friend's house—until I couldn't stop thinking about it. It was the only way I could think of ending the pain and suffering I was enduring.

I started writing myself mantras. I reached out to friends, strangers, and I went to therapy. I was trying to find a sort of light to save me from one of the darkest places I had ever visited. I realized that every day I woke up, I was alive and I had survived another day; that twenty-four hours were an amazing accomplishment and I needed to acknowledge that small success. It wasn't overnight and it wasn't easy, but I started to find courage inside myself that I never knew existed. One day at a time, and one smile at a time, made all the difference. I reminded myself that it was okay to laugh and it was okay to cry.

It took a long time to escape the hell I felt I was living in. I picked up my pieces and put myself back together, in this beautiful mosaic of a woman I have now become.

There were people who helped me rise up from what I thought might have been rock bottom, to become this resilient, bad-ass woman. This is exactly why I choose to share my story. Life is precious, no matter what your belief system or whom you choose to worship. As a nurse, I help deter death and destruction and I aid people in their final days. I've seen life escape from people's eyes and have seen from the outside what true darkness really is. I look back at every smile, every tear, every accomplishment, and every struggle. From that, there is one thing I know for certain: it is not always easy, but I promise, it is worth it.

For any woman out there who has bottomed out and got back up again, putting one foot in front of another, I applaud you.

Everything Changed

By Kathleen Miller

My grandmother, whom I called "Mom Blakeman," let me drape my three-and-a-half-year-old neck and ears with her jewelry and dab my cheeks with her perfume, as my own mother was in the hospital, giving birth to my baby brother. Mom Blakeman had been married at eighteen and a young mother at nineteen—to my own mother— and never wanted to be called "Grandma." She thought it made her sound old. Even into her 70s and early 80s, she stayed up on the latest fashion trends, the newest perfumes, and never let her hair grow gray. Her grandkids would call her Mom until the day she died.

Mom Blakeman was a calming force while my own mother was high energy and go-go-go. Staying at my grandparents' house, my younger sister and I were showered in her attention. Though I was excited to meet my baby brother as Mom Blakeman packed up our belongings and placed us in the car for the ride back home to Minneapolis.

More cars than usual were parked in front of our house as my three aunts and their husbands had come to welcome my new baby brother to our close-knit family. While everyone was talking in the living room, I quietly tiptoed into the nursery.

My baby brother, Mark, was resting in the crib. He was so beautiful and reminded me of my baby doll. I reached out my hand to touch his and his tiny fingers wrapped around mine. I stood there for the longest time as he fell back to sleep, frozen with fear I would wake him up if I moved.

My mother came into the room to check on him and was surprised to see me standing by Mark's crib. We tiptoed out as my new baby brother slept. At three-and-a-half years old I don't remember much about that day, but this one memory, of my baby brother and I meeting in his crib, is so vivid—even now, at seventy-four years old.

After Mark had arrived, our two-bedroom home seemed to shrink and my parents moved us into a new house when Mark was only a few months old. Our new house was a two-story, English Tudor and our neighborhood was filled with children. We had neighborhood ball games, walked to and from school with our friends, played hide-and-seek in the evenings, and ice skated and rode our sleds throughout the winter. The early 1950s were a great time, growing up in Minneapolis with idyllic parents and three siblings, surrounded by my fun-loving aunts and their families, as well as my doting grandparents.

Later in the 1950s, my mother and father made life-changing decisions that would uproot our family. We took family road trips annually from Minneapolis to Florida during the summers. My parents made sure our trips always included a bit of adventure, taking us to New Orleans, Miami, and the Everglades, along with many tourist stops along the drive from Minnesota to Florida.

My parents decided to move our family to Florida permanently after we'd all fallen in love with the beaches and year-round warmth. This was a major decision that would affect all of us—leaving our extended family of grandparents, aunts, uncles, and cousins in Minneapolis for Florida. So, in the summer of 1956, we road-tripped from Minnesota to Florida in a 1948 Buick, without air conditioning, with two adults, four children, and our dog, Hansel. Behind the Buick was a trailer filled with all of the cherished items and furniture we could pack. My most vivid memory of the long trip from Minneapolis to Florida is of my mother crying, as it broke her heart to say goodbye to her aging parents. When my father announced that we had arrived in St. Petersburg, my mother burst into tears once again. I was nine years old and didn't know if I should be happy or sad about this move.

I was miserable for the first year. I missed my relatives and friends in Minnesota. While my parents tried to make the most of it, taking us on the Florida tourist route and spending many days at the beach, I was not a happy nine-year-old. I don't know if anyone noticed that I was unhappy, but I don't recall anyone talking to me about it. The school seemed strange and the neighborhood felt dismal. Then, things changed yet again.

When we were on a neighborhood picnic, Mark couldn't quench his thirst, drinking everything in sight. Everyone remarked on it. And then other symptoms emerged: he lost weight and had difficulty swallowing. My parents promptly took him to our neighborhood doctor and the doctor diagnosed him with diabetes. This was devastating news for my parents. They both educated themselves about childhood diabetes and the prognosis for children (in the 1950s). Now their son, Mark, was one of these children. They began to argue a lot and became distant with each other. They had undergone so many changes in the past two years that this seemed to be too much for them to bear.

Mark was wonderful when it came to adhering to his diabetic diet. He never ate candy or sugary treats, and I never heard him once complain about getting his daily dosage of insulin. My mother had to administer the insulin through a syringe, which was difficult for her. I can remember her practicing putting a syringe into an orange in order to learn how to give an injection. Mark's skin would thicken at the injection site on his arm after a while and my mother would have to administer it on his upper leg. It was a daily routine and he took it so bravely. He followed his strict diabetic diet and it seemed this was a disease he may be able to live with. The future for a diabetic child in the 1950s and 1960s could be frightening. Childhood diabetes could have serious implications on a child's body. We were all made well aware of this. But there weren't any medical emergencies due to Mark's diabetes and so we all slipped back into our daily routines.

Mark was an exceptional child. After school every day, I would go home and pretend that I was a teacher and Mark was my student. I was three and a half years older, and Mark was an eager student for his older sister. He asked me questions that were advanced for his age, which were followed up with discussions between us. By the time he entered grade school, he made the Honor Roll every time. He was the captain of his football team. He would look out for his friends and be the first to defend them if he saw them being bullied. He was the youngest child in our family and seemed to have a close relationship with each of us. When I planned my 13th birthday party, I asked my dad to take Mark to a movie during the party, otherwise, Mark would have been the entertainer of the party, with everyone encircling him and listening to his stories. He was a boy who was full of life, personality, and compassion, drawing everyone to him.

My parents continued to have a difficult time in Florida. I loved both of my parents and thought they were the best mother and father I could have asked for, but they weren't happy together. Finances were tight and it wasn't easy raising four children. They had all of us in private Catholic schools and were trying so hard to give us the best life they could.

We were all looking forward to Christmas in 1960. The house was decorated and the tree was decked out with ornaments, tinsel, and multi-colored lights with wrapped presents for each other beneath it. I asked for a Kodak Brownie camera that year and I was so excited to be able to take pictures. I was fourteen years old and this promised to be a festive holiday season.

As usual, we woke up extremely early on Christmas morning. Mark had asked for a train set and, after he opened up the package with the train, he quickly assembled it in our small living room. My Kodak camera was beneath the tree as well so we were both happily enjoying Christmas Day. I took pictures with the camera right away and one of them was with Mark and his new train set. We stayed up after the rest of the family went back to bed.

Later that morning we all got ready to go to church. Mark got all dressed up in a suit—quite dressy for a ten-year-old. I had my camera with me as we left the house and was able to get a picture of Mark in his suit. What a handsome ten-year-old brother I had. Little did I know that those would be the last two pictures ever taken of my brother.

I can't remember which day it was after Christmas that my father took Mark and me out to dinner. It was just the three of us and I know we ate at a restaurant buffet in downtown St. Petersburg. Both my dad and I helped Mark stick to his diabetic diet as we picked out food.

The next day Mark began to get sick. I will always wonder if the dinner the night before had anything to do with it. My parents took him to the doctor and he came home and went right to bed. The next morning will always be embedded in my memory.

It was a school day, and I remember waking up to a lot of noise in the house. Lights were on and it was very dark outside. My bedroom was right next to Mark's and I could see my mother running back and forth. She came in and asked me to try to get Mark to eat something— he couldn't keep any food down and didn't want to try to eat anything else. She said this was very serious and I should do whatever I could to get him to eat something.

When I went into Mark's bedroom, he looked so sick. I talked to him and told him he needed to try to eat. He took one sip of orange juice and immediately vomited. I had failed.

The rest of the day is a blur. I know I went to school and when I came home my aunt Helene was at the house. She told me they had taken Mark to the hospital and that he was very sick. That night I prayed and prayed to God, begging him to let Mark live.

I awoke in the middle of the night to the phone ringing.

Aunt Helene started crying and then I overheard her say, "Oh no. Mark's gone."

I knew Mark had died. She came into our bedroom after she hung up the phone, as she'd heard my sister and me crying. We cried and cried all night long for the brother we would never see again.

There was a funeral mass at the Catholic church and the entire school attended. As I walked in, I saw all of the navy blue and white uniforms filling pew after pew. I was amazed that the entire school turned out for Mark's funeral. This was totally unexpected and took me by surprise. We walked to the front and took our seats. That is all I remember of that entire day. I know there must have been a mass and we must have gone to the cemetery, but I have no memory of either or anything else that happened afterward.

The days after the funeral seem like a blur to me as I try to recall details of life without Mark in our family. The house felt dismal and bleak. We were all mourning in our own way. I spent many hours in my bedroom, overhearing muted conversations and sporadic crying through my bedroom door. We were all devastated. School was the farthest thing from my mind but I had to go back.

But I remember that first day I had to go back to school so clearly. Overnight, I had changed. I was different from others. My schoolmates were in the class, but I felt like a bystander. It was a parochial school and it would start promptly at 9:00 AM.

"Who can answer this question?" the nun asked as she looked directly at me. The next thing I heard the nun say was, "Kathleen, are you going to answer my question or not?"

I stared ahead, having no idea what she was talking about as my mind was not yet settled into the fact that I was back in school and Mark had died.

"Kathleen, please stand up," the nun said.

I stood up next to my desk.

"Why didn't you turn in your overdue homework?"

This was my first day back at school and I hated being there. I hadn't done any homework while we were mourning the loss of Mark. "I did not complete any of my homework while I was absent."

"Why didn't you do the homework?"

Somehow, I choked out the following words. "My brother just died and I just didn't do the homework." That was the first time I'd said out loud that Mark had died.

"That's not an excuse for not doing your homework. Finish it by tomorrow," the nun demanded.

I fought back the flood of tears and thought, This is my last year at this school. And it was. I went home and told my parents I would not be going back to Catholic school and would be attending public school next year. They didn't argue with my plan.

As I look back, I can see that the only resource I had to get me through this devastation was within myself. I was fourteen years old and as a fourteen-year-old, I felt that God had let me down. He ignored my prayers. The school I attended embarrassed and humiliated me in front of my class, forcing me to vocalize that my brother had died while the nun knew that all along. My parents were dealing with their grief as they had just lost their youngest child and their marriage was falling apart. They were unable to console my siblings and me as they were barely able to survive themselves. My friends were young teen-agers, interested in movies, shopping, and having fun—they weren't about to discuss the death of my brother with me, as they didn't fully grasp it themselves. Mom Blakeman and the family I loved was back home in Minneapolis.

As time passed, I survived. I did a lot of reading and introspec-tion and came to my own conclusions: Mark died, he was gone, but I needed to keep going for the two of us or I should have died, too. While I swore I would never let his memory fade—reminding myself often of his personality, his beautiful green eyes, and the closeness we shared—I had to live.

I named my youngest son "Mark" and made him well aware of his namesake and the uncle he would never know. I have shared all of my childhood stories and memories of Mark with children of my own, children who've grown into adults, children who've been given the gift of life beyond the age of ten. From Mark's death, I learned that everyone is vulnerable—even children. Sometimes, children are taken away before they have a chance to experience the adventures those of us who make it into adulthood take for granted.

I also learned that I was strong and could depend on myself in the most difficult of times. I had survived the death of my brother, my parents' divorce, and the disintegration of my once close-knit and loving family. My memories are a part of me but they could not consume my outlook on life, my future. My parents did the best they could at that time in their lives. Losing a child is horrific. It's some-thing very few marriages survive.

I learned not to feel guilty that I'm still here, still living, and Mark's not. His illness and his death were beyond my control—knowl-edge that did not come easily after that morning, the morning I felt like I'd failed to get him to eat something. I've never forgotten Mark and the short life he lived. I want to remember every detail about him so I don't forget what he looked like, what he sounded like. I have the last two pictures I took of him in my living room. They remind me of that last Christmas I had with Mark, and of the happy ten years I had him in my life, from the moment he wrapped his finger around mine.

We Were Never Meant to Die

By Matiwonesa Munyaradzi

The death of a loved one can burn through your soul; it is a pain so deep that the healing process can take years to "get over." If one can ever really get over death. A series of deaths spelled out a slow crumbling of my foundation. I consider the first death I experienced in my family to be the prelude to the devastation that would shake me, break me down into teeny, tiny little scattered pieces. Pieces that I would somehow have to pick up, or else die myself.

When I was four, my parents separated. My mother moved us from our apartment in Lefrak City—a 4,605-apartment development in Queens—to the place my family would refer to as "the house." My grandmother and her sister, Great Aunt Summer Joy, owned a two-story colonial on a quiet corner in Hollis, Queens. It was a place for family barbecues and dinners—replete with political debates. The kids would sing along to the grooves of Stevie Wonder, Michael Jackson and Prince.

It was the place where everyone would gather for Christmas dinner. I would awake to the sounds of Grandma's favorites—Johnny Mathis's *Merry Christmas* and Aretha Franklin's *Amazing Grace* on vinyl. Our bellies rumbled as the rich aromas of turkey with stuffing,

Grandma's super cheesy mac & cheese, and Aunt Summer Joy's to-die-for sweet potato soufflé curled through every room.

"The house" was also the place where adult children would return home to rebuild after life's setbacks and disappointments, a place where anyone in our family could land, pick ourselves up and—with the family's support—begin again.

And so, when a fire destroyed Great Aunt Jazz's Rochdale home, she came to live with us. I was ten and no one felt the need to explain the situation to me. I soon learned that she had cared for me as a baby, and we fell easily into a close relationship. My mother had to leave for work before sunrise each day. My grandmother worked the nightshift as a switchboard operator in Brooklyn. So, every morning, from ages ten to seventeen, I was responsible for getting myself ready for school. I would make my way downstairs to the kitchen. Great Aunt Jazz and Great Aunt Summer Joy would be in the breakfast nook sharing sections of the *Daily News* while eating steaming bowls of grits and sardines. I would make grits with cheese, chat with my great aunts, and wait for the school bus. Once I left, they would walk to the bus together. Great Aunt Summer Joy traveled west to Manhattan for work. Great Aunt Jazz would head east to her job on Long Island. We wouldn't see each other until after sunset.

After school, the bus would drop me off at Great Aunt Velvet's and Uncle Royal's house. Great Aunt Velvet was my grandmother's eldest sister. She was my teacher, another mother, and a true Southern Belle. She taught me how to be a lady, how to care for a home, how to cook and, more importantly, to dream. She poured her own desires into me, to break away from her working-class lifestyle. With her chin lifted high she would smile at me and say, "Dr. Shona!"

In the evening, my mother or grandmother would pick me up from Great Aunt Velvet and Uncle Royal's to return to "the house," only ten minutes away. On Sundays, Uncle Royal (who was also our Pastor) and Aunt Velvet rode to our house in their shiny, black Cadillac. They drove my grandmother and aunts for church. My mother and I would follow in her car. Church was in Harlem, which was quite a contrast from the quiet streets of suburbia. We spent all day singing praises, learning lessons from the Bible and communing with friends. One of those lessons stuck with me above the rest. It was the statement: "We were never meant to die." The Bible says that Noah lived to 500 years, and that his grandfather, Methuselah, lived to 969 years. Huh? What? Aren't those numbers figurative in some way? Those words left me stunned, even skeptical. Those words also made me think, but not for long. Death hadn't yet come around.

On Sundays after church, we would arrive home in the dark, rejuvenated, exhausted, and ready to collapse onto our beds. That was my life until I went to college.

My freshman year of college, Aunt Jazz, the aunt who cared for me as a baby, called to tell me that she had been diagnosed with cancer. It took a moment for me to digest what she was saying.

"Don't worry," she said.

Was she kidding? How was I not supposed to worry? I did worry. I was afraid. I was 200 miles away, but it felt like thousands.

She went through surgery and chemo. It was tough, but so was she. She went into remission for ten years. I had time to spend with her. Until the day when even her toughness could no longer support the weakening of her body. No one had the energy to care for her. Aunt Jazz made the unspeakable decision to sign herself in to a nursing home, so as not to burden her family.

That meant visits, loads of them. Driven by both guilt and love, Grandma and Aunt Summer Joy went as often as possible. Uncle Royal, her brother-in-law, would go with instructions from Aunt Velvet. "Royal, make sure the doctors are doing this. Bring her that." Aunt Velvet herself could not visit, for her small frame was aching and fragile from years of battling rheumatoid arthritis. She rarely even made it to church.

Now, I hated hospitals, nursing homes, anywhere sick people were. Places where illness roamed the halls and death snaked down the hallways like some dark, evil shadow waiting for the next victim, made me uneasy. When someone was in the hospital I usually sent my sympathy and my apologies, but no way was I stepping foot in there.

That was why when I showed up for my first visit, Aunt Jazz knew that my heart was in it. Five minutes in she gave me permission to go home. She knew me well. I showed up for her even though I wanted to jump out of my skin and run! When the automatic doors opened up for me to leave the hospital, so did the flood of my tears. I let them come, not caring who saw. Four months later, and a few more visits, she was gone.

Three years passed, then suddenly, Aunt Velvet began to fade. She was Uncle Royal's heart, his soulmate. They had been a couple for sixty years. Uncle Royal drove her to appointment after appointment, joined by her sisters. If they did not see each other every single day, they at least spoke over the phone. I spoke to her every day. Then she died, leaving a gaping hole.

Shortly after her passing, a woman pulled me aside in church to warn me. "You know that your uncle will not live very long now that your aunt is gone, right?"

No! I definitely *did not* know that. But those words saved me. When my uncle, our family's patriarch, began to decline, I was prepared—and grateful for the warning.

The guilt of allowing Aunt Jazz to go into a nursing home was fixed in our memories, so we weren't about to let Uncle Royal—or anybody else—go into one without a fight. But Uncle Royal's illness took its toll. Grandma and Aunt Summer Joy, though retired, would get up early as if going to work. They would drive those ten minutes to take care of Uncle Royal. After work, I would show up to do my part. Social life? What was that? Occasionally, I went out with friends. My closest friends would admonish me for the sacrifices I was making. *What are you DOING? Let someone else do it.* But who?

Uncle Royal, my grandmother, and Aunt Summer Joy were my world. I had spent every day with those beautiful people. Yes, I made sacrifices for them, but had they not made sacrifices for me? I prayed about it. I had made the right choice.

Once the deaths began, they kept coming rapidly. My resilient grandmother, my rock, became ill. She was a force like no other. Her parents passed away before she reached age four; yet she raised two brilliant daughters on her own. She was a mother to those who had none. She served on church boards and committees. She never minced words and she was respected for it. She had withstood so many challenges in her life. But this was one challenge that she could not overcome. She died in the summer of 2010. Losing her was devastating. Aunt Summer Joy lost her best friend.

Aunt Summer Joy, although surrounded by family, felt alone. No more phone calls. No more ten minutes away.

Two years passed before Aunt Summer Joy—the middle sister, the moderator and beloved bridge-builder—would tell her daughters that she didn't feel "right." Waiting is always this gnarly rumble-tumble, a bitter journey no one ever wants to take. But, that is where we were again.

Fear gripped us. That all-too-familiar feeling of helplessness.

When we knew that we would lose her, the entire family flocked to her bedside. It was the end of a generation and everyone knew it. The last departure.

Woven throughout those illnesses were job losses. I had the space to care for my family in part because I had nowhere else to go. In between, I sat at my computer and called recruiters in a struggle to find work. Sometimes I would find forgotten glass bottles or piggy banks filled with coins. When unemployment ran out, that was all I had—a piggy bank of dusty coins.

That was my life—jobless, boyfriend-less, childless and caring for elderly people who would ultimately fade away. I had no one. No guy to curl up next to and cry about my situation.

After Aunt Summer Joy's death, when I was thirty-five, I was angry—angry at God, angry at myself. I refused to talk to Him. Had I not followed His will? Why was my life designed this way? Why wasn't I married yet? Why didn't I have children? Why had my career aspirations not come true? Before all of the sickness, I was pursuing all of those things that most people pursue. But I held my family at the center of my life, and now all of them were gone.

One day, I started listening to a female Christian minister who captivated me. The way that she spoke was so interesting that I could not help but watch her videos again and again. Her teachings inspired me to open up the Bible again and read. That was when I began to talk to Him again. The burden that held me down began to lift. I remembered why I loved Him. I began to trust Him again. I could feel Him wrap His arms around me again. It was such a wonderful feeling. Life isn't so heavy when I toss it all up into His hands. Doors opened. I got a job. I started writing again. I started to live again.

I saw that, though nothing is perfect, at least I still have family. I still have my mom who is everything to me now. There are days when I feel such emptiness, like I belong to no one and my foundation is gone. At times, I feel like I am here, but not here. Existing, but not belonging.

We talk about the Great Ones sometimes. Memories so strong it feels like we can resurrect them. The loss of them has left me with a permanent feeling of loss that will never go away. But it has also strengthened my belief that God did not create life to end. I believe that is the reason death is so hard on us. We're not hardwired to lose someone. Yet, even though the death of our loved ones is devastating, I am now able to find some solace in the God who created us and loves us.

For sure, that pesky dude, Death, will come along again. He will come for other family members. I hope not soon. But, like the Biblical story of Methusaleh who lived to be 969 years old, where the promise of eternity is alluded to, I *know,* it's a truth that I feel in my bones—we were never meant to die.

Our Secrets Keep Us Sick

By Liz Nance

Why do we wait to tell our stories?

As I've watched and listened to women in the media coming forward about sexual misconduct, the most common questions I've heard asked are, "Why now?" and "Why did she wait so long?"

Most women we see "just coming forward" aren't new to telling the story. More often than not, we've told our stories already. We told them to someone who was supposed to be trustworthy and safe. When you're shut down, when the people you assume will stand up for you only invalidate your story, why would you want to tell anyone else?

So we lock it up. We convince ourselves that it won't come up again, that it didn't really matter, or that it never really happened. We forget how to be girls, how to be young ladies, and then we don't know how to be women. We forget how to feel human. Then life gets hard, sometimes unexpectedly, and we hit rock bottom.

"Our secrets keep us sick." I can see that sentence in her handwriting when I close my eyes. She wrote it just two weeks before she took her own life. In that same journal a loose piece of paper tucked in the pages reads, "What happened was... I can't ward off the memories anymore. My mind won't sleep, dreams won't quit telling me what is next."

Like my mama, I was raised by a tribe of strong, southern women. I grew up thinking this was what my family was made of and what it was built on. As a child, it seemed to mean something—like bravery, courage, open hearts and open houses. Yet, as an adult, I would find out that earning the title of "strong, southern woman" meant learning how to suppress your feelings and learning to keep quiet about things that might bring shame and ruin the reputation of the family. We weren't a brood of tough freedom fighters at all. Instead, we were generations of women doing our damnedest to keep up appearances.

Around 1 a.m. on November 1, 2010, the world lost a "strong, southern woman" when my mama shot herself in the heart while sitting in her favorite spot on her back porch. In the days and months that followed, a story began to unfold. A story of a woman who had a lot of secrets. A story of a woman who never had a chance to tell her story. A woman who had hit rock bottom without realizing that she could get back up.

When a man takes advantage of his position as head of the household, it is devastating to the entire family. A husband, a father, a patriarch is supposed to give love and support to his household. Fathers of young girls should nurture the fragile nature of being female and provide an example of what she should someday seek in a man. How can a young woman feel strong or empowered if she was raised to feel used and complacent?

When I was in fifth grade, I confided to my mama that a grown man had stuck his tongue in my mouth. Her response was, "Well, he does that to his kids." Telling this story to my sister later in life, I learned that the same man had been inappropriate with her. And she had also told our mother.

Our mother's response to my sister: "One day you'll meet a man who loves you and that will be okay."

We had both been given a very unhealthy response by someone we loved and trusted. Now, I have to say for those who never met my mama—she was loving, caring, funny, and an amazing wife and mother. Everyone who met her loved her. And she loved them back.

But remember, she had known that "our secrets keep us sick." And in some instances, those secrets keep us from being able to react properly to things going on around us.

In my case, and in my sister's case, we had told someone. We told the person that we thought would tell us *what* had happened. We told the person that we thought would tell us *why* it happened. We told the person that we thought would tell us that it wasn't our fault. However, in that moment, in that small, downstairs half-bathroom of that townhouse during the early hours of our big football party, I "tattled" on a grown man who was supposed to be a friend of the family, and I didn't get the response I should have from my mama. If, in that moment, my mama would have admitted that what had just happened to me was wrong, she would have also, in that moment, had to deal with the fact that it had happened to her too.

When my mama passed away, lots of things were unearthed. I felt like I was part of an archeological dig that was exposing the shittyness of humanity. It opened my eyes to picture-perfect families and the realities of the harm that "keeping up appearances" can cause. My mama was a writer. She journaled every day, she took notes, she documented everything. Most families who lose someone to suicide are left with so many unanswered questions. Reading Mama's notebooks and journals opened my eyes to the wild injustices within our family and to a woman who was living in silent terror. She would leave small cries for help in the margins. She wrote the words "quiet strength, inner turmoil" in such beautiful handwriting that you would think it contained a lovely message of hope. Most of her journals were about herself and her daily struggles, about Dad and his work, about how much she loved her kids, and a lot of little stories of sweet memories.

After she died, Dad realized that he couldn't stay in that house without her. I drove down from North Carolina to Georgia to help him go through things and pack up. As dad took apart the dresser in her bedroom, he found another journal—one we hadn't seen. The words inside its covers felt like a hot bullet going straight through my heart. My eyes were opened to a woman who had been molested since the age of four. A woman who was in a sexual relationship with her stepfather—even into adulthood. The part that hurt the most was reading the words, "How could they ever forgive me? How could I ever look him in the eyes again? How will my children trust me again?" She was struggling to keep the secret inside, but struggling even more to figure out how to let it out after she had kept it for so long.

The day after that notebook was found, my sister and I sat down with our family to tell them about all of the horrible things that we had learned. Surely, we "strong, southern women" can work through this together. But that wasn't the response we got. Instead, we found out that other people already knew. We were told, "Well, in another time and place they would have made a great couple."

Turns out the "strong, southern women" had been hard at work keeping this one under wraps. And this started a fight as I attempted to rip off the blinders.

Currently, there are people in my hometown, both friends and family, wondering why I waited so long to share this story. The truth is, I didn't wait. I just tried to share it with the wrong people. I shared it with people that I thought would tell me what happened. I shared it with people that I thought would tell me *why* it happened. I shared it with people that I thought would tell me that it wasn't her fault. I expected healthy, helpful reactions. I didn't expect the fear, the blame, or being told to keep quiet.

Now, I share this story with the people who are closest to me. I share it with the people who need to hear it. I share it with those struggling with similar circumstances. I share it with people who won't make me feel like the guilty party. I share it with people who encourage me to keep going.

Why do so many people in my family not know the truth? It's not because I didn't want to tell them, I just didn't know where to start. You see, those "strong, southern women" wanted to deal with it their way.

Why aren't other people in my family telling this story, or at least trying to? Why did I slow down in my own telling of it? Why didn't I just put it all out there? I feel like I tried. But I shut down due to the reactions of the ones I told. I was confronting them about something that most of them didn't know, something that some of them had suspected, and something that a handful of them already knew. That may have hurt the most. Finding out that someone that my mama loved knew what was happening and never did anything to help her.

They say separating yourself from toxic, negative relationships is good for your mental well-being. That is a lot easier said than done when those relationships are with kin. I guess I assumed that once the secrets were out, the rest would be easy. I guess I didn't realize how hard my family was working to keep that closet door closed—you know, the one with the skeletons. But the rug that everything has been swept under isn't touching the floor anymore.

Running the Obstacle Course

By Puma Perl

I have always been terrified of depression. My father displayed most of the symptoms of bipolarity (called manic-depressive back then) but was never, to my knowledge, treated. I don't even know if he was ever assessed or diagnosed. My uncle, an anesthesiologist, supposedly told my mother that Lithium, the drug of choice at the time, was bad for the kidneys and therefore out of the question, and that seemed to end further discussion. In my family, mental illness was regarded as a weakness, a shameful, dirty secret. My mother, who had personality disorders of her own, sometimes threatened to call Kings County when I was a child; if I yelled or acted up she would say that I was just like my father and that we both needed needed shock treatments.

During manic phases, my father would start businesses or find new jobs, walk the streets all night, his racing thoughts rendering him sleepless. He was charming, engaging and intelligent, but when the mania ended his businesses would crash, the new jobs and friends would disappear, and he'd sink into his chair, chain-smoking and staring into space. As he aged, the manic episodes ended and only the darkness remained. At some point in my early childhood, my parents opened a small neighborhood store. I never realized until much later the courage and stamina my father must have needed to get out of bed and go to work every day.

Depression, as I perceived it, was relentless, without an end or a cure, so I tried as a young woman, with limited success, to outrun all signs of it in myself. Drugs seemed a great way to do it, and maybe they were a temporary solution, for recovery from addiction is better understood and more accessible than recovery from depression. Drugs probably saved my life while also coming close to ending it.

I battled addiction for many years, but this is not the story of the nice Jewish girl from Brooklyn who becomes a heroin addict on the Lower East Side. We have all heard that story and seen the movie— the heroine emerging from street corner shadows and celebrating her first year of recovery with tears and red roses, surrounded by family and friends. There is truth to that story, but it's not the whole truth. Like many addicts, I attempted to fill the void inside me with drugs until the drugs no longer worked. Recovery and abstinence were a relief and my life improved in every way, but I still never felt quite right. I never had, but childhood depression was understood even less than bipolarity so I tried to fit in, and usually wound up hiding. Kids were supposed to play, laugh, act carefree. I was most comfortable alone in my room with a book. People used to tell me that I looked angry all the time and that I should smile more; people seemed to dislike me for my affect and body language. "There is something left out of you," my mother often said. I believed her. "I wish I were dead," I would think, and then I'd feel guilty for having such thoughts.

The first time I felt depressed after getting clean, I was as petrified as I had been when I was younger. I had nothing to refer to, in terms of experience or reading, to make me believe that it would pass, or that people could be helped. It was hard to talk about because I'd always associated it with weakness and failure. I did not want to provide anyone with the ammunition to belittle and shame me. The few people I confided in assured me that the answer was in staying clean, working the twelve steps, and that "more would be revealed." I tried. The periods of depression would lift, but they would return, along with something I'd always experienced but could now name.

Self-loathing. I learned that term in meetings; it was stated in the literature that self-loathing was considered a "character defect," one that could be lifted through prayer and meditation but only if you were willing. I had never thought of it as part of my character; I thought it WAS my character, the same little girl with something left out of her. I was used to thinking of myself as defective, always on the outside, whether sober or actively using. It was enlightening to believe that I could change, but at the same time I felt like a failure because although there was improvement, the general feeling was not lifted. Fortunately, I found a therapist who understood.

Steve had been sober for over twenty-five years and he was aware that all of the answers did not lie in recovery programs and working the steps. And he was on my side, unlike the devil's advocates I always seemed to attract. He did not point out that my parents "did the best they could" or remind me to "look at my part of things" or question my willingness to change. He listened non-judgmentally, which allowed me to share the secrets I'd held my entire life. My life continued to get better and for the first time my sense of self-worth began to be bolstered by my accomplishments; it was no longer based upon the perception of others. I had never before been an independent, self-supporting person, and my self-esteem increased as I found success in the fields I'd chosen to pursue. I became a better friend, a better parent, a better writer. I'd probably never be the "good daughter" my mother would have preferred, but I learned to set boundaries in my dealings with her. My father had died a sad and lonely man, and my mother was always going to be impossible to please. Her sisters told me that "she'd always been different" and that "she needed someone to take things out on." It would have made a difference if one person had taken an interest or let me know that they were aware of the "difference" a few decades earlier but again, family shame and secrecy dominated.

After a few years, I decided to conclude treatment and Steve agreed, with the usual assurances that I could always return. He cautioned me to maintain my awareness that on a daily basis I would struggle with the self-hatred and low self-esteem that had been implanted in my head for so many years. I disagreed. I didn't want to struggle, I wanted to overcome, and I believed that through continuing to take positive actions and using the many tools I'd acquired, I'd find freedom. I hadn't come this far to struggle with the demons every single day for the rest of my life.

It took me about ten years to admit that Steve was right. I do struggle every day, and some days are better than others. In fact, most days are better than the others. I am not bipolar like my father or a borderline personality like my mother. I inherited neither his passivity nor her meanness. I would never speak to anyone the way I was spoken to as a child, except to myself. My immediate reactions to my own imperfections and mistakes can be harsh. I need to constantly remind myself that mistakes are forgivable, even understandable. Sometimes I wake up and the old mantra comes back – *I wish I were dead.* But I've made a pact to live until I die at hands other than my own and I now have references, experiences, and information I can trust to know that these feelings, if not entertained, are not permanent, and the less I chastise myself for having them, the quicker they will pass. My life is more amazing than I'd ever imagined, even though it's missing many of the key ingredients that I always believed one needed: financial security, a decent income, a soulmate, or at least a compatible life partner.

Sometimes, in a single stream of thought, I assess myself: I'm a published writer, I'm an award-winning journalist, I'm alone, I'm too fat, I produce shows, I need hearing aids, musicians write songs for me, my teeth are falling out, I have a band, I love my dog, my kids are great human beings; I want to be out among people, and I want to stay home alone. These conflicting thoughts remind me of a Henry Rollins quote: "I'll never forget how the depression and loneliness felt good and bad at the same time. Still does." I consider my resilience and my mortality. I have not cleared all of my obstacles, but I've survived and even thrived despite them. And I need to remember that on a daily basis—for the rest of my life.

Bent Not Broken

By Taylor Richards

Part I: Honeymoon Ended

A crisp, mulchy autumn fragrance drifted by on a breeze as I signed
the moving company's invoice on the stoop of our new Cobble Hill
brownstone in downtown Brooklyn. I wasn't wearing a jacket that day
and stood barefoot outside. I'm originally from the South and always
preferred not wearing shoes. I drew in a deep breath and smiled as
I gazed up at the golden foliage on our tree-lined block. Home sweet
home. I had a lot on my to-do list that day: call the cable company and
make the switch, go grocery shopping, notify electricity company of
new address, unpack, and get settled.

At seven months pregnant, I wobbled up our front steps and
inside our home. Rubbing my belly, I opened the door to my daughter's nursery and walked slowly around the room. This is the room
where I would soon nurse her, love her, read to her, snuggle her, love
her some more, change her diapers, sing her lullabies, and give even
more love to my little angel. The crib and dresser were positioned
exactly how I wanted them. I got a box cutter and opened all of the
baby shower gifts we'd received from Buy Buy Baby—the bassinet,
humidifier, newborn diaper boxes, breast pump, books, and baby

monitor. I organized diaper creams, soft washcloths, onesies, blankets and mittens neatly into my daughter's drawers. Hours passed by.

I worked all day into the late evening. I never got a chance to start on dinner before my husband arrived home. I didn't get anything accomplished on my to-do list except decorating my daughter's room. I thought my amazing husband would, of course, understand.

My parents divorced at a young age and I was raised in a single-parent home. I cringed every time I'd read the term "broken" being related to "high-risk children" as a result of single-parent homes. Nonetheless, I thought I would never have to worry about those terms being associated with my growing family because I was so thankful and so blessed to be married to an incredible, loving, warm and gentle husband. He protected, provided and professed his love for me. I couldn't ask for anything more.

Later that evening, my husband came home and didn't say anything. I helped him take off his jacket and kissed him on the lips. I was over the moon about our daughter's room and couldn't stop talking about all the decorating I'd done. Guiding him into our daughter's room, I asked him, "Do you like it?" He nodded yes. I flipped the light switch off and pointed out the glow-in-the-dark stars. I measured each glow-in-the-dark star earlier that day, precisely equidistant apart from each other on the walls. He nodded his head, acknowledging that he liked the stars but showing no sign of excitement. Someone must have woken up on the wrong side of the bed that morning, I thought.

He walked into the kitchen and I followed him, still doing all the talking and rubbing my large belly in a circular motion. My daughter kicked a lot during my third trimester. He opened the refrigerator door and didn't see food inside. I told him, "We could just order takeout, I didn't have time to go grocery shopping or cook today." He slammed the refrigerator door. I asked, "How did everything go at work today?" He didn't reply. I suggested he take a shower and I'd order takeout so the food could be delivered by the time he got out. Still nothing. He walked into the bathroom and let the hot water run.

I searched for our box labeled "pajamas" in our bedroom so that he could put on some fresh, comfortable clothes. Our bedroom door was open and I heard him moving furniture around. I yelled down the hallway, "Babe, what are you doing?" He ignored me. When I walked into the living room, he had placed the recliner chair and end table perpendicular to the entertainment center. He moved the couch and love seat sitting directly across from the entertainment center and coffee table in a straight horizontal line, which didn't make any sense. What was he thinking? It was time for "Marcus Stewart" and his interior decorating skills to finally get in the shower. I left his clothes and newly laundered bath towel from the linen closet box on top of the bathroom rack.

He took a long shower, a really, *really* long shower. I rearranged the living room furniture to a more suitable layout before ordering takeout. I wasn't supposed to move anything heavy so late in my pregnancy but I was determined. The shower water turned off and I took a moment to rest on the living room couch, getting in a little reading of Dr. Harvey Karp's *The Happiest Baby on the Block* before the food arrived.

He walked into the living room, looked at the new layout, looked at me, and then back at the layout. What he did next, I didn't see coming. Ever.

He backhanded slapped my face so hard that my pregnant body flew across the couch from his force. I held one hand on my belly and the other on my face in shock and couldn't speak, think, or believe what just happened. He got dressed and didn't say a word as he left the house. The rest of the evening was a blur. The only thing I remember from that point on was crawling into a fetal position on the couch with tears falling down my face. The next morning, my eyes were swollen and burning. My eyelids were too heavy to open from crying.

Part II: It's You, Not Me

Months later, I continued to cook, clean, do laundry and take care of our infant daughter the best way I knew how as a devoted wife, homemaker and mother. I tried not to do anything wrong or to upset him, as he'd recently started a new company and business was going well. My dreams, aspirations and goals were put on hold. No matter how hard I tried to please him, he was still filled with so much hate, anger and rage towards me. My husband beat, choked, slapped and kicked me so many times that I lost count. I lost control of my body once when he was beating me and wet my pants. He told me at that moment, "I would kill you myself if I didn't want to rot in jail." I never called the cops. He isolated me. My support system—my family and friends— were thousands of miles away, back home.

Every time he would abuse me, moments or sometimes days later, he would embrace me in his arms. He was so soft-spoken and gentle when he wasn't being abusive. I asked him to get counseling, but he took no responsibility for anything, always shifting the blame back on me. He always convinced me that I was the problem.

I wanted to leave. But couldn't build up the courage to do so. I didn't tell my family what was going on. I put on a façade for the world to see. The only person I did tell was the one person who knew my husband better than anyone in this world, my mother-in-law. I told her I wanted to leave her son. Now, I cringe at her response: "What are you doing to cause him to be so angry? Separating is not the answer. You don't want to raise your child in a broken home."

Strangely, he was an out-of-this-world, amazing father. He was incredibly tender with our daughter. Yet, at times, I felt he thought I was merely a vessel to birth his children. He wanted to have a second baby right away, but I had a birth control IUD device inserted without telling him so that I couldn't get pregnant. The IUD was safe for preventing pregnancy for five years. I never wanted to have any more children with him because I was afraid he would never change. I knew the abuse would only get worse. I couldn't have my daughter or any additional children see him treat me the way he did. He wasn't sure why I wasn't getting pregnant each month. I pretended I didn't know why either.

I started reading any domestic violence material I could put my hands on and hid the books deep in the coat closet. The knowledge I received from Lundy Bancroft's *Why Does He Do That: Inside the Minds of Controlling and Abusive Men* was empowering. I armed myself with literature. I told him I wanted to go back to graduate school but he went into a rage and said that I should "focus on raising our daughter." He monitored my texts messages, phone calls, e-mails and treated me like his possession—exactly how the book described an abusive person's behavior. Bancroft called out all of his behaviors. All of the things he did to me had names.

Part III: The Affair

Later that summer, my daughter was doing well sleeping through the night. I'd given her a bath, fed her and had playtime together before I rocked her to sleep. Dinner had been ready for hours. The food was simmering as I looked at the clock on the stove. It was 9:37 p.m. when I heard my husband enter the foyer. When he walked into the kitchen, he put his gym bag down and kissed me. He was in a good mood. He worked out at the gym faithfully, every evening after work. (Sidebar, each time I asked for a family membership at the same gym to work out with him, he would go into a rage, accusing me of wanting to look at other men. I had gained an extra forty pounds that I wanted to shed. I ended up ordering a Zumba Fitness and Pilates DVD online and had it delivered in the mail. I went on walks with my little one in her stroller during the day after park time but when I wanted to burn calories I could only exercise at home during the day while he was at work. I hid my DVD's in the coat closet as well so he wouldn't find them.)

As he showered, I heard something vibrating. I looked at the kitchen table but his cell phone wasn't ringing. It wasn't my cell phone, either. The vibration came from his gym bag. I unzipped his bag and found the sound. It was a cell phone I'd never seen before. The password to this new phone was the same as his main one, so I unlocked it. I found text messages, phone calls and emails between him and another woman. There were pictures of them together, meet up times and addresses to hotels. He was having an affair. For months, he claimed he'd been working late. I took as many screenshots as I could and texted them to my cell phone, then edited and deleted the conversation sent to myself. My heart was beating fast. When I heard the shower water turn off, I stood in the kitchen paralyzed. I then placed the cell phone on the kitchen table.

I didn't know what to say to him when he got out, so I held my head down and said nothing at all. Standing at the stove, I made his dinner plate, feeling him behind me, staring at my back, from our kitchen's entrance. I turned around, walking toward him, plate in my hand. He slapped the porcelain plate from underneath my hand. It flew towards the ceiling. When the plate came back to the ground, it shattered into a thousand pieces.

He asked, "What were you doing going through my bag?"

I was scared out of my mind and didn't know what to say. I couldn't think. I should have placed the phone back in the gym bag and not on the kitchen table. I gave myself away. I kept apologizing in fear saying, "I'm sorry, I'm sorry, I'm sorry, I'm sorry." I grabbed a broom from the pantry and swept the glass into a pile. I had my hair in a high bun and as I bent down to place the dustpan and broom near the glass pile I felt something land on my neck. I wasn't sure if it was what I thought it was, so I stood up and faced him, and that's when he did it again. He spit on me repeatedly. I wished for a hand slap. That at least tingles, but goes away. A swollen eye or body part will heal in time. The slaps and kicks I would forget but I will never ever forget the look in his eyes as he spit on me over, and over, and over again.

With all the strength I had in me, I hit him as hard as I could across his head with the broom. New York is not a "Stand Your Ground" state but I had started reading defense laws and knew I had a right to protect myself from harm. I couldn't believe I hit him back. He couldn't believe it either. He was shocked. I was scared shitless about what was going to happen next. I thought he was going to kill me. Instead, he grabbed his bag, holding his eye, and left. I looked out the living room window as he drove away.

Part IV: The Divorce

I stayed strong for my daughter, shielding her from the abuse as I prepared for my escape. I had set up a secret bank account with enough money to start over. I found a place in Queens and signed a lease. I looked into a safe, small daycare in our new neighborhood and started building my case.

I asked my husband to meet me in a public place. I printed a log from our baby monitor, with dates of volume detected and the backed-up recording logs that had been stored on iCloud of his abuse. The baby monitor was connected to our cell phones and iCloud accounts. I printed pictures of my bruises and discolorations on my body. I printed screenshots from the affair. Lastly, I printed an estimate from my lawyer that I would receive in a settlement from his/our business if he gave me any problems in leaving. He was furious. But, I told him, "Lucky for you, I don't want the house, I don't want the memories that come with it, I don't want your money, you started your own business, you deserve every penny, I want nothing from you, I just want to quietly walk away with my daughter."

Part V: Healthy and Happy

He's since remarried. His new wife is stunning and beautiful. He didn't even marry the mistress. My daughter sees her daddy and stepmom on the weekends. She tells me everything and gives minute-by-minute details of what she does when she's with them. She's happy with Mommy during the week and happy with Daddy on the weekends. The new wife doesn't make eye contact with me much. She keeps her head down. There's a very real chance she might be experiencing what I went through. I'm on her side and stand with her. I thought of buying her a broom for Christmas to use on him, just in case. You just never know.

I'm still single and haven't dated in years. I'm taking my time to accomplish the goals I've set for myself. I'm not quite ready for love yet. I am in love with life right now though. I could have moved back home, down South after the divorce, but I put my dreams on hold for my ex-husband. He indirectly taught me a lot about running a business. I started one of my own and registered my company in the State of New York. It's in the beginning stages and doing alright. I'm in graduate school and my daughter and I travel all over the world. We're in a happy home.

Part VI: Reflections

Research indicates babies barely remember the first year of their life. I was glad I left while my daughter was still young. Even if my daughter were older, I would have still made the decision to leave. It's better for a child to be raised in a single-parent home where a child can thrive in a healthy environment and never witness the abuse of a parent as opposed to living in a home with hostility and anger. We divorced before my daughter's first birthday. My daughter has no idea of what I've been through and I wish to keep it that way.

As I write, it's snowing in New York City. My daughter, Yorkshire terrier and I are warm inside our house, cuddling together on the living room couch. On this cozy December afternoon, I reflect on my experiences. Going through something so devastating in life makes the mundane stressors and minor everyday setbacks seem completely irrelevant. I've been belittled, humiliated, and hurt before and I'm sure I will continue to experience life's twists and turns. But, I'm just so thankful right now at how resilient and fearless I've become. I'm amazed that against all odds, I was able to rise out of the ashes. I haven't figured everything out yet. And don't have all the answers. But here's what I do know about single mothers and women in general: we might bend, but we'll never be broken.

The Long Road Home

By Erin Riley

It was my first day at a new school. Around Valentine's Day, in the middle of third grade, my family moved to Boise, Idaho, from Fort Collins, Colorado. My hair was cropped short in a pixie haircut. At nine years old, I was five feet tall with a gender-ambiguous name. Not wanting to be mistaken for a boy, I wore my favorite outfit: an over-sized sweatshirt of Mickey and Minnie Mouse kissing, paired with matching stirrup pants.

"Are you a boy or a girl?" asked a boy with a smile and bratty voice.

My heart sank.

That was the moment I knew I needed to get out of Idaho the first chance I could. I also knew I needed to do everything I could to fit in before that day arrived. In my mind, the way to fit in was to have a boyfriend, which was the ultimate way to prove that I was loved and accepted. I had one significant relationship in high school, but he was older and when he graduated and moved away, I started sleeping with multiple boys in search of the love and affirmation that would prove I was worth something.

I failed out of college after just one semester. My parents felt that I couldn't be trusted on my own and so they moved me out to Seattle where they had relocated and could keep any eye on me. I started working part-time in a bridal shop. Even though I was working my way to become a manager-in-training, I still felt I had failed at my parents' dream of going to college and becoming a successful adult. They were constantly asking what my plans were—if I was going to go back to school, or if I had I thought about a trade school, or anything beyond retail. I quickly slipped back into a deep depression and, once again, had the sense that I needed to get as far away from my family as possible. Running away would give me the chance to change who I was, to start over as a new person.

That was when *Wheel of Fortune* helped play a role in a major life decision. As a family, we would watch the program with my grandpa during the week. One week—military week, in fact—I wanted to make what I thought would be a shocking declaration: I should join the military. Instead of the intended protests, I was met with, "That sounds like a good idea." And so, a month after my twentieth birthday, I found myself in boot camp in Great Lakes, Illinois, preparing for a career in the Navy.

Surprisingly, I had a great time in boot camp. We had three meals a day, got plenty of exercise, attended classes, and hung out with new friends. Everyone imagined traveling the globe and I was no exception. My first choice was to be stationed in Italy, followed by Hawaii, and then Norfolk, Virginia, since I'd never been to the Eastern United States. The powers above overlooked my first two choices, and after boot camp and the two-week school of knot and heavy line tying, I was headed to Norfolk, armed with new skills and a fancy Chicago boyfriend I met during boot camp. We started our relationship by sending notes back and forth to one another through the barrack's mail system, where I was assigned as an extra privilege.

I arrived in Norfolk in January, in the middle of the night. I got to the destroyer that I was assigned to and was quickly escorted to the small women's berthing area, where the sailor on duty shined a flashlight to the top bunk. I was to put my gear and sheets down and unpack in the morning.

What had I gotten myself into?

The same feeling washed over me that I had when I called my mom from SeaTac before boarding the plane to boot camp. Fear gripped my whole body and I wanted to go back to my comfortable life. This was way outside my comfort zone. But I made an agreement with the government and that wasn't easy to break.

When I didn't have weekend duty, I took every chance I could to get off the ship. I would either stay with friends in hotel rooms or someone who had off-base housing.

One night, I found myself in the company of some guys whom I'd met through my boyfriend. We had all spent time together back in Illinois, so why would Virginia be any different? When I first walked in, nothing was out of the ordinary, just some dudes getting drunk on a Saturday. As far as I was concerned, we were just hanging out like old times. But all of a sudden, I found myself in a room alone with two seamen whom I'd met at training school a month prior to that night. The door was closed. The atmosphere had changed. It wasn't light-hearted anymore. One of them had his hand on my breast.

I laughed it off, like so many other times with guys in the past, and swatted his hand away. When I sat down on the edge of a bed, the other man sat down next to me, and grabbed my crotch. Again, I swatted his hand away, and asked what his friend—my boyfriend— would think about him touching me that way. Instead of recognizing how inappropriate this all was, the two of them made their way to the back of the room and began to whisper.

My blood ran cold. Alarms rang in my head. I knew that if I stayed, something really bad was about to happen. I quietly grabbed my things, ran to the lobby of the building, and called my boyfriend. The first thing he said was, "Well what did you think was going to happen? Why did you put yourself in that situation?"

"I don't know... I thought we were just going to hang out... I thought we were friends. I didn't know..."

I ended up calling someone to pick me up and stayed with them on an air mattress, on the floor of what was supposed to be a dining room.

My boyfriend made his way to his new command in Virginia soon after the assault. He took it upon himself to show me how very naïve and dumb I was, insisting that I couldn't be trusted anymore, and that I needed his help to get myself through the world. I had a protector who ended up being my abuser.

The two men were held accountable for what they did to me, and while I didn't feel judged or shamed by my employer, it was a whole different story with my boyfriend, who ended up becoming my fiancé, and then my husband—all in the span of six months.

My "wise" husband introduced me to cocaine right before we were married, and it eventually turned into our therapy drug. It was wonderful to be able to talk through our issues while high—there was no judgment, at least until the drug started to wear off. When we were sobering up, things would turn pretty ugly. This habit ended both of our careers in the Navy, just shy of reaching the three-year mark.

One night, after we had both been kicked out of the military with an "other-than-honorable discharge," my husband and I got into an argument. He pushed my head into the sofa I was sitting on. I called the police. He ran away, but came back fifteen minutes later with a huge gash on the side of his head. I later found out that he had hit himself with his cell phone to make it look like I had beaten him. The police arrested me. But when he saw me in handcuffs, he got himself arrested as well in a drunken, misguided attempt at chivalry. We ended up having to find money, which we didn't have, to bail him out and pay for a lawyer. It turned out he already had an arrest record I didn't know about for the assault and battery of his father.

A month later, we moved to St. John, USVI.

We left for this island adventure convinced that this was just the thing to turn our marriage around. But islands are expensive and small and, as it turns out, there's not much to do there but fall back into old habits. After seven months and a two-day bender, my husband, quite literally, head-butted the sense back into me. I fled to a neighbor's house and called my parents, who immediately bought me a plane ticket. This time I was to join them in Corvallis, Oregon.

I was ready to go home, wherever home was at the time.

It took a full day of traveling across the country to finally be back in Oregon, where I was born in a house just outside of Portland. I ended up staying six years in the state of my birth, but somehow I never felt at home. While still living in Oregon, I spent two summers working at the Grand Canyon. During my last summer there I met a gal from Idaho, where I'd grown up so long ago. She had the state tattooed on her ankle and spoke beautifully about her love for what I still considered my home state.

Once again, I felt the pull to go home. I made a promise to myself that this time would be different, a redemption of sorts—a way to prove that I did fit in and that I did belong. My parents followed within the year and we were back where we started.

I ended up moving closer to downtown Boise, which is much different than the single-family home in the neighborhood that I grew up in. I was nervous about coming back home, and wondered whether I had made the right choice. But I had grown up and I had so much more life experience in my back pocket. I wasn't quite sure if I was going to settle back in Boise or just take time to recollect, spend time with family, and eventually move on. In truth, finances were a big factor that kept me in town, but I had also met some amazing people and finally felt part of a community. I've been back in Boise for five years now.

I have had some rough times—having a boyfriend move out abruptly and disappear, being unemployed for four months, having daily struggles with Post Traumatic Stress Disorder (PTSD). Yet, through those extremely dark times, I found that I had so much support and so much more strength than I ever thought possible.

Within the last year, I have done a lot of self-reflection and focused on personal growth. I found a wonderful therapist and have worked hard at learning to trust again. I realized that I have had some major trust issues—not only with others—but especially with myself. Slowly, and with the help of some intense therapy, I have learned that I can trust myself. It's not something that has come easy, and it takes daily, if not hourly, practice to remember that trust.

It has been easier to speak my truth and not feel shame for what has happened on my path away from then back to Boise. I embrace those experiences and use them in different capacities. I ended up in a local stand-up competition this summer, and it's like a whole new world has opened up. My nearly non-existent self-confidence came back to life on stage, and I'm proud to have found the value and worth I've been looking for; I'm no longer that androgynous little girl, but a woman who has found a way to embrace her own stories and share them without shame or self-judgment. I know that it will not always be easy—I am human, after all. But, without all the darkness and, sometimes, overwhelming pain, I wouldn't be the person I am today.

I am stronger than I've ever been.

The Bad Guy

By Elizabeth Rodgers

Pat screaming. Me backing up. Hands up, like I'm being arrested.

Pat: You don't want to listen to a word. You know everything.

Me: If you could stop yelling, we could talk —

Pat: You can't tell me how to speak! I can say whatever I want to say. You can't tell me —

Me: Please, stop yelling and stop pointing your finger in my face.

Pat: You can't tell me what to do!

Me: Please, you're in my space.

I took one giant step back. Pat stepped into my space and pointed his finger extra close.

Me: I don't respond well to being pointed at.

Pat: *(bending over to gather all of his strength):* FUCK YOU!

Everyone was standing in front of the synagogue. My daughter, 10, watched the confrontation with her friend, Pat's granddaughter, who seemed less invested. The granddaughter skulked away, like an embarrassed teen. She was 8.

Naomi approached with her purple leather purse. I knew she carried a gun in that purse. She never put it down.

Naomi: What's going on?

Pat: You two are trying to tell me what I can and can't say—

Me: *(aside, to Naomi)* I've got to get out of here. He's freaking me out.

I felt bad about leaving Naomi with Pat. I didn't realize how rattled I was even though I was shaking and adrenaline was oozing out of my pores. It's not like there was no one else around. The rabbi walked by. The head of the Hebrew school, too. It was like we were invisible. A crazy man was yelling his head off at two women who kept backing up while he advanced. Not even the rabbi wanted to get involved.

This wasn't the first time I had trouble when I spoke up for myself. I've had differences with lots of people and have argued plenty. It's in my DNA. I never had a problem in college—we were there to argue. We were developing our minds, you know, critical thinking. If you don't like an idea, you counter it with your own idea.

The trouble came after college when the men (always men) I argued with were not having as good a time as I was. Like the time at summer stock when a fellow actor overpowered me and trapped me in my room to try to settle an argument. Or when years later, I told an A-list actor for whom I was writing a script to stop smoking in my presence. I was pregnant. He was offended that I was telling him what to do. I was fired days later.

We moved to Boise from Los Angeles for a better quality of life. I was a screenwriter, so I was blowing up my career—what was left of it. I was in the Writer's Guild, I had representation, but my writing partner and I had separated and I was going nowhere fast. My husband wanted out of my hometown.

We joined the synagogue because it was the only synagogue in town and we like being Jewish. Most Jews who move to Boise aren't seeking Jewish community. You don't move to Idaho to be with the Jews. You have to make it happen. The synagogue is small with a skeleton crew. Members break down the tables and chairs after events, congregants volunteer to teach at Hebrew school, and if you speak up about an issue and if you want anything done, you have to own it—very hands on.

Early on, I had expressed how unadorned and crappy the synagogue looked during the High Holy Days. I owned it. I enlisted the designer from the Anthropologie store downtown to come to the synagogue and suggest design solutions. Ultimately, the synagogue purchased every last yard of muslin in town and we draped the perimeter of the space with the fabric. Like a mini-Christo. And reusable year after year—a practical and beautiful solution.

Pat, a Jew with a seriously Scottish name, was one of the teachers at the Hebrew school and a super-volunteer. He wore shorts, even in winter, with brightly colored novelty knee-socks that looked like cowboy boots or that had sayings like, "I Can't Adult Today." Pat's the guy who had a dog kennel attached to the top of his truck in 2012 when Romney was the Republican nominee for President. He painted his truck's windows: 'Romney's Dog' with arrows to the kennel. It was funny and terrifying. Idaho is a Republican supermajority with open carry gun laws. Pat was unafraid of goading the Idahoans around him.

My kids had been in the school at the synagogue since we came to town. It was Year Six that it occurred to me that my kids were in a glass building, unprotected, on the synagogue campus. I asked if we could have a lockdown drill. A lockdown drill is what you do in preparation for the unimaginable act of an active shooter on campus. I got some pushback, especially from the head of the school. But I had skin in the game. I couldn't not move forward on this once it entered my consciousness.

I connected with Naomi, the head of the security committee. She had been trying to introduce lockdown drills for years, to no avail. We thought it reasonable to conduct lockdown drills during the one night a week when all of our children gather for Jewish education. Pat was not the only one in the synagogue who thought this was a terrible and scary idea. But he was the most vocal. The rabbi is very anti-gun, to the point of wanting to put a sign in the window that says, "Gun Free Zone." Even with my antipathy to guns,

I thought this was not the best idea for a synagogue in Idaho. The one with mostly windows on three sides. "Shalom! We're unarmed!"

Synagogue Director: This is a safe place, Elizabeth.

She grew up in Manhattan. She should know better.

Me: So are the Boise public schools and they run lockdown drills monthly.

Synagogue Director: We are a welcoming community. We can't be scaring people.

Some people saw the idea of a lockdown drill and a welcoming community as mutually exclusive: felt it was off-message for a Jewish place of worship.

I do understand that some people in charge were truly scared. The idea, just the idea of entertaining the possibility of a gunman roaming our halls, killing our children, is chilling and, hopefully, unthinkable. But Naomi and I were the ones who made them think about it—when it wasn't even happening. I think this is how Pat imagined the offense that Naomi and I were terrorizing the children and the community.

Naomi and I did a lot of research. We labeled the lockdown drill a "reverse fire drill" for those offended by the label. We did not care what it was called. For some reason, fire drills are not scary and lockdown drills are. I think it's because they know a gunman is a true possibility, which makes it even crazier that they oppose the lockdowns. Deep down, on a primal level, they know we need to be ready.

None of the lights were on in the front entrance, but it was still light enough that you could see.

Only Naomi was there. We gave each other a hug hello. I saw her purple purse: small, leather and full. She's the only gun owner around whom I feel completely comfortable. She's a trained sharp shooter and extraordinarily level-headed and even-keeled. She's even in the NRA. And a Republican. I have evolved.

Once everyone had arrived a few minutes after the hour, Tracy, the mediator, started the proceedings.

But first, I have to explain Tracy: Tracy's lawyer and a certified mediator. In our first meeting, Tracy told Naomi and me how bad Pat felt about the whole thing. How he loved my kids. I did not think that was an effective mediation strategy. Was she related to Pat?

Tracy sees herself as uniquely qualified to do this mediation at the synagogue because she's the kind of person who believes herself to be as sophisticated and smart as her idea of what a smart, sophisticated Jew is. But that's just it: it's an idea—a ridiculous and ghastly stereotype. I would imagine she feels that way around Black people, too. It's like she's saying, "I know from Jews." Except she doesn't.

Tracy: Pat, you have an apology for Naomi and Elizabeth? Why don't you begin.

Pat: I have been a member in good standing of this synagogue for 40 years...

Pat read from his iPad. To Pat's credit, he started out with a decent apology. That came fairly quickly. Then we had to listen to about fifteen minutes of all the good deeds he's done for the synagogue for the past forty years. He even listed how much money he donated, which was impressive given his profession: school bus driver. And yet, his good deeds were off-topic and exactly what I warned in my initial letter to the leaders of the synagogue, written the night of the incident: "I know [Pat] has built a lot of goodwill in this community through good works. Are those the chits that he gets to cash in so that he can get away with this clearly abusive behavior? I hope not." After speaking about volunteering with the kids, the teens, the ritual committee and on and on, he went back to the apology.

Pat: But I don't think that Elizabeth and Naomi were really afraid. They could have walked away. They are strong women. There were plenty of people around. I know Naomi carries a gun, which makes me afraid of her. Truthfully, I don't believe I did anything wrong other than swear. And for that, I am truly sorry.

It was then that I stopped listening. I glanced at Naomi, who had the look of a startled owl. I looked at the rabbi, the director of the synagogue, the president of the synagogue, the head of education, and Tracy, the mediator: none of them seemed to register that the entire apology had just been retracted. They had stopped listening as well.

Pat finished and put down the iPad. Tracy asked if Naomi and I would accept Pat's apology.

They were so close. I could see it in their eyes: they saw the finish line. They were about to put this whole ugly incident behind them. Sure, Pat was a hothead, but Naomi was a Republican gun nut and Elizabeth was a pushy broad from the big city, a little too demanding and perhaps unlikable.

Me: I'm confused. Pat just said that he didn't think our accusa-
        tion had integrity. That he was falsely accused. The 'fuck you'
        was the least of it.

Naomi nodded.

The other side of the room visibly deflated. I had just snatched momentum from the jaws of victory. Exasperation filled the room on both sides.

Tracy: But he just apologized. Can you accept his apology?
        The world was upside down.

Me: I don't consider that an apology. He said we lied about being
        scared.

Naomi: I agree with Elizabeth.

I had brought the room to a standstill. I knew I wasn't wrong, but still, it's a strange position to be in. Other than Naomi, everyone in the room thought I was the bad guy for not accepting the apology. Naomi didn't accept it either, but I'm the loud mouth.

Tracy: Let's move on to the next issue. Elizabeth, you have been
        telling your story of what happened between you and Pat to
        other people in the synagogue.

Me: Yes.

Tracy: Naomi, you have not been telling your story.

Naomi: No.

Tracy: Elizabeth, when you tell your story, you say that you were scared of Pat. You used the word, "fear."

Me: Yes.

Tracy: The word, "fear," is loaded. When you tell people that you feared Pat, you are casting aspersions on his character. Do you think that's fair? "Fear" is a heavy word.

Me: It's my experience. It happened. I was afraid.

Tracy: Could you perhaps, use the words, "bully behavior" and "intimidate" instead of "fear"?

I thought about it for a moment: words matter to me.

Me: Would you like me to minimize my experience?

The words, "minimize my experience," were so overtly political, that even though I said this in a quiet voice with a smile on my face, I knew I could barely contain my hostility. The rabbi knows what this means. He's a social activist, showing up at the Capitol each year to lobby for LGBTQ+ rights. But I had overestimated Tracy.

Me: Would you like me to minimize my experience?

Tracy: Yes!

Stunned was not the half of it. The worst part was that the rabbi sat there in silence.

In the year that followed, and ever since really, it's been hard for me to attend synagogue. The leadership of the synagogue revealed themselves to me. Anyone can be a mensch on a daily basis, but it's what you do in a crisis that reveals who you really are.

I don't want to turn my kids against Judaism with this story. (It's isolated only to the leadership in our synagogue, right?) I want my children to love being Jewish. To feel connected to their history and their traditions. I want their Judaism to make them feel warm inside. We light candles on Shabbat. I bake challah on Fridays—mostly because there's nowhere to buy it in Boise, but still, I adhere to these traditions because they ground me and inform my identity. My children know what happened, but we don't talk about it at home. And I take them to Hebrew school each week and feel grateful that they still want to go.

Since the shooting at the synagogue in Pittsburgh, there has been more acceptance of security measures, like the lockdown drill and more. Since Naomi and I have long since quit the committee, there are some terrific men, military veterans, who have taken up the cause. We reach out to them to get updates, but otherwise, we are rarely included.

Post-Holocaust Jews are taught that silence is acceptance. Nobel winner Elie Wiesel puts a fine point on it:

> *I swore never to be silent whenever and wherever human beings endure suffering and humiliation. We must always take sides. Neutrality helps the oppressor, never the victim. Silence encourages the tormentor, never the tormented. Sometimes we must interfere.*[1]

About a week after the mediation, I received a letter documenting the meeting. The letter was sent to me, Naomi, Pat, and everyone at the meeting, including the rabbi. The upshot: Pat apologized but Naomi and I refused to accept his apology. And I was asked not to repeat my story and besmirch Pat's reputation, but I refused.

Pat was clean. I was the bad guy.

---

[1] Wiesel, Elie. Acceptance Speech. Nobel Peace Prize, 10 December 1986. Oslo City Hall, Norway.

Devoted to My Magic

By Jasmin Rodriguez

Growing up in New York was tough for a dreamer who grew up in the hood. Both of my parents are Puerto Rican. My dad's first language was Spanish while my mother's first language was English. My dad spent most of his childhood in Puerto Rico before moving to Brooklyn. My mother was born in Hoboken but grew up in Queens. She was this fiery go-getter who worked corporate jobs and went to school, and my dad was a very strict mechanic who specialized in classic car restoration. My mother was my cheerleader and pushed me to follow my dreams, and my father never showed me love and always reminded me that I would never amount to anything. Because of how I was brought up, I was always perplexed as to what to believe for myself. Was I really born a failure who would prove true the opinions of my father, or would I be as successful as my mother said I'd be?

I didn't know. All I knew was that I loved art and it was my life. My passion for art evolved from one medium to another any time I would gain or lose inspiration. I'd do comic illustrations, paintings, sculpting, graphic design, fashion design, and more. This was my escape from the pain I felt as a child who was a loner, who couldn't really connect to people.

Being around so many toxic people growing up tainted my perspective on the world. I'd get bullied by kids in school and then I'd go home to be bullied by my own father. Kids would bully me because I always looked different and wore different things. My father would do it just because, I don't know, maybe he was having a bad day? Those bad days were endless. However, even through fighting one obstacle after another, I was at least strong enough to stick to my guns and stay true to who I am. It was still extremely exhausting and took a toll on my mental health. I just couldn't understand why my dad never liked my artwork, or why it was cool to follow trends and look like everyone else at school when I could create my own identity for myself. I've been told my whole life that I am too much of something, or that I need to water myself down, or that I am just not good enough. I think back on it now and recognize just how brave I was for going against the grain as a child. For not listening to others and for trusting my own intuition. For always being relentless in protecting my magic.

I see today's youth and how vulnerable kids are to negativity and beauty standards and it breaks my heart.

Even with being as determined as I was, I struggled to make space for myself everywhere I went, I struggled to make friends, and I struggled to get people to believe in my visions. That's the reality for people who are different. It's a lonely place, and we are always misunderstood.

It wasn't until I went to high school that people really took a liking to how I expressed myself through fashion and my art. Even if they didn't understand it, they at least tried to because I was so confident about it. This is not to say that kids didn't try to bully me—they tried— but at this point I was ready to go head to head with anyone (including my father, who eventually stopped being emotionally abusive). I felt strong, fearless, and devoted to my magic.

That's when my love of fashion really went full speed ahead and I realized this was what I wanted to transition to (I was doing comic illustration beforehand). My dream was to attend the Fashion Institute of Technology College (F.I.T.) and live the *Sex & The City* dream life all girls wanted at the time. I wanted the brownstone apartment on the Upper East Side, I wanted to either write about fashion or to have my designs in *Vogue*. I wanted to retire early and open a vintage store in the city and be the Iris Apfel of Puerto Rican women. However, when I applied to F.I.T., I was denied—not once, but several times. I did everything I could to get in. And my mother did everything she could to help, like taking money out of her 401K just to send me there to take non-matriculate courses. I raised my GPA, I applied for less competitive degrees, yet nothing I tried worked.

I was heartbroken and thought, "Maybe I just don't have what it takes, or maybe it's the fact that my parents are not wealthy, or maybe it's because I am not white." Walking on campus, I couldn't relate to anyone. There were barely any black or Latina girls. There was not a single person I could really relate to, not even when I took courses there at the time. I was so angry and resentful until one day I had a meeting with my friend Steve, a well-known sneaker designer and all around streetwear mogul from my stomping grounds in Queens. He worked for DC Shoes at the time and I wanted to intern there. I told him how heartbroken I was about not getting into F.I.T and he told me, "You don't need student loans, all you need is a library card." And so the next day I took my ass to the library, learned web design, and started my fashion blog, *Vintage Vandalizm* (VintageVandalizm.com).

By creating my own website, I would be able to talk all things fashion, brand myself as a fashion mogul, and live out my dream as a fashion journalist and designer. At that point, I didn't care where fashion would lead me—I just knew I wanted to be a part of it.

After my first year of blogging, I was already the talk of NYC and being featured in magazines like *Nylon, Gotham Digest, TimeOut NY, Glamour France,* and more. My website became my resume and I never needed one to land any jobs again. I ended up working free-lance modeling and styling gigs as well as corporate positions for amazing designers. I was either backstage at New York Fashion Week working shows or sitting front row talking about them. And it all started with a fashion blog and the relentless belief in my own magic. I am blessed to have had so many great experiences come from start-ing the Vintage Vandalizm empire. None of it would have happened had I given up and conformed to what society wanted me to be.

After years of wearing many hats in the fashion world and helping endless brands find their own voice, I now reside in Las Vegas, Nevada, where I am working on my first ever Vintage Vandalizm clothing line that will be launching this year. I even have a better relationship with my father who finally understands that I know what's best for me. And I understand that when I was a child, he was just projecting his own inner fears of the life I may live.

But he was wrong. I defied the odds. The universe conspired. I now know that this is what I was always meant to do and I hope that the universe will continue to help guide me on the right path. I can only hope that through my own struggles as a Latina designer, I can pave the way and inspire other people of color to be fearless in pursuit of their dreams, of their magic.

Surviving the Underworld

By Monique Rojas

"Mom, I'm not feeling so well."

I had picked up that thousand-pound phone with the desperation of a woman on her deathbed. My mom could tell from the sound of my voice that I was crawling on my knees. She knew I had dealt with bipolar depression and suicide attempts my whole life. But this was the worst nervous breakdown to date.

"Why don't you come out to Iowa?"

"Iowa? I hate that farming fuck place. There is nothing to do there," I scoffed. Even while in the grips of a complete meltdown, I still had standards.

"Well, just consider it, please." I could hear the compassion in my mother's voice. It was like a red ribbon wrapping around me, saving me from the riptide current she knew I was drowning in.

"I'll think about it." I hung up the phone and looked at the empty house.

My small desert home was filled with nothing but deafening echoes and pictures of my father who had passed away the previous month. I could still smell death in the air. I could feel the death seeping into my pores like a tab of acid when you drop it in your eye.

His death was slow and painful. I had taken him to chemo treatments several times a month. Then, we got into a fight over how he treated my dog and never resolved it. We never saw each other again.

Since his death I felt like a dead woman walking. I was ashamed that I had lost everything important to me in my life over the last eleven months. I had finally hit rock bottom. This was just the last straw. The last hit. My final wake-up call. I knew if I didn't make my next move, I was going to commit suicide.

I hit my knees and prayed. Even though I had experienced so much pain and loss, I attributed my survival to a guardian angel or something that has always watched over me.

"God, if you are there, I need help. I am dying and don't know which way to turn. I don't know if this is the right thing to do, but I am asking for your help."

Immediately, a calm came over me and the words I heard were: "If you stay in Los Angeles seven more days, you will die."

I called my mom thirty minutes later and made plans to get out of Los Angeles and move to Iowa within three days. She wired me money because I was so depressed I couldn't work. I put what little furniture I had in storage and what clothes I could fit into my car. Last thing to go into my car was my beloved, obese, long-haired brown Chihuahua named Tooty. He was the only thing left in the world that I would go to jail or take a bullet for. He was spoiled rotten and lived the life of a 17-pound king who huffed and puffed after walking just a few steps. Together we started the 26-hour drive for my survival.

I had never felt freedom like I felt during that first hour driving. It was my first true act of self-care in years.

The window was down and Tooty was resting comfortably behind my neck against the driver's seat. Instead of death breathing down my neck, for the first time in fifteen years I felt life. It was July 7th and I kept driving.

I was leaving behind some serious danger. For the last fifteen years I had worked as an exotic dancer at the largest strip club in Los Angeles, one of the largest and most famous strip clubs in the world. While I chose my path of sex work of my own free will, it was a grueling marathon.

I escorted the entire time I lived in L.A. I was raped in the very beginning. Every time I escorted after that, even though it was consensual, it felt like I was being raped all over again. By the age of twelve, five people had molested me. I was reliving my sexual violations every time I took money for sex. Lap dances were fine but I couldn't handle escorting.

Many girls don't survive what I like to call the "Underworld." The Underworld is full of excitement but it is dangerous. It's a world of black markets, criminal enterprise, hustlers, predators, big money and temptation. So many of my friends have been lost to dancing and the subculture of the Underworld.

In the beginning a few of my friends had committed suicide after abusing drugs. But things got worse as time went on. As I became closer to more dancers, I could see that the Underworld was plagued with mental illness. I had three friends kill themselves in one year—two from schizophrenia and one from bipolar 1 disorder. One committed suicide by enticing the police to shoot her. After getting off her prescribed meds, she had a manic episode and got hold of a gun. She was causing a scene at her house when the police were called. Coming out of her house, she pointed the gun at the cops and was shot multiple times. My friend would have never done this consciously—she was mentally ill and luring the cops to kill her. It seemed like the funerals were never-ending.

Then there were the drug addictions. I thought at first girls did drugs to stay skinny but no one ever does drugs for just that—it's an excuse used to make the addiction more discrete. In the Underworld, people don't always take their meds, so they get aggressive and even psychotic. Some dancers might be struggling with addictions and mental illness, but it becomes deadly when the men around them unleash their demons on the sex workers.

Driving through the iron-rich soil of Utah, the dry desert land wrapped itself around the highway as the ground slowly turned brilliant red. It reminded me of all the blood discretely spilled in these deserts. I thought about my three escort friends who went home with the same guy and were stabbed to death. They just stopped showing up to work. Then, one day we found out why. He decapitated and dismembered them, leaving their bodies in the L.A. desert. He was never caught. His picture was just put up in the office and we were all told not to go home with him. He was identified by the last girl he tried to kill who got away.

My friends were not identified by their fingerprints but only by the serial numbers on their breast implants. He burned all their fingerprints and toe prints off. This wasn't the work of a new killer. Yet, he could easily disappear in the Underworld. Perhaps that's why I stopped getting close to others in the Underworld. Of course, everyone is hustling everyone in L.A.—I could navigate that fairly well. I just couldn't keep watching them disappear, taken by the lure of money and drugs. They would die when their intuition became fuzzy from intoxicants or untreated mental illness.

As I drove, I thought about all the predators, enforcers and hustlers I had worked around over the years. I knew who they were just from looking them in the eyes, and I would sometimes know what girls they controlled as their "enforcer." I chose to never have my own enforcer, as I could protect myself and manage my own business with a mixture of grit and fire. The criminal masterminds never approached me or tried to recruit me—I wasn't weak and I didn't have low self-esteem.

Predators in the Underworld all seemed to follow a simple pattern. They searched for and spotted the girl with the lowest self-esteem. They used a mixture of drugs, sweet talk, and hustling to make them feel special and in need of a man's protection in order to survive in this wild and dangerous place. The predators didn't trouble themselves with powerful women who would question too much and fight back.

Several hours into the drive, the sun was finally setting on the quiet deserted highway. As Tooty fell asleep on my neck and shoulders, I thought about the two times I was almost killed in L.A. The first time I was followed out to my car. We didn't have mandatory valet in the beginning when my club was new. I was twenty-two-years-old. He crept up to me in his car. My guardian angel was working overtime that night. Suddenly, I could feel the man's energy behind me before I could hear him. I grabbed my knife out of my purse and turned around. He was about to pull over and jump from his car toward me with something in his hand. I could see the desire to kill in his eyes but I was ready to fight. My job allowed me to hone certain skills over the years. I can look deep into a man's eyes and immediately know two things about him: his sexual desires and his intentions.

I might have looked like an easy victim from afar—being a petite 5'3" female, in impossibly tall heels, wearing a tight dress, and walking to my car with a purse full of fresh cash. I knew I had to make the first move in order to survive. I walked toward him ready to strike. I dug my heels into the pavement, held up my knife, and snarled, "If you come any closer, I'll stab you in the neck and slice your throat open!" I must have scared this predatory sociopath because he put his hand back down and gassed the car, screeching away. The evil intentions in his eyes were replaced with fear and self-preservation. Predators don't bother with the ones who are too much trouble. For all the evil they inflict, most of them are really just exceptionally selfish, broken and weak. I calmly put my knife back in my purse and walked to my car.

The other guy who tried to kill me lured me to his home. This happened within the first few months after I had moved to L.A. I had a bad night dancing and couldn't afford a hotel room, so he offered to let me sleep on his floor. I should have known his charm was the rope that he wanted to hang me with.

I was new to the Underworld then and I couldn't read people well. It took me a long time to understand who people were and what they wanted from me. When we got back to his apartment he had a large Rhodesian Ridgeback. The man was walking towards me in a very creepy way, staring into my eyes with a sick smile. I felt a chill. He asked if I wanted to "take the dog on a walk." He reached for a thick dark brown leash and started coming toward me instead of toward the dog. The way he said those seemingly innocuous words terrified me. I instantly felt those might have been the last words some girls ever heard.

I could see the truth in his eyes. I knew he was turned on by the thought of killing me, of pulling my flesh from my bones. When I saw his truth, as well as my life on the line, I had to morph into a panther again. I didn't speak a word but I knew in that moment if I didn't stand head to head with this man who was 6'3"—an entire foot taller than me—I was going to die.

I acted quickly, flashing the craziest panther eyes and baring my teeth. I let him know I wasn't going down without a fight. He didn't expect that. Other girls must have not seen murder in his eyes. They must have been blindsided. He backed down in shock, reversing slowly to his room and lying on the bed. Another creepy and strange move that a normal person wouldn't do. I didn't say a word. I didn't have to. He knew I would tear him up. I quickly got my stuff and left. I went to work that day with no money, took a shower and got ready there.

I may have been broke but I was alive. My aggression, grit, power, and ability to fight at the age of twenty-two saved my life. Most of all it was my intuition—my guardian angel—that saved my life.

The sky was dark and the car's headlights pierced the night sky as I entered farmland. The desert gave way to fertile agricultural ground. And I knew it was going to be okay. I started to think back to my nervous breakdown and everything that led up to me getting into this car.

It had started eleven months prior, when my manager, the most powerful man in the Underworld, fired me. To this day I don't know why he picked on me. I was one of the top girls at his club. I was going along with my business as normal. Not one thing had changed. Then he had one of the bouncers, who was also my friend, tell me I was too fat to work his shift. The massive bouncer turned sheet-white, cringing as he broke the news. He knew it wasn't true. I knew it wasn't either. I was the same weight as when I first started. I meticulously kept my body toned and in shape as it was how I earned my living. My manager fired me because I didn't follow the politics of the Underworld. I had never offered him sexual favors and I wasn't going to start now. My world was beginning to unravel. I was hired for another shift but the money wasn't the same. A month later, I broke my arm and was bitten after trying to break up a dogfight. I then lost my house and car because I couldn't work.

Three days later the love of my life, my Boston Terrier named Noodle, died of a severe epileptic seizure. I loved him more than the ocean loves the moon. We had an amazing love story—the kind people write about. No one may ever write a book about my dogs but I have the story in my heart.

I had to stay with my toxic boyfriend at that time because I had gotten into a fight with my dad. He was living with me when Noodle got sick, but he was mean to my dog. That was the last time I ever saw my dad. He said, "You will always be my daughter." And then I slammed the door in his face. I never spoke to him again. He died a few months later.

As I headed east, the road had become the darkest I'd ever seen. L.A. could never get this dark. The darkness was strangely soothing and felt like the journey I had to take in order to venture out of the darkness of the Underworld.

I drove through the night to Iowa. For fifteen years, I didn't see the stars because of the light pollution in L.A. But on that drive, the stars struck me as magnificent and unending.

Growing tired, I stopped at a truck stop and tried to sleep. Even though I was in the midst of Wyoming cowboy country, I felt a peace I had never known before.

Tooty didn't like me to hold him but ever since Noodle died he had grown more affectionate. I picked him up and put him on my chest as I reclined in the driver's seat. I could feel his little heartbeat keeping me alive.

I could see my future. I saw good fortune about to come my way. I believe that every Latina, such as myself, is born with a third eye into the spiritual realm. I knew I was on the right path. I felt fearless. I clung to Tooty. There was no better feeling than him lying on my chest while I clung to dear life. No matter how big of a thug I was, I still needed love.

I slept a little while longer at the truck stop before continuing the drive. I woke up to a sunrise like I had never seen before. I could feel myself getting stronger. And then, I arrived in Iowa on July 8th, not knowing who I was. On that day, I made a promise to myself.

I would start a love affair with myself. I was never going to let anyone abuse me ever again. I had had guns pulled on me by boyfriends, I'd been beaten, I'd done the beating, I'd been cheated on, I'd been nearly killed by an ex throwing me into the middle of traffic. And none of it killed me. I can't be destroyed—I am my own guardian angel and I am the only one who can cause myself to fall.

That's what my nervous breakdown taught me: when you lose everything and hit rock bottom, you have nowhere to go but up.

It was my choice whether I would let life beat me down and make me either bitter or better. I chose to become better.

After I made my way back to Iowa, I took two years off from dancing before I went back. During that time, I went on a spiritual journey. I found a higher power of my own understanding. When I went back to dancing, I had a whole new perspective. I was grateful and happy. We all have our own hustle, but my experience and my scars sculpted me into becoming a visitor of the Underworld—not a victim of it. I can enter it and leave it but am not consumed by it anymore.

I worked my ass off and paid off all my debt. I no longer experience depression or anxiety. While both of my beloved dogs passed away, I now have a cat that I love. My life has taken a 180-degree turn.

I also owe many thanks to Alcoholics Anonymous. I was able to maintain sobriety when guys were attacking me, when I was being raped, when I was being told I was too fat, when I lost both of my dogs, when my dad died a slow and painful death, and when all of my friends disappeared or were murdered or lost to the game. Alcoholics Anonymous taught me to be completely fearless. I know how to be in touch with my emotions to a point that's similar to being under a waterfall, feeling every drop of water on my skin.

Now, I am a complete human being. I know I can handle anything because I have my own higher power behind me. I believe in something bigger than myself—because, when I am alone and all I have is prayer, the unseen is what will save my life.

I have learned to listen to my intuition and not to do anything to cloud it. Drugs, drinks, mental illness, crippling self-esteem, and taking everything and everyone at face value is what destroyed so many of the women I have known. Now that I know my own power, I can never go back to the woman I was before. I carry my experiences to help others along the way. And that includes myself. I am my own guardian angel.

The Crossfire

By Aurélie Rose

As far as I can recall I have always wanted to be a mom. When my sister was born, I was only five years old, but when I held her in my arms for the first time, I felt I had a responsibility towards this little girl who had just arrived in my life. I was as serious as a five-year-old could be about it. The years passed, but that strong draw towards children never ceased to increase, and with it the certainty that one day I would be a mother.

Yet, when I met the person I loved so much that I knew I wanted him to be the father of my children, things did not pan out the way I had dreamed. I dove into the relationship heart first, never looking back, never letting my brain do the slightest bit of thinking. I learned that when a man says, "I do not want marriage or children," do not think that he will change his mind one day, that he needs some time to mature, or that one's love for him is so great that one day he will want the same things. That is the mistake I made—I believed my feelings for him would somehow make his desires line up with mine. In my defense, he married me. So I thought there was room for change—after all, he did not want to get married and here we were, husband and wife. I thought maybe if I were patient, children would come, too.

When I started feeling a real desire for motherhood, I faced a wall. Not that I was ready to have children right then and there, but I needed reassurance from him that one day it would happen. I almost called it quits, but he agreed to seek help, so we did. We had a lot of work ahead of us; there were a lot of things that I had refused to see about him and a lot that we disagreed on. But I was determined to make this marriage work, to compromise, and to give it my all. We finally agreed that we would wait a few more years before starting a family. That was all I wanted: just to know that we were going in the same direction. What I had not counted on and what came as a surprise was the positive pregnancy test that would make my whole world crumble.

When I started feeling that things were a little different in my body, I took a pregnancy test on my own—without telling him about it—and it was negative. It was probably for the best as we were not stable either financially or in our relationship. However, this gut feeling that something was about to change was not leaving me, so a couple weeks later, I took another test. It is said that the tests are more effective first thing in the morning, so at dawn, I locked myself in the bathroom and took another test. I looked at the timer, focused on the seconds slowly passing by, and after exactly two minutes, I looked at that stick again. My breath got short, my heart started beating really fast, and for approximately ten seconds, I think I was happy. *Pregnant.* But then it all quickly came swirling back only to slap me in the face— he did not want me to be pregnant. I started panicking, wondering how to tell him and how he would react. And then I thought, "I took a test a couple weeks ago, it was negative, this one is positive, perhaps this one is wrong." So, I repeated the process right away. The two minutes that followed felt like an eternity, but the result was identical. *Pregnant.*

My heart would not stop pounding, not out of excitement, but out of fear. What was I going to do? I could not keep that from him, not even for a day—it would not be fair to him, so I woke him up. I did not wrap it in a bow, I did not sit him down saying we have to talk—I simply and calmly told him: "I just took a pregnancy test. It is positive. I am pregnant." In that moment, I was hopeful. I thought he would try to keep his composure, try to rationalize, try to talk things through.

But he did not. I completely disappeared in his eyes. He said "Fuck!" over and over, and the more it went on, the angrier he got. Rather than being supported by my husband—by the man I loved—I pushed everything I was feeling deep down, and I took care of him. I managed to calm him down by telling him that sometimes home pregnancy tests are not the most accurate and that I would take another one, just to be sure. I knew two false positive results were highly unlikely, but anything that could buy me time and let the thought sink into his mind seemed like a good idea at the time.

But it only went downhill from there. He was quick to jump to conclusions—after all, I was the one who talked about babies. Never mind that I was on birth control, never mind that it takes two—he alleged that it was my plan all along to trick him into having a child, trapping him into a life he never wanted. I was such an easy bad guy.

He became verbally and emotionally abusive. But I did not care. He could give me his worst—he was the father of my soon-to-be-born child and my husband, and I would find a way to fix it. Little did I know, there was and is no fixing it.

I held on and tried to put myself in his shoes: he did not want a child; his life was being turned upside down and he was angry. I understood. I let him be angry. I let him look at me with disgust. I let him tell me what horrible a person I was. And I let him walk all over me and my baby—his baby.

The first trimester of my pregnancy was nothing but toxic. Instead of taking care of myself, I tried to please him, to help him, to calm him down. That is when I started seeing who he really was: a narcissist, a selfish man-boy. And still, I had hopes that it was temporary, that it was just anger, that it would pass.

One day, he bluntly told me that he could not respect me anymore. And that was when something broke in me. He could resent me, he could be angry, he could be mean all he wanted—he could not show me respect. But hearing that he did not respect me, from his mouth, was the last straw. I left. Out of self-respect, and in order to preserve the rest of my pregnancy, I had to go.

From that moment on, I went through the pregnancy on my own. There is no point in sugarcoating it: it sucked. I did not have the opportunity to enjoy my pregnancy because I had nobody to connect with about it on an emotional level. When I felt my baby kick for the first time, I wanted someone to share it with, but I was alone. So, I busied myself as much as possible and acted as if I were not expecting. Do not get me wrong—I already deeply loved my baby and never did anything that would hurt him; I went to all of my doctor's appointments, took my daily vitamins, nested as pregnant women do, and was thrilled to hear I was having a boy. I even had a baby shower.

But something was missing. I was unable to be happy. I was terrified to go through pregnancy, labor, childbirth and raising a child on my own. What had happened to my dreams of motherhood? What had happened to my marriage? I had failed at everything and was convinced I was a bad person—I had been a bad wife and I was petrified at the idea of being a bad mom. So, I did the only thing I knew how to do: I kept my mind occupied with work and with research for the baby to come. I was determined to have my baby in the most natural way possible, so I signed up for a private natural childbirth workshop, and found it to be one of the best decisions I had ever made. I met couples with due dates that were close to mine. More than that, I connected with other families and felt safe enough to unload some of my burden by sharing my story with them. I cried my fair share—we all did. We were all working through things that were scary or difficult. And that was when things started shifting for me, at least emotionally. I had finally found a group of people I could open up to and was slowly finding my happy place.

When I felt that I had failed at life, there were very few people I felt comfortable reaching out to, including my closest friends. I was embarrassed not only for what had already happened but also for still having hope that my husband would turn things around. I did not want to hear anyone say that he would not come back, that he was showing his true colors, or that I should get out of the relationship. Looking back, I wish I *had* reached out to my closest friends. I wish they had told me all of the things I feared hearing. And I wish I had faced my fears and heard them.

I gave three years of my time, energy and myself to that man, even after he reacted the way he did and said the things he said. Three years. Three years from the time I moved out, I still held out hope that we could mend our relationship. I visited him, with his child, on a regular basis. For the first year, he barely looked at his own son. For me, my son was and still is the most beautiful miracle baby: a gorgeous little boy, full of life, eager to explore the world. I thought he would surely melt his father's heart and change his mind. But his father was angry—he was angry with me, possibly with God, and maybe the rest of the world, too. He never showed anger towards my son—just indifference. He certainly did not want to be called "Dad" and he could not even call me his son's "mom." I was the "Lady" and his son was the "Kid."

Picking our son's name was quite revealing, too. My husband did not participate in naming him and that was difficult for me. I was responsible for choosing his name, at least his first and middle names, but what about his last name? Was I to assert myself, thereby risking losing my son's father for good, by giving him my last name? Or was I to remain hopeful, offer him an olive branch, and give my son his father's last name? I asked him what he wanted to do, to which he asked to meet with a social worker in order to know if not giving the baby his last name would free him of his responsibilities as a father. His question was quickly answered: *Yep, man, he is your son, a part of you, no matter what his name is, and that will never change.* So, my husband figured, since it does not change anything, he might as well wear his name. I saw this as a good sign. How dumb was I? I thought it meant that he was finally admitting, recognizing and accepting that the baby was his.

Reflecting back on that decision, I see myself as weak. I was blind and I was stupid. I was repeating the mistakes I had made in my marriage to him. And today, I can only weep. I did not want to open my eyes, and I did not want my eyes opened, for that matter. I tried to create a relationship between father and son and I tried to heal my marriage. I could not divorce him, as I saw divorce as a failure. But I know now that divorce is *not* a failure. It was the hardest thing I have ever had to do—it took guts and it took me almost three years to get there. It took another guy—a neighbor—showing kindness to me to realize what I needed to do.

When we agreed to divorce, he was very clear that he would only divorce through the "do your own divorce" route. However, when I noticed how pushy he was about it, I decided to hire a lawyer, just to be safe, to have someone in my corner, to tell me when he was trying to get his way and do things in his sole best interest. By hiring a lawyer, I unleashed a beast I had not seen before. He hired the biggest, scariest, most expensive attorney out there, and started his quest for custody. That's right—*custody!*

He went to the court asking for overnights and legal custody. He and his whole family ganged up on me, describing me as a mentally unstable, drug and alcohol abusing, suicidal maniac. He asked that my baby be taken away from me, claiming I was a danger to him, and that if I were to have any time with him, it should be through supervised visitations. I had taken care of my baby this whole time, without my husband's help. My baby was happy and healthy. And he was taken away from me and given to a father who was indifferent to him.

It has been over a year since our case started. We are officially divorced. And he was granted full legal custody. In other words, I have no say in any decision-making concerning my little boy and only share physical custody three to four days at a time. Since my pregnancy, my road has been paved with challenges and rude awakenings. People whom I thought I could count on did not show up. The deepest, darkest times in your lifetime can give so much insight about the people who surround you. This journey has shone a light on who my real friends were and I am so thankful for the people who have supported me. They have gone above and beyond for me. I never thought I deserved much. And never thought I would be so blessed to have such amazing people in my corner.

If one is to take one thing from my story, please, please, please do not let anybody treat you poorly. Do not think your partner just slipped, that it was temporary, or that they will change. If they are not willing to see that their behavior is wrong and seek help, they will likely not change. Chances are, things will get worse if they do not accept responsibility for their abuse. When a partner shows signs as clear as my ex-husband's signs, do not ignore them. It was scary and difficult to leave and to be alone, but I was so much better off alone than stuck with a spouse who was not good for me. I feel horrible for not leaving when I had the chance—he even gave me the chance, and I did not take it. Now, my little boy is caught in the crossfire and that is the worst thing for a mother to witness.

Be true to yourself, do not let anybody take your happiness and shine from you. You are worth so much more than you know. The minute you have doubts about someone, take the time to reflect, and for once let your brain do the work. Letting your heart guide you is not a bad thing in life, but as soon as your whole being seems to scream at you that you are in a situation that contradicts your heart, then listen, stop, and think. Nobody is worth the aggravation. The people in your life should help you be the best you that you can be. They should bring you happiness and fill your days with joy. If it is not the case, or ceases to be the case, think long and hard. The way I now try to think about it is by asking myself: would I want this for my son? Is that the example I want him to follow? Is that the way anybody should treat him? If the answer is no, I have my answer.

I Am Not a Writer

By Emily Rose

Staring at the blank pages in front of me, having read short stories by masterful journalists and novelists, I am struck with this simple fact: I am not a writer. To one who never fancied himself or herself a writer, this piece of information might skim across the conscious mind unencumbered by shame. But just moments ago and for my whole life prior, I very much identified myself as a writer. Alas, I am not. This sobering truth can be witnessed by many—as an otherwise straight "A" student, nearly all the courses toward my creative writing minor wilt as low as B's. And while I have a book on the market that has self-helped thousands, I am self-published, as anyone with the Internet and an online account can be today.

I have failed at being the very thing I aimed to be since child-hood. The irony is that judging oneself as a failure lives in the realm of story—as anything only ever happens or does not—and while my prose is subpar, apparently my storytelling is captivating to the most important critic in the room: myself. I sat down weeks ago to write about "bottoming out" and wound up discovering momentary stories wrapped in lifelong stories—breakdown moments triggered by lived-in lies, built upon other moments that marked my character and after tens of thousands of words transcribed, identified me as the woman I am today: not a writer.

I am sure as you read this you're wondering how I could even think I'm not a writer—I'm writing to you at this very moment, aren't I? But what defines me as a writer and what you define as a writer is guaranteed to differ, and in my eyes what I've just done is run full speed ahead at a destiny that was never mine to fulfill, and so I've fallen with each word I type as I plummet to my demise in front of your eyes. Can't you tell this is nonsense? Hogwash? Malarkey? Would a real writer turn to the thesaurus to find more words to describe their own gibberish? I think not.

But there are other things I think, too. Like how admitting that I am not a writer is one of the most liberating things I've ever just done. I'm not a writer—it's the first thing I said to you here. And if this is true it means that my entire life has been compensating for this deep shame.

If I am not a writer, I am not expected to produce anything worth reading. I can blather about the page and word-by-word discover what wants to be written. When I admit to myself that I am not a writer, I see not my life as a failure, but my failed attempt at writing a provocative piece as just and only that. The meaning is removed. It truly means nothing that I am not a writer. When I am not a writer I have a blank slate from which to produce. Instead of an empty page chiding me, it invited me. So I told it the truth: I am not a writer. And with that truth I became one.

Surviving Myself

By Cheryl Slavin

I've been told that mental illness recovery takes two years. I am a
notorious overachiever. I did it in about five. In some ways I am still
recovering, as the prognosis for my diseases is a lifetime. It's been over
a decade since I was hospitalized. This is some of what I remember.
The staff did not directly tell me that I was suffering from bipolar
disorder in addition to my primary disorder, obsessive-compulsive
disorder (OCD). They also failed to mention that I was delusional,
as this likely would have upset me. My primary psychiatrist in the
hospital simply told me that since my outpatient medication manager
was starting to experiment with bipolar meds, that we would simply
continue along that course of treatment. It took a few years to see the
patterns and cycles that would determine that I was indeed suffering
from comorbid disorders.

Upon intake, the gentleman who interviewed me told me
that I would be responsible for all damages (for example, if I were
to get angry and throw a chair). I assured him there would be no
chair-throwing or acts of melodrama on my part. My struggle was
internal—becoming outwardly angry never was my style. We were all
there for harm or violence done to ourselves or others.

While hospitalized, I sang songs from Broadway musicals at the top of my lungs while restless and wandering the halls. I was suddenly in a place where fear of performing was insignificant compared to all of my other fears.

The staff was very concerned about not having belts, pencils, or other sharp things around in order to limit the potential degree of harm and self-harm, but the water for the tea was SCALDING hot.

My husband gave me roses, and a member of the staff cut a 7-Up bottle in half and let me keep the roses in my room. I was told repeatedly by patients and staff how lucky I was to keep them because I could have hurt myself with the thorns.

They had a shampoo/body wash combo in the showers that didn't work very well. Every time I am in a hotel with shampoo and body wash dispensers it reminds me of my stay in the hospital.

I kept trying to concentrate enough to read or write but couldn't manage, even though reading and writing were once thought to be my strong suits. I don't know whether this was from my deteriorated mental state or from the massive doses of drugs they were administering.

I have never been much for puzzles, but I found them a relaxing pastime between groups. It was as if the puzzles helped me put the pieces of my brain back together, to try and figure out why I had behaved the way I did.

A lady diagnosed with schizophrenia told me of one of her frequent hallucinations during dinner. She said that sometimes, when she chewed, it felt like there were four mouths chewing simultaneously inside of her mouth.

Another content-looking younger gentleman told me, as he smiled wistfully in his rocking chair, that he suffered from bipolar disorder and was recovering from an overdose on Trazodone.

There was one little lady who could predict when it was time for her to go back into the hospital. She would pack herself a few little suitcases. She had magazines with horses in them that she brought specifically for arts and crafts. Another particularly articulate gentleman told me he coped with his bipolar disorder by using street drugs for six months and then going to the hospital for the other six months of the year.

And of course, I remember talking to my three-year-old son on the phone while in the hospital. "Mamma, you need to come home." My son was insistent. "I miss you, Mamma, and you need to come home." I told him that I loved him very much and that I missed him, but that I wasn't able to come home yet. I did not tell him the logistics—of how I needed to prove to the doctors that I was no longer a danger to myself or others.

I was immersed in delusion and telling the psychiatric hospital staff what they wanted to hear in order to gain my freedom. I had put myself into a self-constructed prison. The locked ward was simply a physical manifestation of my state of mind. I was extremely paranoid. I spent my days thinking I was hiding from the law. Every knock at the door was the police coming to get me for some imagined crime. I also spent my days in denial that I had been blessed with a dual diagnosis—OCD and bipolar disorder I.

Years passed, I was released, and I was assigned to a new psychiatrist in Wyoming. I was kept on extremely high doses of medicine. Those years that followed my hospitalization were a nightmare. Balancing medications, for me, was particularly challenging with a dual diagnosis. One drug, though psychiatrically beneficial, caused me to gain sixty pounds in a few months. I remember eating a five-pound bag of gummi bears, in two days, by myself. I eventually adjusted the meds myself in defiance of the psychiatrist, which is something I do not recommend. A lower dose of a tricyclic antidepressant was all I needed to survive without intrusive thinking and extreme obsessions.

I depend on those medications for not only my quality of life, but for my survival. I struggle to afford my medications post-divorce—drugs the experts seem to think are necessary to prevent relapse. My co-payment for my tricyclic antidepressant, with full benefits, is currently $250 for a 90-day supply. It is more than I can comfortably afford. But I know that without it, I will go back to that locked ward.

Despite the other logistical struggles, my actions in and out of the hospital have started to make some sense. Reading is fundamental, especially when you're reading about your own mental illnesses. I read everything I could find on my disorders. Gradually, I came to the point where I was no longer controlled by compulsion and guilt. I even learned, somehow, to forgive myself for what I had done.

Or so I tell myself.

I have good days and I have exceptionally bad ones. Even on my medications, I find myself obsessing. I put the full weight of my body against my apartment door after locking it. I triple check the burners before leaving for the day, and all of my appliances in my kitchen remain unplugged. And then there is the social anxiety, a condition with which I continue to struggle. I have these classic foot-in-mouth moments when socializing that cause me to never want to go out in public again. Each of these brings on a rush of new obsessions. Some of these spells last for days and make me think I should self-admit to the hospital. But now that I am somewhat on my own, I have no choice but to carry on as though nothing is amiss. Despite my social phobias, I do occasionally get out. I go to comedy clubs and a variety of other performances. I can even be seen doing the occasional bit of karaoke. Someday, I will sing in front of others without fear of being judged, as I did while pacing the halls of that locked ward.

I work now, in a call center where I caption telephone calls for the deaf and hard-of-hearing. Behind the scenes, I am barely acknowledged. How I long to have the confidence to be myself in public, or to even make friends at my place of work.

I dream. And in my dreams, I am still shackled. I dream about everything from divorcing my ex to the sheer horrors of filthy public restrooms. I also have school anxiety dreams, perhaps reflective of the fact that I am constantly learning and adapting while awake.

But though I had a break, I am not broken. My old dreams of performing and writing are starting to come true. Though I have struggled emotionally and financially since my divorce, I am living in a dream. I am so deliriously happy that at times I fear I'm going manic. I am proof that one can live a happy and productive life even with comorbid disorders.

I have survived my own worst critic—myself. And I love being a part of the world instead of allowing my illnesses to estrange me from it. My mind still threatens hell at times. But I have never enjoyed such freedom.

Lotus

By Jessica Steindorff

I struggled with depression during my teenage years and most of my twenties. By thirteen, I had already been sent to rehab. I was suicidal and out of control.

In my early twenties I went to an upscale facility in West Hollywood, run by a doctor repeatedly featured on CNN speaking of such matters as I was going through.

I reached out for help and they willingly admitted me.

Manipulative and entitled, it was only a matter of time before I had the staff wrapped around my finger. I knew where all of the bodies were buried. I picked fights and made out with fellow patients.

It was beautiful at said facility. We had our own private chef, attended daily groups where we got to talk about ourselves for hours, engaged in private therapy sessions and wicked fun activities. You could even earn car privileges.

My two small dogs came with me and I actually loved being at the facility. I loved my therapist. I had friends. I had my pets and a beautiful room with maid service.

That is, until the owner sent me to a hotel for the first time. I won't go in to detail because, quite frankly, I'm not ready to be public about it. But let's just say #MeToo.

For a few years, I became a prisoner—of the facility, the owner and the rehab. I fell into a downward spiral. I hated myself. I was out of control in totally different ways: I was cutting my inner thighs with blades, having meltdowns in group therapy, and breaking furniture. I didn't have a voice yet. I couldn't even muster up the courage to tell my own therapist what was happening, a therapist who is still in my life to this day.

One day I was told "no" by a staff member. I had direct access to the head honcho. *No one says "no" to me.* I raged and my inner anger came out in an explosion. I took my dogs, got into my car (I had "earned" car privileges), and drove to a friend's house. I grabbed a bottle of wine and cried and raged with her.

Within an hour a staff member was there to pick me up. I kicked, screamed, and even pulled a fire alarm. I was an *adult,* in my mid-twenties—they couldn't do this to me. But they did. I ran into an upscale dining facility on Highland and Melrose and screamed for help. I was wearing a bathrobe and looked insane.

No one helped.

Then I ran to a gas station. And no one helped.

Next thing I knew, I was back in the car. The door was locked. I tried to roll down my window. It went back up. I needed air. *Give me air.* The staff member allowed me to crack my window.

I propelled my body out of the car backwards.

The rest is a blur.

I woke up in an MRI machine, unable to move. My hand was broken, my ACL was torn, and my shoulder, hip and cheekbone all had large amounts of skin missing.

One witness of the accident who I happened to know said that he watched me go flying, and then get up and try to run away with my knee bent backwards.

A few years later I was working with a woman who asked me to help her raise money for this charity in Cambodia. I said yes. A few months later, that charity was on the cover of magazines for fraudulent activity. The people who had donated asked me where the money went.

I didn't know.

A week later I landed in Cambodia. My mother always said it was the trip when my heart chakra opened. On our way to meet over sixty children, ages two and up, I started to feel car-sick. It was a dirt road and bouncy as hell. I was clutching my stomach in pain, waiting to arrive.

When we finally pulled up to what looked like an overgrown field, I had to get out. I instantly started throwing up and crying.

There's no way in hell I can go into this center filled with children who had been sex trafficked and face that kind of despair and trauma. *There's no fucking way.* It made me physically sick even thinking about.

I refused to see the children and went right into the nurses' station. I couldn't stop throwing up. The nurse gave me some medicine and I fell asleep.

When I woke up, I was surrounded by tiny angel faces. One of them had water for me, the other had tissues, and another had a snack.

They smiled from their hearts and it pierced my soul. Little did I know these children would help me more than I would ever be able to help them.

They helped me find my voice with their bravery. I discovered gratitude from seeing theirs. And slowly, with each trip I took, I found self-love in a way I never knew existed. My heart beat then, and still beats now, for these children.

It's been many years now and many, many visits to Cambodia. Sometimes I go alone. And sometimes I go with a handpicked group of friends I want to share the experience with.

These children are beyond grateful because their basic needs are met: food, water, shelter and access to education. It's that simple. Because they have those things, everything after that is just a gift. During my own difficult years, I looked outside for answers. Little did I know, I had everything inside of me to heal, to overcome, and to learn how to love myself. Through these children, I have been taught a new way of thinking. I love myself. I love my life. And I have found my purpose.

Bardo

By Mary Stewart

There was no notice.
No sickness or decline or final farewells,
just a phone call:
"Your son passed away this morning."
I repeated the words, so loud
everyone in the restaurant
stopped talking and looked up.
My friend Mark caught me
before I slid to the floor.
He walked me to the hotel lobby
across the street
where we sat on cushioned armchairs,
waiting for the car to arrive.

I stared into my own disbelief
as though I might find something there to grasp.
Finally, I said to him,
"This is not going to break me,"
as if to convince myself.

I only meant that I would survive,
I would flourish
no matter what shatters or gets lost
or ceases to exist. I knew this, even though
the tunnel of grief that lay ahead
would envelop me, nearly entomb me,
I knew this one thing
and had to say it before
the walls of my world ruptured.
In that state,
I ceased to be, I de-ceased
and went with fmy man-child
to a place beyond death.

Months later,
I walked out of the rubble
with one scrap of lucidity,
like a madwoman who's discovered
the secret of the universe,
only I had:
that loss is a gift, an unstoppable vortex
trenching canyons into your being
and gyring you into open space
so that you are not the person
you once were
but more—
able to embrace more, feel more, be more—
more than the tight identity
you once held so snug inside.

    Do not pity the bereaved mothers
    for they are as adept at losing
    as they are at having it all,
    and sometimes scarcely
    know the difference.

After All, She Deserves a Celebration

By Samantha L. Taylor

I searched for home in all the wrong places,
I searched for home when the walls of my childhood home became
the things of nightmares,
I searched for home in arms that grew restless with the passing
    months
I searched for home in between mint colored sheets
and afternoons spent holding on to what-ifs that wavered when the
    silence
became too much to bare
I searched for home in other people, through unequal parcels of
    love hoping
to find solid ground and peace of mind.
When the home you've grown up in holds too many memories
of loss,
death,
decay,
broken promises,
and prayers that went unanswered by God
you start to wonder if you ever knew what it felt like to be at *home*.

In the presence of hardships and many of life's tribulations
we go searching for a place of comfort, familiarity, and security.
When I opened my heart to another, I had searched for a home in
     him,
while leaving a crumbling foundation behind
I held on to any little warmth I could get from spending most
     Sundays
with him,
in his home,
on his foundation,
hoping that I could find a place of refuge, love, and a place to lay my
head at night in the midst of running away from a war.
The home that I would eventually build with him would be the place
I would eventually come to avoid
when the betrayal got uncovered,
when the heartache sank in,
when the depression forced its way in,
intrusive.
Violent.
Inevitable torment.
The arms that kept me safe and warm started to
loosen around me and crumble before my eyes,
I was exposed and left without a home.
I became one of many women who go looking for a place to call *home*,
a place and environment of love, solitude, and stability,
when we've faced many losses and feel defeated
it's important that we understand that if we come out on the other
     end
stronger and more resilient
we can reassure ourselves that through the battles we face
there is a place inside each woman that refuses to be
demolished,
defeated.
All this time we go searching for home when we come from
foundations that once crumbled or no longer hold a place of solitude
and realize that the *home* we seek has always been inside of us all
     along.

You will fight external and internal wars,
confront them,
deal with them,
bleed along the way,
heal from it over time,
and overcome.
The same place that holds the most epic wars also hold
grounds for healing and transforming beyond what we ever
    thought we
were capable of.
Home takes on a new meaning when we learn to find peace in
    ourselves,
Home takes on new meaning when we achieve emotional security
Home takes on a new meaning when we understand how transforma-
    tive personal
solitude can be.
Home takes on a new meaning when we become the place we seek
    the most
in love,
in solace,
in comfort,
in light,
and transcendence.
May we take time to celebrate the woman that stands before us,
may we celebrate the woman who has fought many battles and,
regardless of battle scars, comes out victorious.
May we celebrate the woman who is made stronger because of
how much she's overcome.
We have the ability to rebuild and turn any place that has been run
    down
into something homely and beautiful.
A Home is found here,
a Home is found inside of us.

Innie

By Awet Teame

I'm oddly shaped. I have skinny arms, skinny legs and a wide midsection. But I have a cute face and good hair. God's got to give you something to work with.

I fall into the "exotic" category. If my name hasn't given it away already, I was born in Eritrea, East Africa. When I was born, Eritrea was in the middle of a war with Ethiopia. I was three years old when the battle came to our city, Dekemhare. My mother was an activist and had an "in" with the soldiers. They made sure they got us out before Dekemhare became a warzone. It was a rough escape but we had it easier than most. We were driven in the middle of the night to Keren, Afa-abet (then Port of Sudan), where we either camped out under trees or stayed in houses provided by EPLF (Eritrean People Liberation Front) with others fleeing the conflict. When we camped out, we slept in a circle, with the parents on the outside and children on the inside, to protect us from animals. But we were already pretty safe as we were protected by Eritrean soldiers every step of the way. The only scary setback was that both my mother and I were bitten by something and needed treatment. My mother got sicker than I, as she had also contracted malaria. After she received treatment, the soldiers flew us to Khartoum, Sudan. We were the only two civilians on the flight.

My father, also an Eritrean, was living in Italy at the time. After a few months, he arranged a flight for my mother and me to Italy. My mother assumed we'd finally be a family but to her surprise, my father had other plans and wanted a divorce. I believe that truly shattered my mother's heart. Sadly, whenever Wham's song "Careless Whisper" came on the radio, with the lyrics "I'm never gonna dance again," permeating the room, she turned the volume up! She never remarried.

My mother is a diehard believer in abiding by ancient Eritrean rules that just don't apply to modern women. However, looking back, that may have been for the best, as it resulted in more freedom for me.

When things went south with my father, my mother met some Eritrean friends at a local café in Italy, and they suggested she should move to America. We were granted refuge by the Catholic Church and flown to Maryland. The transition was seamless—we were given Social Security cards and became legal aliens almost immediately.

And so began my journey in America.

The early years left me feeling awkward, as if I belonged nowhere. Each group at school taught me different ways to try to fit in. For instance, when I arrived I only spoke my native language, Tigrinya, and Italian. I was ridiculed in elementary school for pairing pink and purple flowered pants with a blue and black stripe shirt and pink shoes. My Black friends immediately pointed out that my outfit "didn't match" and that I also needed a training bra. I wanted to belong, so I made my mother buy me a bra and solid colored shirts. Then my Puerto Rican friends suggested I shave my legs and start messing around with boys. I wanted no part of that and quickly became the odd ball for having half-shaved legs and waiting for what they considered forever to kiss a boy.

My mother didn't make much money as a maid at the Colonnade Hotel. We lived on Hemenway Street, near Berklee College of Music, and the Colonnade wasn't a far walk from home. She worked until 11 p.m., so I was alone every night during the week. She had a coin purse full of dimes so she could call me every hour from a payphone at work. Before three-way calling existed, she would ask the phone operator to interrupt my calls if I was already on the line. I used to talk to my best friend for hours but then be interrupted by this terrifying operator who'd yell into the phone, "Young lady! Your mother is trying to get a hold of you, I'm terminating this call!"

My voice trembled, "Okay."

Then, the operator would patch my mother through. My friends never heard the operator, thank God.

Eritreans are a tight community and so I spent most of my younger years insulated by them. The culture is very similar to the Greeks in *My Big Fat Greek Wedding*—the Eritrean community prefers that we only marry other Eritreans. My family's religion is Orthodox Christianity. I've been baptized but I don't practice. I believe in the Universe. One of the many reasons my mother and I clash.

Eritreans expect you to follow your parents' religion and be submissive. I've always rejected the protocol and gone my own way. And after reading a million self-help books, I was way too confident to find chauvinistic control freaks attractive.

Having said all of this, I'm sure it's understandable when I say that it's been my experience that Eritreans never ask you what you want, they *tell* you what you want. When my family finally did ask what I wanted, I told them, "I want what Oprah has!"

They said, "Oprah?" *(with an Eritrean accent)*

I said, "Yeah, Oprah!" *(with an American accent)*

They said, "Okay!"

I thought, "Okay? They're okay with the whole long-term non-marriage thing? This is great!"

But they misunderstood. And found me an Eritrean who looked like Stedman. I told them that wasn't what I meant. But, their finding was impressive, so I asked if I could put in an order for an Eritrean who looked like a Hugh Jackman, Chadwick Boseman, or a Bradley Cooper. The best they could find was a Sheldon Cooper looking Eritrean. Again, I was impressed, because I discovered that all engineers really do look alike!

Spiritually, I believe we choose our parents. And I can see why I chose my mother. I'd prefer her over any other Eritrean mother. But no one's perfect. I do wish she wasn't as traditional as she is—she's basically a slave to cultural rituals.

My mother agreed to have me circumcised forty days after I was born. Eritreans do everything after forty days—such as celebrating a person's death forty days after they die and fasting for forty days before Easter. While the country ended female circumcision over twenty years ago, I'm pissed it ever existed.

When I asked my mother why she allowed it to happen, she just shrugged and said, "It's the culture."

When I was older, we had a deeper discussion and she explained, "They did it to keep women from being too sexual."

I asked, "But didn't it happen to you? And didn't you figure out that wasn't true?"

She shrugged again but this time she didn't know what to say. She sensed my resentment, which I still haven't released. I think it's even worse that she did it to mark me as a "pure" or "proper" Eritrean girl. I'm even angrier that no one was there to advocate for me, to stop her, to stop the midwife who cut me. They don't stitch you up after. My mother told me that the wound supposedly heals on its own when you urinate, which sounds ridiculously painful.

As a kid, I knew something "down there" wasn't right. At times, my skin felt tight. And sensation felt dulled, as if there could have been more. But, I'm sure whoever started the practice would hate to learn that we—women who have undergone female genital mutilation (FGM)—still orgasm and have sex recreationally.

Although this was something that happened to me, I still feel ashamed and embarrassed by it, as a grown woman. I feel insecure, as if I am less desirable than other women. Maybe that was their goal, too?

This is one of the many reasons I view my culture negatively. Its traditions have not only violated my right to choose what happens to my body, but I also find it to be judgmental, competitive, disrespectful and intrusive. People in the community often act as if they're entitled to an opinion of you, who you're in relationships with, where you go, what you do, and especially how much money you have. They arrange marriages and frenemies! Oftentimes, the men are possessive and the women are controlling and competitive. So, I learned to push back.

Being raised by an immigrant mother is confusing. I'm a grown woman yet she yells at me like I'm twelve, constantly insults me but then does my laundry and cooks all of my meals. Even at age twelve, I wondered why I was being yelled at all the time and physically beaten. Well, that ended the day she charged at me with a high-heeled shoe. Instinct made me kick her in the stomach. I had a feeling that would have caused brain damage. Then I told her to stop hitting me. That was the first time I had ever stood up for myself. She never hit me again.

But the emotional and mental abuse continued.

Physical wounds heal but verbal, mental and emotional leave long-lasting scars. Scars that can shape beliefs of how you look and what you deserve. All false and untrue. I'm still a work in progress but these experiences have taught me a thing or two about protecting myself and creating boundaries.

Even though bringing me to America was her last resort to escape a failed marriage, my mother's bold decision turned out to be the greatest blessing in disguise. Here I can rebuild. I'm an Emerson College graduate. I've been living the dream as a stand-up comic (still haven't made any real money at it, but love it nonetheless), striving to work as a voice-over artist, writer, actor, recent Cyber Security Apprentice and more. I have the freedom to be who I want to be in this country. I don't take for granted that I can be myself here and feel respected.

Forgiveness is the last step in healing from the pain I experienced as a survivor of FGM—but forgiveness takes time. I've only told about three people, outside of the men I've slept with, but they don't count, as most of them weren't even paying attention. When men have noticed, I just tell them I have an "innie" and they buy it.

Coming out about my "innie" is a huge deal for me, but it is time to take my power back from all of these people who've tried to take it away from me, since the day they cut me. Yes, something very precious was taken from me but the rest of me has somehow compensated, somehow become empowered despite my scars.

Frank

By AK Turner

2012

I receive a phone call that my ex-stepfather has died in a plane crash.

Relief washes through me in warm waves.

He is gone. And I am relieved.

Anger soon follows. I am not angry with him or the plane or the mechanical error that led to this phone call.

I am livid with myself.

He was, after all, a human. A life ended violently when the '64 Beechcraft Musketeer crashed along the tree line not far from the runway. I hope his death was instant and painless, but still, what kind of person feels relief at such news?

I wait for grief. A sense of loss. Where is the mourning?

2010

I don't want to answer the phone, but I do. He's living in a van near the airport. His health is not good. He's nudging me for an invitation. He wants me to save him. He is, after all, a father figure, though he and my mother have long since divorced.

I know the words he craves. They go like this: "Gosh, Frank. I'm so sorry. Why don't you come live with us? We have plenty of room."

But I have two daughters. They are one and three years of age. I will not expose them to him.

But can I let him continue living in a van? Will he freeze when the mornings turn to frost and then sleet and feet of snow? Will he be the news story no one wants to be? The forgotten figure who dies alone and broken? At age seventy-seven, is this where life will leave him?

Is this where *I* will leave him?

But I have two daughters.

2000

He is fit and spry at sixty-seven. He flies across the country to visit, to see where my husband and I have made a home as we attempt to figure out what it is to be young and married.

I tell myself that it's fine and the past is past. He is simply a visiting family member. I am an adult. We sit, he and I. My husband is there, as is a friend. I warned her about him, as a good friend does.

We drink wine.

I ask about an old neighbor, attempting conversation about someone we both know.

"Did I ever tell you about the time she asked about *us?*" he asks.

There's something unsettling here. I know it's coming. I've been here before, heart racing, on alert.

He chuckles and continues. "She asked if you and I ever *got together.*" He laughs harder. *"Isn't it funny?"*

My mind grapples with this. So much of it is unbelievable:

That a neighbor would inquire if he's had a sexual relationship with his stepdaughter.

That he would think it funny.

That he would give voice to it.

That he would do so to me, to my husband, to my friend.

It's not fine. The past is not past.

1994

Frank's apartment in Baltimore is a short drive from my dorm room. I'm expected to visit often over the next four years. He buys me my first car to make sure I do. It's a generous act with strings attached and a purchase he cannot afford.

He lives in an expensive, spacious loft in an historic building. He pretends not to owe hundreds of thousands of dollars to the IRS. This reality will eventually lead him to life in the van.

His giant waterbed is at the center of the apartment, a bedroom on display. Shiny packets of condoms form a foil caterpillar along the headboard.

There will be times when he'll leave VHS tapes lying around. They are all pornographic, save for *Romancing the Stone*.

I visit and he kisses me hello and goodbye, licking his lips before he does so. He is skilled and experienced, always thwarting my efforts to offer only a cheek.

I visit and he shows me a contraption that straps to the back of his hand. He plugs in the attached cord and his hand vibrates. He's showing me his latest sex toy.

I plead with my friend to accompany me on these visits, but he insists on kissing her hello and goodbye as well, and she's had enough of him licking his lips before he does so.

1981

I want to talk to Mom. I hear her voice. She's standing in the doorway of the bathroom. She's talking to Frank, who just took a shower.

I wait behind Mom. I want to be good and patient and not interrupt because I've learned that that's a rude thing to do. Mom doesn't know I'm standing behind her because I'm quiet and good. I peer around her and see Frank standing naked. I see what a naked man looks like. Frank sees me. I see Frank. He doesn't reach for a towel. He takes his time letting Mom know that I'm there. When she sees me, she quickly shuts the door.

This is the man who does certain stepfatherly things:

"Pedal, pedal, pedal!" he encourages, running alongside my bike and keeping me upright when I first shed training wheels.

"I'll get it!" he shouts, sprinting the length of the backyard to grasp the string of the kite that got away from me.

He runs in earnest on my behalf, trying in these moments to build a familial relationship. These moments are few, though, and dwarfed by a thousand instances in which he destroys any chance of normalcy.

He runs for me.

I'll spend decades running from him.

2012

My relief makes me inappropriate. It feeds shame and guilt. He was human. I should be mourning instead of breathing easy.

Maybe I can forgive him for being who he was.

I'm fairly certain that I cannot forgive him for shaping my view of men, for believing them seedy and manipulative and opportunistic and without honor.

I'm confident I can forgive myself for that shock of relief. Maybe I already have.

It's that warm wave sweeping through me again, an undeniable physical sensation. He is gone. The burden of him is gone. I still have two daughters, and he has not touched them.

I am relieved.

Spilt Milk

By Erika Warner

I could hear the laughs and comments behind me as I tried to clean the milk I had just spilt on the kitchen floor. I had made the mistake of asking them for a wringer, to which they sneeringly replied that I could find it at the end of my arms. Suddenly I remembered my grandmother wringing the mop with her own hands and I realized that such a modern tool as a wringer was not very popular among these Colombian women, who pride themselves on being cleaning wizards.

Wringing the mop with my own hands was harder than I thought and they delighted in my inability by providing me with commentary.

"Wow, you are going to be a terrible wife!" said one woman with her hand on her hip.

"How have you survived all of these years?" asked another woman in an accusatory tone.

"A true Colombian woman knows how to clean!" said another woman, looking proud.

And, finally, they said the sentence I needed to hear, the one that woke me up: "Your mom did you no favor at all by not teaching you how to clean!"

My mom!? My *mom!?* The one who has taught me all of my life *not* to let people label me because of my gender or my race? The one who told me that a woman's role goes beyond household duties? The one who sold all of her possessions and bought a one-way ticket from Colombia to Europe in hopes of offering us a better future? The one who, by the way, did teach me how to cook and clean but reminded me that my biggest pursuit in life should be my education. That mom? How dare you talk about her? How dare you!

Of course, such a blatant reply only happened in my head. I would never dare to such audacity, especially because I felt pity for them. My mom had taken me from a tumultuous Colombia (in the 1990s) to Spain as a child and given me a comfortable life and a good education. But these women were not as privileged as I was—they had to stay and endure a very hard life.

But, in 2013, I was back in Colombia for a simple reason: love. My boyfriend had just graduated college and had been offered a volunteer opportunity in Colombia's coffee region. We had been in a long-distance relationship for two years so I decided to go with him. I saw it as the perfect opportunity to be with him and to reconnect with my Colombian roots.

My boyfriend would be a teacher in a rural school in the small town of Quimbaya, Colombia. In return, he was offered room and board in a beautiful eco-hotel nearby. Surrounded by bamboo forests, banana trees and beautiful streams, this rustic hotel was the epitome of serenity. He went first and I would join him later. My plan was to find my own apartment and get a job in the same town.

But upon arriving in Quimbaya, my boyfriend discovered that the hotel's receptionist had just quit. I had given my boyfriend copies of my resume to carry around in case he saw job openings, and he immediately handed one to the hotel owner. Coincidentally, I had a hospitality management degree, considerable customer service experience, and English skills. The owner, a lively and uncompli- cated man called Don Guillermo, offered me the job on the spot. He would also let my boyfriend share his room with me. Before I had even set foot in Colombia, I had a job and a place to live. I was ecstatic!

Little did I know that I would pay dearly for my good fortune. The fact that I didn't have to go through an interview didn't sit well among the hotel staff, which consisted primarily of evil-tongued ladies whose major recreation was gossip and conflict. My lack of participation in their daily routine of gossip and complaints enraged them and gave them even more reasons to dislike me. They would try to provoke me by making up gossip about my sweet boyfriend, who was possibly the most honest and completely transparent human in the world. They would tell me that they had seen him with women in town, or that he was hitting on them, to which I commented: "I am very sorry that those are the only kind of men you know."

They made me their mark. They wouldn't serve me food during our meals, they gave me the worst shifts, they blamed me for any mistake. I really didn't care. I made up excuses in my mind for their behavior. After all, they had difficult lives. They hadn't been in school, they all bore children as teenagers, some of them woke up at 4 a.m. to make food to sell in town before coming to work a twelve-hour shift at the hotel. Every single month, our salaries would be delayed, sometimes for weeks at a time. I could see how they might find some joy in tormenting me. After all, misery loves company.

It took them a while to crack me. I was madly in love with my boyfriend, and he was the picture of happiness. He would spend all day teaching in a one-room school of twenty-five students. The only other teacher was a saintly woman named Oliva who had dedicated her whole life to educating these children. The kids were kind, ingenious, and well-behaved, so my boyfriend loved every day.

He would spend the afternoons doing yoga and wandering around on a scrappy, undersized bike he had bought for twenty bucks. He would come home excited about the adventures of the day and we would walk around the picturesque setting, laughing and in love. I hadn't told him about my continual state of war with my coworkers. I didn't want to burst his bubble and I didn't think they would eventually get to me.

However, that day in the kitchen, the day of the mop, they succeeded. They got to me. They had dared to insult my mother and that was totally unacceptable. I left the kitchen knowing that my days at the hotel were numbered.

I sat in the shade of a tree and started to think about my mom. I knew she would be disappointed because I hadn't defended myself. She was a confrontation enthusiast. She relished a good fight, but I have always had my own style. I like to hide my sadness or anger and retire to a quiet spot to analyze my feelings before taking action.

With tears in my eyes, I started a dialogue with myself. This has always been my way of sorting a difficult situation.

"Why am I so sad? This isn't the first time someone has offended me or told me that I am not good enough—I have endured far worse! Remember when Spanish kids would tell me to go back to 'my' jungle? Or when I was studying in the U.S. and people would assume I was a cleaning lady?"

"I know," I told myself. "Then why is this getting under my skin, why does this hurt?"

"This hurts more because these are my own people rejecting me, that's why. My own people."

Yes, I had endured rejection as an immigrant in Spain and the U.S. But somehow I never thought that I would receive it from my fellow Colombians. I was neither Spanish nor American, and now apparently, I was not a good Colombian either. A sunray slipped through the tree branches. I felt its warmth on my face and then in my heart when I remembered the only place in my life I had felt one-hundred percent part of something that was me, completely me: an ESL classroom.

While I was living in Colorado, a friend asked me to volunteer in her ESL classroom. My English was very good and I loved grammar, so she thought I could be a great help. The class had people from all over the world, and they were just trying to survive in their new home. I had been in school all of my life, but these people were new to the whole school thing. They were blue-collar workers, grandmothers, homemakers, adults who had not even finished high school. They put so much effort in their learning; I fell in love with their resilience. That was the day I found my vocation.

Since that day, I started to dream about becoming an ESL teacher so I could help hard-working individuals achieve their dreams. I had put my own dreams on hold because, well, life happens. Fortunately, dreams can't ever really be put on hold—they always find their way out of their hiding places and surface even stronger than before.

These ladies had just granted me a moment of lucidity, and now my dream was out there, begging to be fulfilled.

I stood up from under the tree, full of confidence and conviction, and I walked towards my room. I started rehearsing a speech in my head. I was going to tell my boyfriend that I loved him with all my heart but that I wasn't happy there. It was time for me to start taking steps towards my own dream. I was going to ask him to consider leaving that place. I entered the room and there he was as cheerful as always.

"I am not happy here," I said.

He looked into my eyes, read my entire speech and said, "Say no more, we can leave tomorrow."

We could have indeed left the next day, but I wanted to be respectful so I gave two weeks' notice at the hotel. No one was surprised. They all knew I didn't belong there.

In the months to follow, I finished a Teaching English as a Foreign Language (TEFL) certification, enrolled in online school to attain an English degree, and applied for ESL jobs all over the world. I got a job in Moscow, Russia, the first place that gave me an opportunity to teach without being a native English speaker. I worked there for two years and gained priceless experience while continuing my online classes and getting only A+'s.

Then, when we finally were married and moved back to the U.S., I had a good resume and plenty of experience to have my own classroom. And, on that first day when I walked into my classroom and looked around, my heart filled with joy and pride and I couldn't help but think, "Do not ever cry over spilt milk."

Luck to Cluck About

By Christy Wicks

My mouth is small.

Keeping it open for extended periods is painful. I grind my teeth to the point of having a very thin veneer of porcelain on my otherwise healthy but well-worn teeth. Every hygienist I have ever seen always feels the need to gasp and comment on their poor state. In hushed tones, they ask me if I was cognizant of my teeth's condition. Since I'm fifty, and the damage had occurred by the time I was twenty-four, I'm used to having my teeth berated. I check myself before sighing, because that would require a deep breath. In my current situation— with my head down and my feet in the air, my mouth open to what feels like a silent scream, and my eyes blinded by a glaring light—I can only breathe shallow gasps. Instead, I reassure the kind soul in garbled grunts that I'm well aware.

With each new dentist comes the new stress of explaining my quirks. This goes along with the full disclosure of my medical health history. For the most part, I get to check "no" on the boxes. All except when it comes to asthma, migraines, and cancer. I hate being reminded, but I take a deep breath. It's been eight years, and I take care of myself.

Today, I wait for the new dentist, wishing I was swimming with the fish in the tank instead.

A young woman with long, raven hair calls me back. She takes me to a beige lounge chair, gestures for me to sit down, and hands me a pair of sunglasses.

"I'm going to take a full set of photos today for our records since you are brand new, okay?" She speaks with a slight lisp, and I wonder how long she's had braces.

I smile and nod my head as I clench the glasses in my lap. My thoughts are on the plasticky things they jam into your mouth for imaging because they always pinch.

She catches my eye, and her face gets all serious.

"I see on your health form you had breast cancer."

I nod, then stop. It's not unexpected that she's bringing this up, but I'm caught off-guard because I had moved onto the pictures and I'm mad at myself for not being ready. I nod again, hoping she's going to keep this short.

"You were one of the lucky ones." She holds eye contact to make sure that she knows she has my attention.

My fingernails dig into my hands.

"Cancer is terrible, truly terrible. I worked with a woman who had breast cancer at my last job."

My jaw tightens with the pressure of my teeth, settling against one another. She launches into her story, and I know she's going to be one of those.

"It was a couple of years ago."

She watches me intently as she speaks. I position my face into what, I hope, is an expression of neutrality. My expressive face has gotten me into trouble my whole life. I can never lie because even strangers can tell when I'm not happy. But over the years, I've come up with a way of freezing my features, so today I slip my face into this mask.

"She had a cough, but she ignored it." She's nodding like she wants me to nod along, and after a pause she continues, "And, you know you're just so lucky. She didn't make it like you. But she was over-weight. She was older."

Well, naturally, I think. Of course, it's her fault. I wonder if I can gracefully exit to the bathroom. The birds in my tummy are flapping away, churning up my lunch and stomach acid in equal measure.

"She should have gone to the doctor sooner. It was so, so sad."

Bobbing my head, my hands twist restlessly in my lap as I tug, pull, and poke, expressing emotions with my hands that I don't dare with my voice. I want to shout at this woman to shut up. I don't want to hear her death story, and I certainly don't want to be reminded of my own experience. My heart shreds for the woman who died and who is being remembered in such a crappy way.

And I don't like this twenty-year-old telling me to feel lucky.

Now that she's safely confronted death, she leaves the room to procure what I can assume are the instruments of brutality that she will soon ram into my mouth. I quickly wipe a tear from under the sunglasses I shoved on. Then, another.

I don't want her to see that she got to me.

The hygienist comes back into the room, and this time she's wearing a mask over the lower part of her face. I'm hoping it will stop her from talking. She asks me to open my mouth and I acquiesce.

"Open wider, please."

I try to stretch my mouth to accommodate the rigid spacers.

"How long ago did you have cancer?"

"Yate yars ago." I say. Saliva drips down my chin. She deftly wipes the drool with the bib around my neck and I feel like a small child.

"Oh, you were so young," she tuts. "Did they find it through a routine exam?"

I nod as she positions the camera close to my cheek. This is not exactly the truth, but I'm not in the position to delve into the specifics. As if, I would want to.

"Bite down and hold still."

I bite back a glare. What I desperately want to do is climb up out of the chair, a heroine of my own making and run through the office. Dental equipment flung in my wake, inspiring other patients to stand in solidarity and join me in a slow-motion montage to escape. The entire event paired with a peppy ear-worm song celebrating our freedom.

Instead, I do as she commands. She exits the room, leaving me frozen in the chair. The camera starts its snapping and clacking. I try to swallow but my throat is too dry.

She bustles back into the room. "Did you have a family history of cancer?" Her brown eyes wait for an answer.

What she really wants to know is if there is a reason I got cancer.

I quickly wipe my mouth with the napkin to prevent her from getting to my dripping chin first. I shake my head "no." There is no explanation to provide.

She frowns slightly, before efficiently plugging the spacers into the other side of my mouth. She pushes too hard and it jabs into my gums. I flinch.

"Well, you're just so lucky they caught it. Almost done here. Sit tight."

I'm never quite sure what I'm supposed to get from these cancer conversations people feel inclined to initiate with me. Their stories frighten me. They're a reminder that next time I might be the one in the ground. Someday, someone will be telling a cavalier anecdote about me.

I choose to live like I did before cancer. However, when I'm forced to examine my health, my choices strike at me like chickens pecking at corn. *Did I need that chocolate chip cookie at lunch? Should I have had that glass of wine with dinner? I probably should have gone for a walk today.*

I mean, I know better, I know I'm going to die. Still, I could make wiser decisions. But it takes a lot of energy to pump myself up. Even though my shelf-life has been revised, I'm not ready to be discarded quite yet.

Having cancer is scary business, but it's not the vortex upon which my life revolves. I'd like to have the opportunity to move past my health history and be more than someone who just "got lucky." Technically, I got lucky when I fell out of the top of the tree and caught myself on a branch before hitting the ground. I also got lucky when I couldn't get out of work early and missed getting caught up in a ten-car pileup on the Ninety-Nine bridge. And, there was the time I got lucky, when I got a bad vibe from a guy I got into a car with once at a bar and decided to scramble back out. Life is full of near misses.

At last the hygienist goes away, and the dentist comes into the room. He's friendly, but not overly talkative. The instrument he's holding looks sharp as the point nears my face. He asks me to open my mouth. I tense, waiting for recriminations or pain. Neither happens as he gently taps on each tooth.

"Looks like you have a broken filling here."

I smile sheepishly, trapping his fingers, and he quickly removes them, so I can speak. "I know. Every time it gets filled, I end up chipping it off because of my strong bite."

He nods.

I increase the wattage of my smile. "I don't mind it. I find I floss my teeth more often." I'm hoping not to get chastised for my strong jaw strength. It's happened before and I cringe in my seat, waiting for his response.

"Well, I don't believe in doing unnecessary work. If you're fine with a little gap, I don't see any reason to fix it unless it starts causing you problems."

I'm speechless.

He gestures for me to open my mouth again and continues making comments to his assistant as he makes notes about my teeth. My body collapses into the dental chair with stunned relief.

But there's no time to relax. He's finished and shaking my hand, telling me to come back in a year. As he leaves the room, I'm giddy at this turn of events. A weight has been lifted, because my body is good enough.

As I leave the office, I realize I do feel lucky. Lucky to have escaped the clutches of the dentist for another year.

I Promise I'm a Friend

Mae B. Yu

I began troubling you when you were thirteen. When other girls showed off their shaved legs, I made you shudder at the sight of the blade. You were too young to understand my corruption, had no clue where you got these ideas, but your urge to put blade to vein kept you from putting it to skin completely. So girls taunted you while boys scrunched their noses at your unappealing growth, and I'd punish you by saying I told you so.

Though you were invincible, most days. You could conquer anything, believed you were meant for greatness. There was never a warning of when I'd shatter it all. I never destroyed you slowly either. You'd always crumble all at once.

Suddenly, you'd be a burden to everyone in your life. You had no purpose, no abilities, no value. Not only were you worthless, you were the reason for everyone's unhappiness. I made you believe they'd be better off if you were gone.

I didn't make sense, I know. If I did this all the time, it would have been easier to understand. My nature wasn't you. You were confident, productive, lively. I was not.

At fifteen, you fell in love. He was kind and adventurous, pushed you to do things you'd never done before. You wanted to be as brave as he was, but every time you got close, I told you he'd never want you. Not with me around. So you loved him from a distance, watching as he turned his heart to someone else. Someone with courage and grace and life. Someone who didn't have me. She wasn't you, and you envied her for it.

At eighteen, I wandered places I'd never been before. I became specific, offering you ways to disappear. This frightened you. You decided to seek help, desperate for someone to save you from me. She was kind, though overwhelmed. She couldn't seem to figure out what was wrong. Eventually, she turned you to someone more qualified. Wrote their name on a piece of paper with directions to their office. You couldn't blame her. How does one fix a problem that can't be understood?

You tossed the paper in your desk drawer, so close to getting the help you needed. You were close, but I decided you were weak, that others had it worse and you were being narcissistic and ungrateful. I made you desperate to be fixed, all the while making you believe you did not deserve fixing.

At twenty, the one you loved told you he'd visit you. You were thrilled. You thought perhaps he'd finally accepted me, that he could care for you despite my presence.

You waited. And waited.

When he didn't show, I became angry. I told you that you were foolish for believing he meant it, for believing he could ever want us.

And then you saw the news. No. It couldn't be. He loved her so dearly. It was hard to accept the unfairness, the breath in her lungs ripped from her despite how much she cherished it. You hated yourself for having envied her. You couldn't comprehend why she was gone while you were still around. You swore never to let me get to you again, promised to stay for her, just to be half the person she was, to love life as much as she did. And in your pain, you let him go.

From ages twenty-one to twenty-five, you could not stop crying. Though I didn't make you disappear, you didn't quite know how to enjoy your stay. You took on jobs that allowed you to set your own schedule or work from home. Your fear of me misbehaving in a workplace prevented you from living up to your potential, while not living up to your potential made me misbehave even more. It was a cycle you couldn't break.

Your new love was as patient as anyone could be. He'd hold you tight while you wept, assuring you it'd all be okay and reminding you of your worth. It didn't make sense that someone would want you. I began to feed you lies. You'd believe me at first, accusing him of doing things he'd never do, only to wake up wondering where it all came from. There wasn't enough patience in the world that could deal with me.

You decided to jot everything down, record everything I made you believe, every feeling I gave you. You tracked me every day for a year, made note of my best and worst.

That's when you noticed the pattern. I'd only hurt you during certain weeks of the month. You didn't know what this meant, but you at least knew when to expect my antics.

With new knowledge, you began grad school. You learned how to operate with me. You got a hold of syllabi before semesters began, getting head starts on assignments so you could afford to be in bed when they were due. You couldn't beat me, but you could stay steps ahead. When I came around to tell you that you couldn't do something, you'd already done it. You consistently raised your hand during weeks I behaved, so you could stay quieter during weeks I didn't cooperate. Occasionally, you'd cry in front of your colleagues but if you found the right words, they'd consider you empathetic.

It didn't fix everything. At twenty-six, your love grew weary, no longer eager to fix what he knew he could not. He feared he could no longer deal with me, and you knew only you could make yourself better, only you could break this cycle.

You began researching my habits, marking the symptoms and patterns. How I yearned for adventure on certain days and didn't allow you out of bed on others, how I wanted everything and nothing, the aches of your body and soul.

And suddenly, a name.

You found that premenstrual dysphoric disorder (PMDD) affected one in twenty women. It caused both extreme physical and mental symptoms during parts of their cycles. Those suffering from it often experienced anxiety, depression, hopelessness, difficulty concentrating, and thoughts of ending one's life.

The establishment of the disorder was so new, there was no official cure despite how many it affected. Only theories, self-help books, and stories from other sufferers existed.

You marched yourself to doctor after doctor, meeting two, three, four. Over and over you heard the same thing. They'd never heard of me and wouldn't know what to do if they did. You felt defeated, but I told you to try again, promised you could beat me now that you knew what I was. You thought of the endless sobbing, the constant pain in your chest, the wondrous things that could be yours.

The gynecologist's curled mustache quivered as he glazed over your file. You handed him your records of me, describing everything I said and made you believe. You asked him if he'd heard of the disorder, seemingly deciding that he had not. He smiled at you, a sympathetic twinkle in his eye.

"Oh boy, have I," he told us.

Like that, a heavy loneliness left your chest. Someone understood me, knew it wasn't your fault, knew you could be fixed. He confirmed your diagnosis, scribbled supplements on a Post-it and asked you to try them.

Could it be that the solution to your turmoil—the harmful urges, the endless arguments, the loss of half your days—was small enough to fit on a Post-it? The thought made you laugh through your tears.

And so, you learned it wasn't you at all. Your body made you this way and you could change my behavior by taking the right substances. Two, three, four months went by without me hurting you. You didn't know if it was forever, but it was enough to make you hopeful. You aimed for higher-paying jobs, shared your disorder with those closest to you, and claimed your time alone when you needed it. Bit by bit, you defined your worth and learned to love yourself as much as others loved you.

I began troubling you when you were thirteen. At twenty-seven, you learned my name.

I'm sorry I made you question things. Your relationships, your potential. I shouldn't have made you believe you were undeserving of love. I forgot to remind you that you are not the only one with faults, but that others have their own, and that you are not less than anyone else.

I'm sorry I never stayed still. Never stayed quiet enough for you to sleep soundly, while only becoming louder when you tried to shut me out.

I'm sorry I was so unkind. It wasn't me. It wasn't me. It wasn't you.

I know it seems like I was out to destroy you, but I have always loved you.

You see, everything else was me, too. I completed your assignments ahead of time, recorded your symptoms, researched my own blemishes, and continued to seek help no matter how many turned you away. It was me who held onto her grace, me who your new love fell for, me who seeped fragments of brilliance you were so desperate to keep.

I may have been your worst enemy, but I was also your best friend. In the deepest, tiniest cracks of me I knew you were meant for something greater, knew you could make magic and see beauty in unexpected places. You'll carve your name into revolutions, teach the ways of a wounded queen, and build a kingdom where no one ever has to feel alone.

I promise I'm a friend. I've kept you here, haven't I?

Note: *The writer would like to encourage anyone who has experienced similar symptoms to seek help from a psychologist or gynecologist, as cures vary per person. She would also like to share the resources that have helped her during her healing process:*

iapmd.org

viciouscyclepmdd.wordpress.com

facebook.com/groups/iapmd/

facebook.com/groups/PMDDinfo/

instagram.com/pmddsupport/

instagram.com/pmdd.memes/

Contributors' Biographies

Zara Ali is a Jefferson and Echols Scholar at the University of Virginia. She has worked extensively with the ACLU and in the Homicide Unit with the Department of Justice. She aspires to be a lawyer and best-selling author someday.

Rebecca Andrew grew up in a small corner of England, which bears a passing resemblance to Hogwarts and claims Mary, Queen of Scots, as the local ghost. Whilst working in finance she has spent time living in Milan, London and New York and has consequently nurtured a love of pizza.

Dr. Leonora Anyango is a language, culture and education expert of international repute. She specializes in language teaching and learning, multilingual writing, and translation. She invests in working with diverse groups of students to use language as a tool to advance their scholarship.

Sunshine Valus Arnold is a private therapist and the CEO of CASA, an emergency shelter and outreach for survivors of domestic violence. She received both her BSW and MSW from Florida State University after serving in the United States Marine Corps in support of Operations Enduring Freedom and Iraqi Freedom.

Eli Beagle was born in Hunan, China, and adopted around ten months of age. Her main passion is writing, but she also enjoys drawing, animals, and theater. She hopes one day to professionally publish novels, but she'll have to actually finish writing one for that to happen.

Shersy Benson has lived many lifetimes and had more than her share of heartbreak and failure; she keeps getting back up again with enthusiasm and love. She earned her MBA from California State University and is completing her second Master's degree in Extension Studies with a concentration in Journalism from Harvard University.

Sherry Briscoe is an award-winning author who loves all things supernatural. She comes from a long line of storytellers in her Cajun and Native American heritage. She is a world traveler, U.S. Army veteran, founder of the Idaho Screenwriters Association, active board member of the Idaho Writers Guild, and professional speaker. She lives in Idaho with her temperamental and often argumentative Russian Blue, Nika. (sherrybriscoe.com)

Michele Brito is a Los Angeles-based artist and writer with a background in filmmaking. After graduating from CUNY Brooklyn with a degree in Film Studies and Production, Michele spent the next few years working on film sets before transferring to distribution. She's currently developing a digital children's show.

Dawn Brockett lives in Idaho with her wife and their dog, Coco. After completing six academic degrees and certificates, she mustered the courage to write something that was not assigned. Dawn recently completed the manuscript of her first book, a memoir titled *Content(e): The Woman I (was) Meant to Be.* Mountains of exceptional height, coffee of profound depth and conversations of extraordinary length reliably lure her from her writing chair. (dawnbrockett.com)

Laura Bruno is a multifaceted author and an avid polo player. She is currently completing her Master's in Extension Studies, with a concentration in Journalism, at Harvard University and preparing her PhD proposal.

Nancy Buffington holds a PhD in English from the University of Arizona. After teaching English for 20+ years at the University of Delaware, Stanford and a couple places in between, she left academia and moved to Boise, Idaho, where she's worked as a public speaking coach since 2010. (nancybuffington.net)

Lindsey Byars is the Communications Liaison for her alma matter, Concord University, in Athens, West Virginia. A mother of three amazing kiddos, she is pursuing a master's degree in her free time through Harvard Extension in Creative Writing and Literature. Her writing can be found in regional publications, and more recently in *Pangyrus Literary Magazine.*

Kate Flanigan Canute is a semi-retired rock star, shameless geek, and lover of broken and geriatric dogs. In 2013, a four-month hospitalization with meningitis and encephalitis led to her diagnosis with ICL—a super-rare immune deficiency. Although she returned to music after re-learning how to walk and speak in full sentences, the struggle to keep her immune system at a passable level has pushed performing onto the back burner.

Ana Cristina Cash is an acclaimed Cuban-American singer/songwriter who was raised in Miami and is based in Nashville. She will graduate with her Master's Degree from Harvard University in Creative Writing and Literature, Extension Studies in 2021. Ana started her music career as a child, performing on the longtime running variety show Sabado Gigante; she signed her first professional recording deal at the age of 16 with Sony Music Latin. Since then, Ana has recorded several records in both Spanish and English, was nominated for a Premio Lo Nuestro Award, and has performed in venues ranging from the White House to the Country Music Hall of Fame. She lives with her daughter and husband, John Carter Cash, with whom she co-owns Cash Cabin Enterprises.

Rachel Cassidy is a Canadian horror and dark fiction writer. Her work has appeared in *PseudoPod, Deciduous Tales, Dark Moon Digest, The Molotov Cocktail* (Pushcart-nominated), and others, in which she has inflicted countless tortures on the subject of this memoir. She highly recommends creative writing as a coping mechanism. (rachelcassidy.com)

Patricia Chamburs lives in Gainesville, Florida, and Bryson City, North Carolina, enjoying the best of both worlds—summertime in the Smoky Mountains and winters in North Central Florida. She cherishes precious time spent with her family and is grateful for life and the many blessings she has been fortunate enough to enjoy.

Emily Charles believes that with age, comes wisdom. She grew up in a small, structured world, but was lucky to have the opportunity to move from that world to other parts of the world that offered her many different experiences, interactions and, most importantly, meaningful relationships. It took her many years to find her voice and real identity but it was well worth the time spent.

Natalie Clark is a Scottish singer/songwriter who made headlines in the U.K. when Sir Richard Branson unexpectedly invited her to sing on-stage at a BBC event in Glasgow. She has since moved to the Los Angeles where she was handpicked to open for the Grammy award-winning Indigo Girls tour and released an EP.

Darla Eden is a special education teacher who lives with a cat in her very own place in Simi Valley, California. She would be the first to tell you things didn't quite turn out according to the plan she had in mind when she was growing up. However, she would also add that she wouldn't want it any other way because our experiences shape the people we grow to be.

Alane Ferguson is the author of over thirty books and the recipient of numerous awards, including the 1990 Edgar Allan Poe Award. She co-authored a series, *Wolf Stalker,* for National Geographic with her mother. It was the first work of fiction *National Geographic* had published in its, as of then, 109-year history. She was born in Cumberland, Maryland, and attended the University of Utah and Westminster College, where she studied journalism.

Lauren Flores is a Recruiter at Google in Austin, Texas. She has a passion for writing and spending time with her boyfriend, Logan, as well as friends, family, and her cat, Zoey. She is passionate about suicide prevention and awareness after losing her younger brother, Zach, to suicide in 2018. (on Facebook: fb.me/zrffoundation)

Kerry Garvin is Harvard University's 2020 Thomas Small Prize Recipient. She graduated in 2020 with her Master's of Liberal Arts in Extension Studies (Concentration: Creative Writing and Literature) from Harvard University. She works as a writer, editor and teacher of creative writing in Western North Carolina.

Sarah Graalman is a writer, makeup artist, and performer based in Brooklyn, New York, though she is very proud to have grown up in Oklahoma. She's worked as a makeup artist for over fifteen years, doing everything from editorial to beauty and commercial work. Graalman is currently writing a book about women, makeup and beauty rituals, after interviewing women across America for the past few years.

Janelle Gray is the founder, editor, and producer of Echoes Media, a company dedicated to eradicating discrimination by promoting platforms to unseen communities. After the release of her first novel, *Echoes of the Struggle,* about the United States Civil Rights Movement, Gray felt a calling to educate people about the continued civil rights issues in our society today. She is based in Dallas, Texas.

Kristiana Gregory is the author of more than thirty children's books. This story is excerpted from her memoir, *Longhand: The Rise and Fall and Rise of My Career as a Children's Author.* Her first novel, *Jenny of the Tetons,* is still in print with Harcourt after thirty years.

Gillian Hill is a Scot who currently lives in Boise, Idaho, with her husband and two boys who, despite her best efforts, do not sound remotely Scottish. She is a part-time freelance writer and editor, and she writes a blog called *Outdoors Mama.* (on Instagram: @outdoorsmamablog)

Diane Hughes prides herself on being one badass mother and consummate truth-teller. Diane grew up in southwest Baltimore where her dad taught her what it meant to live life on her own terms while her mom showed her the magical powers of true friendship. She now lives in Boise with her husband and their two girls.

Elizabeth Hunter is just a woman in her late thirties still trying to figure out this thing called "life." She resides in the beautiful Santa Ynez Valley where she is a Massage Therapist and Reiki Practitioner. She has always loved writing and is thankful to share a chapter of her life with you.

Natalie Komlos-Zeiler grew up in Appleton, Wisconsin where she fell in love with music and words and long car rides with her dad. After college she moved to the San Francisco Bay area, got married, and had numerous jobs that had nothing to do with her history degree. She lives in Boise, Idaho, where motherhood serves to distract her from a permanent existential crisis.

Kristine Hope Kowalski is a writer and celebrity entertainment news journalist from New Jersey. She earned her BA from Rutgers University in 2011, and MA from NYU in 2013. She is currently pursuing her second Master's in Journalism at Harvard, because why not?

Amber Paige Lee grew up on a farm in South Georgia and currently lives in Atlanta. She earned a Bachelor's degree in English: Writing/Publishing from The University of North Georgia, while simultaneously working seasonally for Disney. She is currently pursuing a Master's degree in Creative Writing and Literature through Harvard University's Extension School.

Rochelle Lierz is a coach, writer and mother. She founded and operated two coaching businesses, integrating her experience in business, systems, and social psychology. She collaborates with others who are actively pursuing social change. She stumbled on writing as a coach, and uses it to inspire change toward a more conscious future.

Bethanie MacDonald likes to read and travel with her family. She takes way too many photos of her dogs but never actually posts them online. She's proud of her family and actually likes her life. Her biggest goal is to parent without screwing up.

Angela McCall received a B.A. in English and Professional Writing from Appalachian State University. She always dreamed of living in California and traveling the world. One of those dreams finally came true when she moved to Lake Tahoe with her best friend, boyfriend, and partner, Micah.

Elisabeth Sharp McKetta is a writer, teacher, and mother of two. She teaches writing and fairy tales for Harvard Extension School and has authored nine books, including five poetry collections, a writing guide, a children's book, and the biography *Energy*. Her first novel, *She Never Told Me About the Ocean*, was published by Paul Dry Books in 2021. In 2019 she gave a TEDx talk titled "Edit your life like a poem." (elisabethsharpmcketta.com)

Isla McKetta is the author of *Polska, 1994* (Éditions Checkpointed) and co-author of *Clear Out the Static in Your Attic: A Writer's Guide for Turning Artifacts into Art* (Write Bloody). She earned a Master of Fine Arts in Creative Writing at Goddard College in Port Townsend, Washington. Isla makes her home in Seattle where she writes fiction, poetry, and book reviews. (Twitter: @islais-reading | islamcketta.com)

Mage McManus was born in California and raised in New York City. She has spent the last decade in the medical and non-profit worlds. She enjoys opportunities that her city provides her with to push herself educationally. When she isn't traveling, her time is spent with her husband and their dog on the Upper West Side of Manhattan.

Breanna McPhillips is a queer AMAB woman still discovering herself. She is a qualified accountant, working in finance for the last fifteen years, having qualified with a MA in Accountancy and Finance. She lives in London and loves the full diversity, quirkiness and color of the city.

Melanie Mendenhall received an MA in English literature from the University of Illinois at Urbana-Champaign, where her story "School Day" won the Bresee Memorial Award for Graduate Fiction. She also graduated with honors from Emory University School of Law. As a freelance editor, she enjoys editing long works of fiction and provocative legal essays. (melaniejmendenhall.com | on Instagram @wordblerg)

Kelly Mercer has been raising hell in the Sunshine State of Florida since birth and is a veteran of the U.S. Army. She works in a cardiovascular ICU as a registered nurse. When she's not saving lives, you can find her searching for a new fur baby to rescue, drinking wine with her best friends at the local bottle shop, or binge watching Netflix with a box of Girl Scout Cookies in bed.

Kathleen Miller was born in Minneapolis and moved to St. Petersburg, Florida, when she was nine. She raised five children, foregoing a career to become a stay- at-home mom. She served as President of Parents, Family and Friends of Gay, Lesbian, Bisexual and Transgendered Persons (PFLAG) in Pinellas County, Florida, for twelve years.

Matiwonesa Munyaradzi was born and raised in New York City and has been writing since she was nine. Her life and her work reflect her African American upbringing, which says put God first and highly value extended family. As a child, Shona loved to read. One day she realized that mostly men were praised for their writing. That day she decided that she would write her own stories.

Liz Nance is from a time and place in Georgia where women did what they were told and held back tears to hold families together. It didn't take her long to realize that just wasn't her. Leaving behind the idea that you can't talk about the skeletons in the closet, she started writing to expose them in the form of song. Liz resides in Bryson City, North Carolina, with her husband.

Puma Perl is a writer and the author of five solo poetry collections. Since 2012 she's presented *Puma Perl's Pandemonium,* merging spoken word with rock and roll. She's received three awards from the New York Press Association in recognition of her journalism as well as the 2016 Acker Award in the category of writing.

Taylor Richards is an American writer and native of Savannah, Georgia. She holds a B.S. in Psychology and is working on an M.A. in Literature and Creative Writing. Richards is fascinated with Alice Walker, Maya Angelou and all things James Baldwin. When Richards isn't writing, she enjoys theater, Bikram yoga and horseback riding. She lives in NYC with her daughter and dog.

Erin Riley is a storyteller. Her stories often span decades and she would travel the globe in search of a satisfying narrative. She is a three-time featured storyteller at Story Story Night in Boise and an accomplished podcaster and comedian as co-host of *Atheist Nomads*. Erin is a Navy veteran, college graduate, and community organizer. She is also a former addict and survivor of domestic violence. Her stories are eclectic. They are resilient. And they are hers.

Elizabeth Rodgers is a writer and filmmaker. She has written for Paramount Pictures, Carsey-Werner and Showtime, among others. Her documentaries have appeared nationally on PBS and on educational television worldwide. Until now, she has never written about her personal experience.

Jasmin Rodriguez is a Puerto Rican bombshell and native New Yorker, raised by a breakdancing fashionista from Queens and a Brooklyn-based racecar driver. She is the woman behind the wildly successful *Vintage Vandalizm* blog and clothing brand, bringing her retro-style expertise and sinfully seductive style to hundreds of thousands of followers worldwide.

Monique Rojas is a simple woman, from Mexico and the West Coast. The encounters she has had with glittery people have all lacked emotional connection, like sand thirsty for water. She does not believe she's the most interesting woman in the world, but she's loved someone else more than she loved herself. She wishes you the same gift.

Aurélie Rose is a mother and immigrant living and surviving in America.

Emily Rose is a women's transformational life coach at TheFearlessFeminine. com. With a degree in Psychology from Harvard University and a bestselling relationship book, Emily is fulfilling her mission to facilitate women into power in their personal and professional lives.

Cheryl Slavin was a performer and a military spouse in her former lives. Now, she is a defunct diva and a former idealist. She lives in Boise, Idaho, with her lovely daughter and her comorbid disorders—obsessive-compulsive disorder (OCD) and bipolar I. Hoping to destigmatize mental illness, she authors a personal blog detailing her life with her disorders.

Jessica Steindorff grew up where the mountains and the ocean meet in California. She is an active board member of Afesip and Together 1 Heart and frequents Cambodia a handful of times each year. She currently lives on a horse ranch in Malibu where she runs her talent management company.

Once upon a time, **Mary Stewart** joined a writer's workshop and received First Place for her short story from the Space Coast Writer's Guild. Since then, for the past thirty years, she has lived in the mountains of Western North Carolina, working as a General Contractor and custom homebuilder.

Samantha L. Taylor is an Afro-Guyanese poet and writer who was born and raised in Queens, New York, by her father after the passing of her mother. Over the course of eight years, Taylor has developed a collection of poetry, "The Gold Collective Poetry Series." Instagram: @thegoldcollectiveseries

Awet Teame is an Eritrean-American comedian, actress, voice-over artist, writer, radio host and front-end web developer. She graduated from Emerson College and was a 2019 Hack Diversity Fellow. She has performed standup comedy from Boston to Los Angeles, as well at universities, for the past fifteen years.

AK Turner is a *New York Times* bestselling author of multiple book series. Her work has appeared in *Money Inc, The Huffington Post, Folio Literary Magazine,* and *Artocratic,* among other publications, and in numerous anthologies. She is the recipient of Independent Publishing Awards, Foreword INDIES Awards, a *Publishers Weekly* starred review, and inclusion in *PW's* Top 5 Indie Books of 2014. (AKTurner.com)

Erika Warner was born in Colombia and has lived, studied, and worked in Spain, Ireland, Russia, and the United States. She now lives in Boise, Idaho, with her husband. She is currently working on her second bachelor's degree while working as an adult educator at a local nonprofit called The Learning Lab.

Christy Wicks lives in Seattle where she wrangles her teenage boys. Her mind is constantly running and finds her best inspiration comes from a fear of normal things gone wrong. While death is an inevitable part of life, it mystifies her and she's constantly looking to discover the answer of what happens next.

Mae B. Yu is a published author and poet. On days she can't get out of bed, her emotional support dog helps by sitting on top of her head. She still talks to herself, but the words are a little kinder now.

The following essays were previously published:

Harvard Summer Review (2017): "Loss and Lonerdom" retitled "Rescue"

Longhand: The Rise & Fall & Rise of My Career as a Children's Book Author (2017): "Rescuing Jeff and David"

Option B (2017): "The Two Jizos"

The editors would like to thank Jodi Eichelberger, whose Pleiades project inspired several of these stories in earlier drafts; and Stan Pottinger, Sarah Tregay, and Craig Lambert—who guided us along the way.

Made in the USA
Las Vegas, NV
12 August 2021